the
pacific
northwest
garden
tour

D0961883

the pacific northwest garden tour

The 60 best gardens to
visit in Oregon, Washington,
and British Columbia

DONALD OLSON

TIMBER PRESS
PORTLAND | LONDON

Frontispiece: A perennial border inspired by English landscape gardener
Gertrude Jekyll runs along the fence at Deepwood Estate in Salem, Oregon.

Photo credits appear on page 289.

The Haseltine Building   6a Lonsdale Road
133 S.W. Second Avenue, Suite 450   London NW6 6RD
Portland, Oregon 97204-3527   timberpress.co.uk
timberpress.com

Printed in China
Cover and text design by Laken Wright

Library of Congress Cataloging-in-Publication Data

Olson, Donald.
  The Pacific Northwest garden tour: the 60 best gardens to visit in Oregon,
Washington, and British Columbia/Donald Olson.
      pages   cm
  Includes bibliographical references and index.
  ISBN 978-1-60469-451-2
  1. Gardens—Northwest, Pacific—Guidebooks. 2. Northwest, Pacific—
Guidebooks. I. Title.
  SB466.U65N767 2014
  635.09795—dc23
                    2013043425

To the gardeners who created the gardens and
to the gardeners who keep them growing, I doff my
hat, raise my trowel, and dedicate this book.

A field of rare Himalayan blue poppies
is one of the springtime highlights at
the Rhododendron Species Botanical
Garden in Federal Way, Washington.

contents

Introduction   8

OREGON   23

Portland & Vicinity   25
Cistus Nursery   26
Crystal Springs Rhododendron Garden   30
Elk Rock Garden of the Bishop's Close   34
The Grotto   38
Hoyt Arboretum   42
International Rose Test Garden   46
Jenkins Estate   50
Joy Creek Nursery   54
Ladd's Addition Gardens   58
Lan Su Chinese Garden   62
Leach Botanical Garden   66
Peninsula Park Rose Garden   70
Pittock Mansion   74
Portland Japanese Garden   78

Salem & Vicinity   82
Adelman Peony Garden   84
Cecil and Molly Smith
    Rhododendron Garden   88

Dancing Oaks Nursery   92
Deepwood Estate   96
The Oregon Garden   100
Schreiner's Iris Gardens   104
Sebright Gardens   108

Eugene, Central Oregon &
the Oregon Coast   112
Castle Crest Wildflower Garden   114
Connie Hansen Garden   118
Hendricks Park   122
Shore Acres State Park   126

WASHINGTON   131

Seattle & Vicinity   132
Bellevue Botanical Garden   134
Bloedel Reserve   138
Dunn Gardens   142
Elisabeth Carey Miller Botanical
    Garden   146
Evergreen Arboretum and Gardens   151
Heronswood   154
Kruckeberg Botanic Garden   158

Kubota Garden	162
Meerkerk Rhododendron Gardens	166
RoozenGaarde	170
Seattle Japanese Garden	174
South Seattle Community College Arboretum and Seattle Chinese Garden	178
Volunteer Park Conservatory	182
Washington Park Arboretum	186
Woodland Park Rose Garden	190

Tacoma & Vicinity — 194

Chase Garden	196
Lake Wilderness Arboretum	200
Lakewold	202
Pacific Rim Bonsai Collection	206
Point Defiance Park	210
Powellswood	214
Rhododendron Species Botanical Garden	218
Soos Creek Botanical Garden	222
W. W. Seymour Botanical Conservatory and Wright Park	226

Central, Eastern & Southern Washington — 230

Fort Vancouver Heritage Garden	232
Hulda Klager Lilac Gardens	236
Manito Park	240
Ohme Gardens	244

BRITISH COLUMBIA — 248

Vancouver & Vicinity — 250

Dr. Sun Yat-Sen Classical Chinese Garden	252
Queen Elizabeth Park	256
Stanley Park	260
UBC Botanical Garden	264
VanDusen Botanical Garden	268

Victoria & Vicinity — 272

Abkhazi Garden	274
The Butchart Gardens	278
Milner Gardens and Woodland	284

Acknowledgments	288
Photo Credits	289
Index	290

Beautiful in all seasons, the Seattle Japanese Garden is particularly magnificent in autumn.

introduction

When I first moved to the Pacific Northwest, it was the gardens that immediately caught my eye. I'd come from a place where gardens, when they weren't buried under snowdrifts, were yards with mowed grass, shade trees, a few hardy shrubs, and not much else—except for mosquitoes.

What a different world it was in the Northwest, where I couldn't turn around without confronting a rose or a rhododendron, and where the pungent smell of bark dust was always floating in the air. Plants I'd read about but never seen grew with a kind of luxurious abandon. If I kept my eyes open, I could always find something in bloom, even in fall (autumn cyclamen and crocuses) and winter (witch hazels). And to top it all off, the natural landscapes of this region, where Native Americans had lived for more than ten thousand years and European settlers for fewer than two hundred, had a beauty and a grandeur that astounded me then and continue to astound me today.

Yes, it's true, from November through May there is rain, lots of it, in every form you can imagine. And yes, the skies are sometimes dark and gray for weeks on end. All I can say to that is, so what? If you're a plant, or a gardener, this is paradise.

PACIFIC NORTHWEST GARDEN GEOGRAPHY AND VARIETY

In this guide you will meet sixty of the most noteworthy public gardens, parks, and arboreta in the Pacific Northwest, a region that includes Oregon, Washington, and British Columbia. Nearly all of the gardens are cradled in the moist, temperate zones west of the Cascade Mountains. Within this area are innumerable topographical features that create a surprisingly large number of mini-microclimates. That's just another way of saying, if you can find the right spot for it, you can grow almost anything from the temperate world.

A couple of the featured gardens in Oregon are right next to the Pacific Ocean, but most of them are in the fertile Willamette Valley between the Cascades and the Coast Range, an area that includes Portland, one of the three great garden cities of the Northwest. One of the gardens—the Castle Crest Wildflower Garden—is in Crater Lake National Park in central Oregon.

The International Rose Test Garden in Portland's Washington Park is among the most popular tourist attractions in the City of Roses.

In Washington, the gardens are mostly on or near the shores of Puget Sound, although a couple of notable exceptions are located in central and eastern Washington, where the climate is considerably hotter in the summer, colder in the winter, and drier all year round. Seattle is the second great garden city in the Pacific Northwest. Several exceptional and still relatively unknown gardens are located in the South Sound area in and around Tacoma.

The beautiful gardens in British Columbia, including those on Vancouver Island and in Vancouver, the Northwest's third great garden city, are situated on or near bays, fjords, inlets, or straits.

The common denominator in most of these gardens is that they get a lot of rain for six to eight months of the year, rarely experience searing extremes of temperature, and sit in relatively sheltered locales. But they're definitely not immune to surprise attacks by ice storms, snow, and fierce winds. The Columbus Day storm of 1962 and the ice storm of 2013 wreaked havoc in gardens and parks in Oregon and Washington, and a windstorm in 2006 toppled ten thousand trees in Stanley Park in Vancouver, British Columbia.

I've been both inclusive and selective in my garden choices, presenting a wide array of different garden types for you to explore and enjoy, and weeding out those that aren't worthy of an hour or

A reminder of an earlier age, the bust of playwright Henrik Ibsen stands among the rhododendrons in Tacoma's Wright Park.

two of your time. You may be surprised at the variety of gardens you'll find here, each one an outstanding example of the gardener's or landscape designer's art. Of course, all the big show-off display gardens, the ones that celebrate floral abundance and civic pride, are included, but so are some smaller and simpler heritage gardens. There are also a number of once-private estate gardens that are now open to the public. Many of these are English or European-style landscape gardens that required a designer and a cadre of gardeners to do the hard work, but you'll find as well some wonderful smaller gardens created around smaller houses where the owners were the ones wielding shovel and trowel.

The region is blessed with many century-old parks that are gorgeous in and of themselves but that also contain display gardens and/or world-class arboreta within them. Superb Japanese and Chinese gardens and noteworthy botanical gardens created by plant-loving individuals are among those covered here as well. And because the Pacific Northwest is home to a multibillion-dollar nursery industry, I've also included commercial nurseries and specialty growers that have exceptional display gardens.

Gardens are showcases for plants, of course, but sometimes they also serve as venues for outdoor sculpture. And many of the gardens in this book have architectural components—grand homes, delicate teahouses, ornate pavilions, bridges, pergolas, arbors, handmade fences, carriage houses, stairways, rock work, and, in one instance, a stockade fort. These picturesque human elements add immeasurably to the enjoyment and interest a garden provides. And one thing more: at many of these gardens you will find unique and unusual plants from the garden for sale. When you buy a plant, you're helping to support the garden.

A SHORT PRIMER ON PACIFIC NORTHWEST GARDEN HISTORY

I have to admit I was still something of a garden snob when I first moved to Portland. I knew more about the gardens and gardeners of England than I did about the gardens and gardeners of the Pacific Northwest. But as I began to explore and write about Oregon, Washington, and British Columbia, my love and appreciation for the gardens, garden history, and gardening culture of the Pacific Northwest grew.

No, we didn't have any aristocratic gardeners like Vita Sackville-West, who created the magnificent gardens at Sissinghurst in

New Gardens in a New Land

The gardens of the Pacific Northwest are new gardens, relatively speaking. The first and oldest garden in the region was planted in the 1820s at Fort Vancouver, a British Hudson's Bay Company fur-trading fort in today's Vancouver, Washington. Back then, the Pacific Northwest was still called the Oregon Country and ownership was disputed between the United States and Great Britain. There were no gardens before that time, at least that we know of (the Native Americans harvested roots, fruits, nuts, and berries but did not plant gardens), and the plants we know and cultivate today were completely unknown. Seeds from the Royal Horticultural Society in London were sent by ship to Fort Vancouver to see if they would grow. It was virgin territory as far as planted gardens were concerned. The garden at Fort Vancouver was a kitchen garden meant to grow food, but a few ornamental plants were part of it, including the first dahlias from Hawaii.

Camassia leichtlinii blooms in early May above the perennial flower beds at the Connie Hansen Garden on the Oregon coast.

Kent—but we did have Belle Ainsworth, a turn-of-the-century Portland heiress who moved to the country, built an enormous Arts and Crafts–style palazzo called Lolomi, and surrounded it with gardens and an imposing elm allee (all of which can be seen at Jenkins Estate in Beaverton, Oregon). No, we didn't have any great landscape parks like the one Capability Brown designed at Warwick Castle in Warwickshire—but we did have Bloedel Reserve, a pretty sublime garden-park created by Prentice Bloedel on Bainbridge Island in Washington. And no, we didn't have any botanical gardens with the royal pedigree of Kew—but we did have the outstanding collections at VanDusen Botanical Garden and UBC Botanical Garden in Vancouver, British Columbia.

The diverse and colorful flower gardens Pacific Northwesterners create and enjoy today had very humble beginnings indeed. Imagine a pioneer woman of the 1840s or 1850s leaving her home in "the States" and bringing flower seeds or a cutting from a beloved rose or lilac overland for 2,500 miles so that she could plant it as a reminder of the home and family she would never see again. Picture a pioneer farmer hauling fruit trees westward in his wagon because he wanted to start an orchard where none existed. Those transplanted seeds, cuttings, and saplings marked the beginning of gardening in the Pacific Northwest. You can pay your respects to scions of these earliest pioneer plants in Seattle's Woodland Park Rose Garden and at the Pioneer Orchard behind the historic James F. Bybee House on Sauvie Island near Portland.

The Post-Pioneer Garden Era

Starting in the late 1880s and lasting into the 1920s, garden awareness and garden construction surged throughout the Pacific Northwest. This was the post-pioneer period, when "resource extraction" was in full swing, railroad and shipping lines were expanding, fortunes were being made, and cities in the Pacific Northwest were starting to flex their economic muscle. The pressures of rapid urbanization and the concomitant need for public parks to provide recreation, enjoyment, and physical and mental health were acknowledged by civic leaders. The City Beautiful movement espoused at the Chicago World's Fair of 1893 gained momentum during this period, and the Olmsted Brothers landscape design firm exerted enormous influence throughout the region with plans for naturalistic city parks and arboreta. (The parks got built but the arboreta weren't planted for another two decades.)

13

Seattle's Volunteer Park dates from this time, as does Portland's Washington Park, Wright Park in Tacoma, Hendricks Park in Eugene, and Manito Park in Spokane. If you like conservatory gardens from this era, two of the oldest and finest glasshouses on the West Coast are the Volunteer Park Conservatory in Seattle and the W. W. Seymour Botanical Conservatory in Tacoma's Wright Park. These now-iconic but still functioning relics of a bygone age gave Americans of the time their first opportunities to examine tropical, semi-tropical, and desert plants.

It was the Gilded Age, and then the Jazz Age, but it was also the Rose Era. Roses became floral emblems of the Northwest, civic boosters got Portland named the City of Roses, and big public rose gardens like the formal Peninsula Park Rose Garden and the International Rose Test Garden, both in Portland, and Woodland Park Rose Garden in Seattle, were planted. Georgiana Pittock, who'd trekked overland on the Oregon Trail and married at fifteen the man who would become the millionaire editor of the *Oregonian*, was instrumental in founding the very first chapter of the American Rose Society in Portland in 1888.

Some of the parks from this post-pioneer period were built on land donated by rich, civic-minded citizens, often pioneers who had cashed in on the seemingly endless opportunities in the Northwest. Private fortunes also went into creating private estate gardens that eventually became some of our most fascinating public gardens.

Shore Acres, now a state park on the central Oregon coast, Deepwood Estate in Salem, Jenkins Estate in Beaverton, Elk Rock Garden of the Bishop's Close in Portland, Dunn Gardens in Seattle, and The Butchart Gardens near Victoria are among the once-private estate gardens that have since gone public and now allow visitors to see how the one percent lived and gardened. At all of them, you'll see that the predominant design influence came from England (where Gertrude Jekyll was the reigning queen of mixed borders) and the East Coast of the United States (where Olmsted Brothers was headquartered).

Public Works Gardens of the Great Depression

Gardens everywhere rise and fall with the economy. During the Great Depression of the 1930s, creating ornamental gardens wasn't at the top of anyone's must-do list. But we can thank garden clubs and city bureaucrats for remembering and pushing ahead with

The Olmsted Influence

It's impossible to overestimate the importance of Frederick Law Olmsted (1822–1903) in the history of American landscape design. The creator of New York City's Central Park was one of those seminal thinkers whose ideas—in this case, how public parks and green spaces are essential to human health and well-being—reshaped cities across the United States and continue to resonate today. After his death, Olmsted's legacy was carried on by his sons, John Charles and Frederick Law Jr., who formed the Olmsted Brothers landscape architecture firm in 1898. Based in Brookline, Massachusetts, Olmsted Brothers quickly became the pre-eminent landscape design firm in the United States.

The Olmsteds' presence was soon felt in the Pacific Northwest, where they designed park plans for Portland, Seattle, Bellingham, Spokane, and Walla Walla, and landscaped Oak Bay, a residential neighborhood in Victoria, British Columbia. They also prepared plans for the grounds of Reed College in Portland, the University of Oregon in Eugene, and the Washington State Capitol in Olympia, and they designed private estate gardens. Their best-known private estate gardens are Dunn Gardens in Seattle and Elk Rock Garden of the Bishop's Close in Portland.

twenty-year-old plans to create Hoyt Arboretum in Portland and Washington Park Arboretum in Seattle. How did they do it? Civic-minded citizens coughed up the design fees and sometimes paid for the plants, and Franklin D. Roosevelt's Works Progress Administration (WPA) program provided the manpower. We wouldn't have our noteworthy "tree museums" today if it weren't for the labor of formerly unemployed men.

The Japanese Influence

An enormous shift in garden design and plant material occurred in the late 1950s and early 1960s. Japanese design expertise resulted in the creation of four outstanding gardens: the Seattle Japanese Garden, Kubota Garden in Seattle, Portland Japanese Garden, and Nitobe Memorial Garden in Vancouver, British Columbia. All four of these gardens were designed by Japanese garden masters.

How did this all come about? Cross-cultural ties between the Pacific Northwest and Japan had existed for some time. From about 1868 until they were banned from entering in 1924, Japanese immigrants arrived in the United States in a steady stream, and

many of them worked on farms and in orchards throughout Oregon, Washington, and British Columbia. American travelers to Japan, meanwhile, were exposed to an ancient culture with ancient gardens—especially the temple gardens in Kyoto. After World War II, various organizations made efforts to rebuild relations between the two countries, and the building of Japanese gardens was part of this cultural exchange. Japan and the Pacific Northwest are neighbors, after all, even if they are separated by the Pacific Ocean. Another incentive was the Seattle World's Fair of 1962, which provided an opportunity to show visitors the meticulous, miniaturized, Zen-infused style and spirit of Japanese gardening.

Gardeners on the lookout for new plant material suddenly realized that plants from Japan, China, and southeast Asia would

A dazzling palette of autumn color adds magic to The Butchart Gardens.

not only grow in the Pacific Northwest but thrive here. Today, cherry blossoms are part of the springtime pleasures of Portland, Seattle, and Vancouver, British Columbia, and dwarf or low-growing conifers and elegant Japanese iris are used in many Northwest gardens. It wasn't always that way.

The art of bonsai was also pretty much unknown until the Japanese influences of the mid-twentieth century increased awareness of this ancient art form. Now you can visit one of the world's great collections of bonsai at the Pacific Rim Bonsai Collection in Federal Way, Washington.

Mid-Century Modern Gardens

The Japanese gardens built during the 1950s and early 1960s gave gardeners a whole new garden world to explore and had an impact on other gardens that were being created in the Pacific Northwest during this period. A shift occurred in thinking about Northwest garden design, and the size and placement of a house or building within the garden. European-style manor houses like those you see at Bloedel Reserve on Bainbridge Island, Lakewold in Lakewood, and Elk Rock Garden of the Bishop's Close in Portland broadcast status and add romantic appeal to grand estate gardens. You look at such houses and the gardens around them, and you think "servants." But starting in the late 1940s, a new kind of house design appeared that blended in more unobtrusively with the garden planted around it.

You'll see these Mid-Century Modern houses and gardens at Abkhazi Garden in Victoria, Bellevue Botanical Garden in Bellevue, and Chase Garden in Orting, Washington, all of them private, middle-class properties that became not-for-profits in order to save their unique gardens. Low-slung, unpretentious, made of local wood and stone, with big windows and rooms that are open and flowing, these places may look like suburban "ranches," but they were in the vanguard of a new home and garden aesthetic influenced more by Japan than by England or Europe. They are, in fact, the first examples of a unique Northwest style.

You may be surprised by the number of gardens that date from the 1950s and 1960s. Since this was the period of my childhood, none of these places seem particularly old to me, but in terms of Pacific Northwest garden history, they can be considered heritage gardens with heritage plant collections.

Enter the Rhododendron

If the late nineteenth and early twentieth centuries were the Rose Era, the 1950s and 1960s can be called the Rhododendron Period. As every gardener knows, the Pacific Northwest is rhodie heaven because the temperate climate, slightly acidic soil, and abundant tree cover provide near-perfect growing conditions for these colorful denizens of the forest understory. But, believe it or not, nobody in the Pacific Northwest had ever seen a rhododendron, except in its native form, until 1905, when an English nursery shipped some plants over to display at the Lewis and Clark Exposition in Portland.

It's hard to believe now, when you can find hideous hybrid versions of rhododendrons at any garden outlet, just how rare and exotic these first rhodies were. It would be almost another half century, however, before they became part of the plant consciousness of Pacific Northwest gardeners.

Rhodies, like roses, had their boosters. The genus *Rhododendron* had fascinated plant collectors since intrepid Victorian botanists from Great Britain first encountered them in China in the mid-nineteenth century and started rhododendron collections at some of the great gardens in England and Scotland. In 1945, the first chapter of the American Rhododendron Society was founded in Portland, and the first stirrings of rhodie fever took hold in the Pacific Northwest. These exotic, woody plants with their diversity of habit, leaves, and flowers had tremendous appeal to regional plant collectors and hybridizers. The result is that the Pacific Northwest is now one of the greatest repositories of rhododendron species and hybrids in the world.

Crystal Springs Rhododendron Garden in Portland, originally a rhododendron test garden, opened to the public in 1956 and is now one of the springtime wonders of the city. (Crystal Springs has a rhodie of unknown provenance that is estimated to be about a hundred years old, which makes me wonder if it's one of those very first rhodies seen at the Lewis and Clark Exposition in 1905.) Other spectacular rhodie collections can be seen at the Cecil and Molly Smith Rhododendron Garden near Salem, Jenkins Estate in Beaverton, Meerkerk Gardens on Whidbey Island, Bloedel Reserve on Bainbridge Island, Lakewold in Lakewood, and Point Defiance Park in North Tacoma. But the absolute Louvre of rhodie gardens is the Rhododendron Species Botanical Garden in Federal Way, Washington, which counts some seven hundred of the approximately one thousand known rhododendron species in its collection.

More Recent Garden Trends

Given the new focus on and interest in China, it's no wonder the Pacific Northwest now has two fine Chinese gardens (Lan Su Chinese Garden in Portland, and the Dr. Sun Yat-Sen Classical Chinese Garden in Vancouver, British Columbia), with a third one on the way (Seattle Chinese Garden). In form and style, if not spiritual content, Chinese gardens are very different from Japanese gardens, and they are worlds apart from our Western gardens, where plants predominate. Chinese gardens are very much built environments, and complex architectural elements, such as pavilions, walls, walkways, and bridges, are as important as the plants used.

One trend I hope will become more popular involves rescuing old gardens and outstanding plant collections from death by backhoe. The sad truth is that gardens rarely outlive their owners. New owners or developers who don't have a clue about gardens or any kind of emotional attachment to the plants growing on their newly purchased property come in with bulldozers and chainsaws and obliterate in a couple of hours plants and trees that were

The Duncan Garden in Spokane's Manito Park dates from 1912, placing it among the oldest formal gardens in the Pacific Northwest.

carefully nurtured and enjoyed for decades. Every once-private garden in this guide survives today only because garden lovers rallied to save it, or because the owners made some legal provision for its continuance. In the case of Lake Wilderness Arboretum in Maple Valley, Washington, master gardeners and local garden lovers not only banded together to turn an old landing strip into a lovely, informal garden, they also figured out ways to move entire collections of genetically important heritage plants to a new home. Without a dedicated corps of volunteers, many of the gardens in this guidebook simply could not exist.

As the climate changes and the earth warms, it seems inevitable that the gardens of the Pacific Northwest will change, too. In friends' gardens and in plant nurseries where horticultural trends begin, we are already seeing a slow but steady increase in the number of plants once considered unsuitable or ungrowable in the Pacific Northwest. (Bananas, not my favorite plant, seem to be proliferating.) As water becomes more of an issue, we will see more and more emphasis on xeriscape and native plant gardens. You'll encounter aesthetically pleasing solutions to the changing realities of our brave new gardens at places like Evergreen Arboretum and Gardens in Everett, Washington; The Oregon Garden in Silverton, Oregon; Bellevue Botanical Garden; and PowellsWood, the newest private garden to open its gates to visitors, in South Tacoma.

VISITING THE GARDENS

I laughed when I read a story in the Science section of the *New York Times* that described the health benefits of walking in a park or garden. Wasn't that stating the obvious? Anyone who has an ounce of common sense and a minimal appreciation of nature, and who likes to stroll through a garden or ramble through a park, knows intuitively, without having their brainwaves measured, how good it is for the body and the spirit.

Gardens refresh us. If we let them, they help us unplug from the stress that is one of our rewards for creating an increasingly artificial world in which technology intrudes on every aspect of our public and private life. So much of the time we ignore the natural world entirely. We let our kids stare at screens for hours at a time instead of taking them out to look at trees and introduce them to plants. We have commercialized consciousness itself and are on the verge of alienating ourselves from the very Earth that supports us.

A different kind of truth is to be found in a garden or a park. It doesn't have a voice, except in birdsong and the sound of wind in the trees. It doesn't have a face, but you can recognize it in the bark of a tree and the petals of a flower. Without saying a word, and in the most profound way possible, a garden connects us to the eternal rhythms and infinite variety to be found in nature. A garden is nature controlled, and every garden is a testament to our profound need to connect with the natural world around us.

You don't need to be a trained botanist, horticulturist, historian, or landscape designer to appreciate any one of these gardens. Just walk through it. Enjoy it. That's what the gardeners who created them did, and that's all you have to do.

Every garden, park, or arboretum I've included in this book is open to the public, and most but not all of them are free. For each one of them I've supplied the essential information you'll need to plan a visit. Take note, though: hours and opening dates can change year to year, so please call or check the Web site before you head off on your garden adventure. If you can, plan at least some of your garden visits from mid-April through June. This is, in general, the most spectacular time of year in Pacific Northwest gardens.

I hope my enthusiasm for the gardens of the Pacific Northwest is evident in this guidebook, and I hope that you, whether you're a resident or a visitor, will find it an enjoyable and useful introduction to some very remarkable places.

oregon

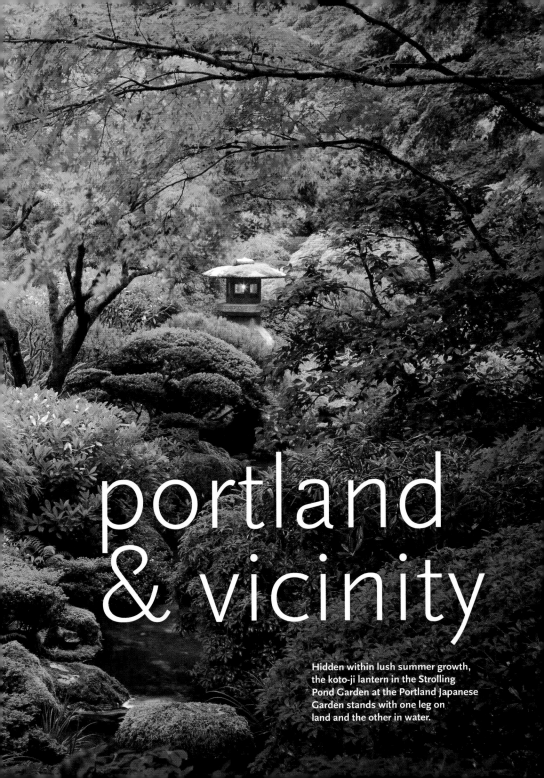

portland
& vicinity

Hidden within lush summer growth,
the koto-ji lantern in the Strolling
Pond Garden at the Portland Japanese
Garden stands with one leg on
land and the other in water.

cistus nursery

22711 NW Gillihan Road, Sauvie Island, OR 97231
cistus.com
Visit spring and summer

....

- 📞 (503) 621-2233
- 🕐 Open daily 10am–5pm
- $ Admission free
- 🐕 Dogs on leash

A multicultural lexicon of eye-catching shapes, sizes, colors, and textures

Zonal denial. Ever heard of it?

As you stroll through the display gardens surrounding Cistus, you may wonder if you've somehow been transported from the Pacific Northwest to the Mediterranean, or South America, or the American Southwest—a place where eucalyptus trees scent the air and matilija poppies *(Romneya coulterii)* flutter like giant white butterflies. Trees and shrubs associated with drier and hotter zones—yuccas, mahonias, olives—share the space with water-reliant Northwest natives. This multicultural lexicon of eye-catching shapes, sizes, colors, and textures looks as if it's been growing here, in happy harmony, for decades. In fact, the entire area was bare until 2003, when Sean Hogan moved his nursery to this location. His display garden is a reminder that contrary to popular belief, the climate in the Willamette Valley is not a year-round rain festival. It is, in fact, similar to a Mediterranean climate, wet from late fall into spring but generally dry and warm from July through September and sometimes October. The range of plants that can be grown here is larger and more diverse than most people realize.

Cistus is a place that promotes new possibilities for your garden, whether that's a small, shady backyard, a sunny suburban lot, or a planter on a windy balcony. Though they come from all over the world, the plants available here all thrive in the Willamette

The display gardens at Cistus Nursery feature trees, shrubs, and plants that extend the zonal boundary of what is typically grown in the Portland area.

Valley and beyond. Plant connoisseurs looking for out-of-the-ordinary specimens will love browsing at Cistus. It's like going to a good art gallery where you can actually afford the works of art.

Sean Hogan, the man behind Cistus, is a plant collector, landscape designer, and horticultural writer whose encyclopedic enthusiasm for plants literally knows no boundaries. To that end, the retail side of Cistus is divided into ten distinct areas, each named for the kinds of plants you'll find there or the growing conditions they require. In the Mediterranean section, for example, you'll find aboriginal and West Coast natives (arbutus, ceanothus, cypress, sequoia, and mahonia) along with nonnatives from winter-wet/summer-dry climates (olives, eucalyptus, rhamnus)

and heat-loving herbs. The Fetish area is stocked with a tongue-in-cheek assortment of fun and unusual plants like aspidistras and prehistoric-looking tree ferns. Dramatic and colorful accent shrubs and plants from Chile, South Africa, Australia, and New Zealand (phormiums, hebes, leptospermums) occupy the Araucana section. Drought-resistant agaves, yuccas, sedums, and sticky-pricky desert plants of all kinds fill the Xerophyte area. In Zonal Denial you'll find plants with bold foliage and a tropical feel—hardy palms, bananas, bamboos, grasses, gunnera, and many more. And under The Big Top, surrounded by their pet plants (abutilons, hardy impatiens, banksias), you'll find the information desk and a staff member to help get you started on a new plant adventure.

The Pioneer Orchard behind the James F. Bybee House on Sauvie Island preserves scions of the oldest apple trees in the Pacific Northwest.

James F. Bybee House and Pioneer Orchard

You can easily combine a trip to Cistus Nursery with a stop at one of the region's most historic houses and orchards. Completed in 1858, the Greek Revival James F. Bybee House on Sauvie Island is surrounded by some of the oldest cultivated land in Oregon. The nine-room house with its stern white façade and inviting back porch is unfortunately not open to the public, but you're free to stroll around the grounds. The Pioneer Orchard behind the house preserves a collection of the oldest apple and fruit trees in Oregon. Each tree was grown from a cutting taken from a tree known to have arrived in Oregon via wagon train or shipped around Cape Horn. These scions of 160-year-old pioneer stock were planted in the 1970s by the Oregon Historical Society and are descendants of the oldest fruit trees in the West. 13901 NW Howell Park Road, Sauvie Island.

Blue Heron Herbary

Did you know that the Pacific Northwest is one of the most productive lavender-growing areas in the world, second only to Provence in France? *Lavandula* lovers visiting Sauvie Island won't want to miss Blue Heron Herbary, a five-minute drive from Cistus Nursery. Here you'll find more than a hundred varieties of lavender in an amazing range of colors—purple, pink, white, mauve, lavender, even yellow—and many other medicinal and culinary herbs for your garden. 27731 NW Reeder Road, Sauvie Island. blueheronherbary.com.

crystal springs rhododendron garden

6015 SE 28th Avenue (28th Avenue and Woodstock Boulevard), Portland, OR 97202
rhodies.org
Visit April through June, with peak bloom around Mother's Day

📞 (503) 771-8386
🕐 Open daily Apr–Sep 6am–10pm, Oct–Mar 6am–6pm
$ Admission fee Thurs–Sun Mar–Labor Day, otherwise free
🚌 Public transportation
🐕 Dogs on leash

Memorable lakeside garden-park stuffed with rhododendrons and azaleas

Lovely year-round, this 7-acre garden in the Eastmoreland neighborhood of southeast Portland turns spectacular from April through June. That's when two thousand–plus species and hybrid rhododendrons and azaleas burst into bloom. Right around Mother's Day there's such an abundance of bloom, color, and fragrance it can make your head swim.

If you live in the Pacific Northwest, you may think that all those rhododendrons you see blooming everywhere in the springtime are native to the region. They're not. Until 1905, only two native species—one on Mount Hood and the other in southern Oregon—were known in Oregon, and since neither one grew in the Willamette Valley, the genus *Rhododendron* was unfamiliar and unavailable to plant lovers. The Lewis and Clark Exposition of 1905 changed all that. At that huge fair—held in Portland to celebrate the one-hundredth anniversary of Lewis and Clark's arrival in Oregon—visitors saw nonnative rhododendrons for the first time. The plants had been shipped over by Waterer Nursery in England. Suddenly, these flowering, shade-loving exotic shrubs native to Asia and a couple of mountainous places in the United States and Europe could be imported and planted in Northwest gardens.

In 1945, rhodie enthusiasts in Portland founded the very first chapter of the American Rhododendron Society (ARS), further increasing the visibility and viability of rhododendrons in the Northwest. The Portland chapter immediately began searching for land where they could test rhododendrons according to the rules of the newly formed ARS.

Claude Sersanous, the first president of the Portland chapter, and Paul Keyser, the superintendent of parks, decided Shakespeare Island, an abandoned island in Crystal Springs Lake where students from neighboring Reed College had once staged the bard's plays, should be the site of the new garden. The land had once been part of a vast farm owned by William Sargent Ladd, two-time mayor of Portland in the 1850s and the man behind Ladd's Addition. The new garden-park was established in 1950 and opened to the public six years later.

Rhododendrons in full bloom frame a glimpse of the North Lagoon in Crystal Springs Rhododendron Garden.

From the parking area, visitors pass through a gatehouse and enter the northern—and newer—section of the garden. A wide ramp loops down past banks of azaleas to the High Bridge, which spans a bright, rushing stream and overlooks a waterfall ravine to the left and the North Lagoon and Peninsula to the right.

There are many ways to tour the garden from this point but I'd suggest that you cross the High Bridge and continue on to the Low Bridge that separates the South Lagoon from Crystal Springs Lake and leads to the original Shakespeare Island garden. The bridge is an excellent spot to bird-watch—or duck-watch, as the case may be. The margins of the lagoon and the lake are planted with reeds, sedges, and water plants that provide shelter and nesting habitat for coots, widgeons, scaups, wood ducks, mallards, and Canada geese, plus occasional herons and cormorants. Paddison Fountain, installed in the 1980s, shoots a geyser of water into the lagoon.

Once you're off the bridge, follow the path along Crystal Springs Lake and keep an eye out for a stake with the number 6. Right behind it is the oldest rhodie in the garden. No one knows the name or origin of this vigorous, tree-sized centurion; all that's known is that it was planted on what was Ladd's Farm sometime before 1917 and has been producing masses of pink springtime flowers ever since. Perhaps it's one of those plants shipped over from England for the Lewis and Clark Exposition. Continuing along the lake you'll come to a dawn redwood (*Metasequoia glyptostroboides*), a deciduous redwood that was thought to be extinct until a stand of them was discovered in a remote valley in China in 1944. John Bacher, the garden's first chairman, acquired a seed in 1947 and donated the sapling to the garden.

Continue along the waterside path all the way around the east side of the island and head back on the path that leads to the Meadow, an open lawn area. The original landscaping for the island was done by Ruth Hansen, a landscape architect and secretary of the ARS, in 1950. Head over to have a look at the tree-sized rhododendrons to the right of the far bench. These are called the Cynthias *(Rhododendron* 'Cynthia'), and they were among the very first rhododendrons planted in the garden in 1950. Donated by Paul Keyser and taken from his garden, they were forty years old at the time.

The path just beyond and to the left takes you to a lovely grove of species rhododendrons and a stand of huge 'Loderi' hybrids with unusually sculpted trunks and white flowers with pink throats.

The Low Bridge separating Crystal Springs Lake and the South Lagoon is a favorite haunt of bird-watchers.

Retracing your steps back across the Low Bridge brings you to the Peninsula, an area landscaped in 1977 by Portland landscape architect Wallace Huntington. If you follow the waterside path to the end of the Peninsula and round the bend, you'll come to a deciduous magnolia (*Magnolia sprengeri* 'Diva') that produces enormous pink flowers in March before it leafs out. The low concrete bridge at the south end of the Peninsula brings you to the Fern Wall and crosses over to the Floweree Waterfall Garden that stretches along the east side of the North Lagoon. Another path at the end of the concrete span leads into the Jane R. Martin Waterfall Garden. Here, in the ravine beneath the High Bridge, you'll find the third of the garden's waterfalls—and still more of the rhododendrons and azaleas that greet you at every turn in this memorable retreat.

elk rock garden of the bishop's close

The oldest, largest, and most intact Olmsted-designed private estate garden in Oregon

Completed in 1916, Peter Kerr's house sits in an English-style landscape garden designed by Olmsted Brothers.

11800 SW Military Lane, Portland, OR 97219
elkrockgarden.org
Visit April through May for blooming magnolias, rhododendrons, viburnums, and trilliums

··

- 📞 (800) 452-2562 or (503) 636-5613
- 🕐 Open daily 8am–5pm; closed Christmas
- 💲 Admission free
- 🚌 Public transportation
- ♿ Cliffside steps and paths make part of the garden unsuitable for wheelchairs
- 🐕 Dogs on leash

This is a garden to fall in love with—or in. Hidden away on a high bluff overlooking Elk Rock Island, the Willamette River, and Mount Hood, it woos visitors with charm, character, and a personality as rugged and refined as the man who created it.

The setting, with its graveled paths and rock steps (built by Adolph Meyer, a Swiss-trained landscape architect) meandering up and down the cliffside gardens, adds a sense of drama and discovery at every turn. Benches placed strategically provide quiet places to sit and admire the river and iconic Mount Hood, though trees now obscure parts of the once-unobstructed view. Rustic touches, including a rock-lined pool, are offset by more formal areas, such as a Japanesque nook with a stream and a wooden bridge, and the rather severe Italianate boxwood allee that stretches across the northernmost section of the property just west of the house.

Peter Kerr, the original owner of this 13-acre riverside estate, was born in Scotland in 1862. He worked for an uncle's import business in London before traveling to Portland in 1888 and establishing a successful grain-exporting business. The property that

Cliffside trails at Elk Rock Garden offer panoramic views of the Willamette River and east Portland.

is now Elk Rock Garden was purchased jointly by Kerr and two partners in 1897. After his marriage to Laurie King in 1905, Kerr bought out the interests of the other two owners and began plans for the present house and garden.

An avid amateur gardener (unlike his wife, who preferred golf), Kerr hired the influential landscape designer John C. Olmsted of the Olmsted Brothers firm in Brookline, Massachusetts, to draft a plan for the garden in 1909. (This is one of only two private-estate gardens designed by Olmsted Brothers that is open to the public; the other is Dunn Gardens in Seattle.) In 1914 Kerr commissioned Portland architect Ellis Lawrence to design the house. Completed in 1916, it resembles a somewhat dour Scottish manor and looks out over a lush, undulating sweep of lawn edged with a stately assortment of elms, redwoods, and Douglas-firs underplanted with witch hazels, viburnums, and other ornamental shrubs. This cultivated, English-style landscaping contrasts sharply with the more natural woodland gardens planted to the south of the house.

During the 1920s, using Olmsted's basic plan augmented by suggestions from Emanuel T. Mische, Portland's first superintendent of parks, Kerr began creating the gardens visitors see today, continually adding plants obtained during his world travels. But Kerr didn't rely solely on imported botanical treasures to adorn his estate. Elk Rock was one of the first gardens in the Northwest to use native trees and plants—madrone, Douglas-fir, western dogwood, and Oregon grape—in a cultivated landscape. Interspersed with the native flora are imported exotics such as weeping Atlas cedars, Japanese snowball shrubs, dawn redwoods, and numerous magnolias. It's this mixture of familiar and foreign that makes Elk Rock such a pleasure to visit and stamps it with Kerr's distinctive personality.

When Kerr died in 1957 at age ninety-five he had spent sixty years developing his garden. Some of its paths he had built himself. In 1959 his daughters donated the house and land to the Episcopal Diocese of Portland with the stipulation that their father's once-private Eden be open to the public. Hence the formal name, Elk Rock, Garden of the Bishop's Close. (In England, the term *close* means the enclosed, parklike area around a church.) Some Portlanders call this garden Elk Rock, others call it Bishop's Close. Whatever you call it, Peter Kerr's garden is not a place you're likely to forget.

the grotto

A clifftop forest-garden sanctuary
and Catholic shrine

8840 NE Skidmore Street (entrance NE 85th and Sandy Boulevard), Portland, OR 97220
thegrotto.org
Visit year-round

....

- 📞 (503) 254-7371
- 🕐 Open daily from 9am; closing time changes seasonally; closed Thanksgiving and Christmas
- 💲 No fee for lower-level gardens; elevator fee required to visit upper gardens
- 🚌 Public transportation
- 🐕 No dogs

Shrines and sanctuaries have played an important role in human cultures and consciousness since time immemorial. They were often places of healing, dedicated to a god or goddess whose aid was invoked through ritual, meditation, and prayer. The holy place did not have to be within a temple; it might be a clear, bubbling spring, or a cave, or a grove of trees. The point was to connect with the mysterious healing power of nature.

This ancient notion of creating a sacred place devoted to devotion—Catholic devotion, in this case—is what The Grotto is all about. But let me hasten to add that you don't have to be a Roman Catholic or even a Christian to enjoy this clifftop haven.

The Grotto—its official name is The National Sanctuary of Our Sorrowful Mother—was created to fulfill a personal vow made by Father Ambrose Mayer, a priest of the Servite (Servants of Mary) Order. In 1923 he made a down payment

The small chapel on the forested grounds of The Grotto in northeast Portland is often used for weddings.

on a 62-acre parcel of land in northeast Portland that was owned by Union Pacific Railroad and slated for residential development. The parcel included the northern slope and top of Rocky Butte, a volcanic uplift with far-ranging views of the Columbia River and the Washington Cascades. A national campaign raised the balance of the funds to buy the land, and in 1924 the archbishop of Portland dedicated the land as the Sanctuary of Our Sorrowful Mother. A grotto was hewn out of the basalt on the lower level to become an outdoor altar where Mass could be said in the summer months (a tradition that continues today).

The upper gardens, reached by an elevator, are laid out along paths that wind through impressive stands of Douglas-fir and western red cedar interspersed with small, quiet meadows. Before exploring the gardens, step into the modern Rose Moyer Memorial Chapel perched on the edge of the cliff near the elevator and enjoy the far-reaching view of the Columbia River and Cascade peaks in Washington.

The plantings in the upper gardens feature a roster of flowering trees, shrubs, ground covers, spring bulbs, and hardy perennials familiar to Pacific Northwest gardens and gardeners. Something's always in bloom: hellebores and camellias in January; pieris in February; viburnums, forsythia, daffodils, and sweet-scented daphne in March; trilliums, rhododendrons, magnolias, and dogwoods in April; astilbe, bleeding heart, and Solomon's seal in May; roses in June; daylilies, daisies, and annuals from July through September. Fall brings color to the Japanese maples.

As you stroll the quiet paths you'll pass shrines, statues, and bas-relief panels illustrating stories from the Bible, most of them relating to Mary. You'll also pass a monastery for Servite friars built in 1936, a pond, and, most interesting of all, a replica of the large, circular pavement labyrinth built at Chartres Cathedral in the thirteenth century.

A statue of peaceful, nature-loving Saint Francis, here with a rhodie in his hair, stands in a meadow at The Grotto.

hoyt arboretum

4000 SW Fairview Boulevard, Portland, OR 97221
hoytarboretum.org
Visit year-round, April through May for magnolia and
cherry blossoms

- 📞 (503) 865-8733
- 🕐 Grounds open daily 6am–10pm; visitor center open
  Mon–Fri 9am–4pm, Sat 11am–3pm
- 💲 Admission free
- ♿ Hilly terrain, trails can be muddy in wet weather; a
  special two-mile trail near the visitor center is suitable
  for wheelchairs
- 🐕 Dogs on leash

Grove after grove of fascinating trees from far-flung corners of the globe

More than a thousand species of trees (and six hundred cultivars) from around the world, all grown from seed or collected in
the wild, are found along the 12 miles of trails that wind through
Hoyt Arboretum. This living museum is best known for its well-
established stands of magnolias, maples, oaks, hawthorns, and
cherries, and for the most extensive conifer collection in the
United States, including a dawn redwood near Bray Lane that's
part of the Oregon Heritage Tree Program. From April through
June, visitors can enjoy a bonanza of colorful blossoms; in the fall,
the tree-covered hillsides and trails blaze red, orange, and yellow.
At any time of year, you can wander for hours and discover grove
after grove of fascinating trees from far-flung corners of the globe.

The short Overlook Trail just south of the Washington Park
light-rail station leads to the visitor center (you can also drive
there), where you'll find maps and booklets for self-guided tours;
you can also download a map from the arboretum's Web site.

When you hike any of the trails in this spectacularly beautiful
arboretum, you're treading on ground that was once home to the
native Atfalati tribe. For centuries they and their predecessors

A peaceful retreat with twenty-one different hiking trails, Hoyt Arboretum is located just minutes from downtown Portland.

used controlled burning to create meadows and grasslands within the ancient fir forest that covered the hilly terrain. This same land was later farmed and logged by pioneers who obtained it through the Donation Land Act of 1850, but their homesteads failed and by 1865 the land was owned by Multnomah County. In 1889, a forest fire raged through the west hills, burning every tree and building to the ground. Part of the ravaged acreage was used to construct a county poor farm and sanitarium that was closed in 1910 when its shocking living conditions were revealed. And that's just the beginning of Hoyt Arboretum's backstory.

Fourteen years after the fire, in 1903, the newly formed Portland Parks Board commissioned Olmsted Brothers of Brookline, Massachusetts, the most famous landscape architecture firm in the country, to draw up a parks plan for the city. With that, the seed for what would become Washington Park was planted. But it took another three decades before that seed, or any other seedling or sapling, could be planted in what would eventually become the 187-acre Hoyt Arboretum at the south end of Washington Park.

An arboretum didn't figure into Olmsted Brothers' original parks plan, but the brothers' famous father, Frederick Law Olmsted, had designed New York's Central Park and Harvard's Arnold Arboretum, the oldest and most prestigious arboretum in the country. In doing so, he created an arboretum prototype that his son, John C. Olmsted, probably talked about when he unveiled his plan for Portland parks. Civic leaders took note and finally, in 1922, Multnomah County deeded the space to the City of Portland for use as a public park dedicated to growing and conserving tree species from around the world.

It was another nine years before any trees were planted.

John W. Duncan, a Scotsman who'd worked his way up from gardening on private estates to become superintendent of parks in Spokane, was commissioned to design a plan for Portland's new arboretum. Duncan's plan, completed in 1930, provided specific locations for nearly forty families of conifers and flowering trees planted in a naturalistic landscape where open meadows alternated with taxonomically organized groves of trees.

But before the plan could be implemented, the site had to be cleared of the dense second-growth forest that had sprouted up after the fire of 1889. WPA work crews cleared the forest and built the roads and paths that wind through the arboretum. Some of the thirty-year-old trees—Douglas-firs, western red cedars, western hemlocks, and bigleaf (or Oregon) maples—were left, creating the mixture of native and planted trees found in the arboretum today.

Finally, in 1931, arborists began planting the specimen trees specified in Duncan's plan. Planting continued until 1944, by which time Duncan's entire catalog of plant families were in the ground and growing. Many of the specimen trees had to be replaced after the devastating Columbus Day storm of 1962.

The trees visitors admire in this gem of an arboretum tell a compelling story without uttering a word. You can enjoy them without knowing a thing about where they came from or the history of the land they grow on. But sometimes it's good to remember that great parks and places like Hoyt Arboretum don't just happen by accident. They are hard-won gifts of nature that have been shaped by human hands and given to us so that we can refresh our spirits.

Designed by the Portland landscape architecture firm of Walker Macy and dedicated in 1987, the Vietnam Veterans of Oregon Memorial is located in the southwest corner of Hoyt Arboretum.

international rose test garden

**400 SW Kingston Avenue, Washington Park,
Portland, OR 97205**
portlandonline.com/parks
Visit late May through July for peak blooms

- 📞 (503) 823-7529
- 🕐 Open daily 7:30am–9pm
- $ Admission free
- 🚌 Public transportation
- 🐕 No dogs

Thousands of roses in colorful, fragrant terraces overlooking downtown Portland and Mount Hood

Portlanders love their roses, and they've got a lot of them to love, as a visit to this famous rose garden will attest. As you might expect, the International Rose Test Garden is a major tourist attraction in the City of Roses—the place where Portlanders always take their out-of-town guests and where visitors often get their first glimpse of Portland's scenic and botanical bounty. Other cities have rose gardens, of course, but none of them has quite the wow factor that Portland's does.

Portland's fondness for the genus *Rosa* goes back a long way. Pioneers coming overland on the Oregon Trail sometimes brought with them seeds or cuttings of hardy, old-fashioned roses, and it became apparent early on that the mild winters and warm, dry summers of the Willamette Valley offered rosy growing conditions for the rose. As the city grew, so did its population of roses. In 1888 the Portland Rose Society, the oldest such group in the United States, was founded in Portland. In 1907, rose-loving citizens successfully campaigned to nickname Portland the City of Roses; adoption of that moniker came about the same year as the first Portland Rose Festival. Held every June to coincide with the flowers' peak blooming period, this fourteen-day, two-parade festival is among the largest floral-themed extravaganzas in the country.

In 1917, ten years after the first Rose Festival, the rose garden in Washington Park opened. The International Rose Test Garden is the oldest test garden in the United States, and among the largest rose gardens in the world, but it is not the oldest public rose garden in Portland. That honor goes to Peninsula Park Rose Garden, a sunken formal rose garden in north Portland that celebrated its centennial in 2013.

Today, more than seven thousand roses representing 610 species grow in the International Rose Test Garden in fragrant formal

The magnificent International Rose Test Garden in Washington Park is the oldest rose test garden in the United States and one of the largest.

Other Attractions in Washington Park: Oregon Zoo and World Forestry Center

The International Rose Test Garden and the Portland Japanese Garden are the two must-see attractions for garden lovers visiting Washington Park, but this enormous and enormously beautiful park just minutes from downtown Portland is also home to Hoyt Arboretum, the Oregon Zoo, and the World Forestry Center. The Oregon Zoo is the most popular tourist attraction in the state and home to some twenty-two hundred animals representing some 260 species, including many that are endangered and threatened. The World Forestry Center is a museum and educational facility (supported by timber companies) with two floors of exhibits relating to the world's forests and the essential role they play in our lives. MAX, Portland's light-rail system, stops at Washington Park, providing easy access from downtown; in the summer a narrow-gauge excursion train runs between the rose garden and the zoo. oregonzoo.org; worldforestry.org.

terraces overlooking downtown Portland and Mount Hood. Since 1940 the rose garden in Washington Park has been one of the official testing gardens for what is now called American Garden Rose Selections (AGRS) and one of five test gardens for miniature roses.

The rose garden is located below the Portland Japanese Garden, the other major showcase garden in Washington Park. From the parking lot, steps descend to an information kiosk surrounded by elevated beds of miniature roses. Extending east and covering two broad terraces is the AGRS Test Garden. The roses being tested here are given a code number rather than a name; four plants of each variety are evaluated for two years by an official judge using thirteen different criteria. The City of Portland annually awards the best-performing roses with a gold or silver medal. Winners are then given fanciful (or sometimes awful) names and moved to the Gold Award Garden, located on the terraces below the Beach Memorial Fountain. The fountain, a walk-through stainless-steel sculpture created by Portland artist Lee Kelley in 1974, is named for Frank E. Beach, who spearheaded those efforts to nickname Portland the City of Roses.

You can't help but smell the roses at the International Rose Test Garden, where more than seven thousand roses of every size, shape, and color perfume the air.

Queens' Walk, on the lowest promenade, is inset with bronze markers for every Rose Festival queen since 1907. Annual and perennial flowers named in Shakespeare's plays are planted in the Shakespeare Garden, in the lower southeast corner of the rose garden.

jenkins estate

8005 SW Grabhorn Road, Beaverton, Oregon 97007
thprd.org/facilities/jenkins/home.cfm
Visit May through June for rhododendrons, anytime
for a walk

- 📞 (503) 629-6355
- 🕐 Open daily year-round 6am–4pm
- $ Admission free
- 🐕 Dogs on leash

A once-private estate with English-style gardens, historic buildings, and trails

I've never aspired to own a big estate (too much work and expense), but I do love visiting them to snoop around the houses and gardens. Historic Jenkins Estate in Beaverton is worth a trip for a peek at a bygone era when Old Portland society could enjoy (and afford) a life of genteel country living.

When wealthy Americans of the nineteenth and early twentieth centuries built grand houses and gardens, they generally took as their stylistic models the historic homes and landscape gardens of the English aristocracy. That was what Belle Ainsworth and her husband, Ralph Jenkins, did when they bought 68 acres of land tucked into the northwest corner of Cooper Mountain. The parcel, which overlooks the Tualatin Valley and surrounding mountains, was one of Oregon's earliest land claims (1845, extended in 1859).

Belle was the daughter of Captain J. C. Ainsworth, a prominent Portland shipping magnate and financier. (Ainsworth Street, Ainsworth School, and the Ainsworth neighborhood in northeast Portland were named after him.) Belle loved horses and met her husband, a station agent for the railroad, at a riding stable on SW Canyon Road. The horsey heiress found city life too confining and decided that a secluded country house would be more to her liking. The Jenkins's new home, a "rustic" seven-bedroom log palazzo completed in 1912 and called Lolomi (a Native American

Lolomi, Belle Ainsworth's rustic palazzo, is seen through the Rhododendron Garden at Jenkins Estate.

word meaning "peace and quiet"), was reputedly modeled after a hunting lodge built for the English royal family.

If the Arts and Crafts–style house is open when you're there (check with the office), step inside for a look at the solid maple floors, the ornate light fixtures, and the call box in the kitchen, which Belle used to summon her staff. And a sizeable staff it was, for in addition to the house there was a carriage house, a stable (with hardwood floors), a covered riding arena, a teahouse, a farmhouse, and a greenhouse. This "English country house" collection of intact, century-old buildings is rare in the Pacific Northwest.

Strolling around the grounds and English-style gardens takes a half hour to forty-five minutes. A path lined with giant white hydrangeas leads from the main house to the teahouse, a low cabinlike building that sits beneath giant firs with a small ornamental pond and wooden bridge to one side. It's a charming spot.

Perennial borders, wildflower meadows, and water features highlight other areas on the grounds. The Herb Garden, created in 1985 with help from the Oregon School for the Blind, contains a Braille Garden planted with fragrant lavender, French thyme, and rosemary. The large Rhododendron Garden, the first garden

The charming garden beside the teahouse at Jenkins Estate is a springtime delight.

you come to after passing through the iron gates, is the showpiece of Jenkins Estate.

A magnificent avenue of elms (*Ulnus americana*) is also noteworthy. The stately trees were planted by Belle Ainsworth between the original farmhouse on the property and her new Lolomi. Although elm trees were among the most popular street trees in the early twentieth century, Dutch elm disease has greatly reduced their numbers. These octogenarian elms are in remarkably healthy condition and have been designated Oregon Historic Trees.

joy creek nursery

Lush display gardens in a vortex
of conflicting microclimates

The display gardens at Joy Creek Nursery overlook a landscape of low forested hills near the confluence of the Willamette and Columbia rivers.

20300 NW Watson Road, Scappoose, OR 97056
joycreek.com
Visit when the display gardens and nursery are open

📞 (503) 543-7474
🕐 Open Mar–Oct daily 9am–5pm, or by appointment
$ Admission free
🐕 Dogs on leash

For years, discerning gardeners have been making their way to this fine nursery with its display gardens overlooking the Joy Creek Valley to find unusual plants that larger commercial nursery outlets don't carry. You can order plants online from Joy Creek, but some of their choicest gems are available in such limited quantities that they're not listed in the online catalog. That's why visiting here is such a pleasure—you never know what you might find in the sales area, and a stroll through Joy Creek's wonderful display gardens will give you lots of ideas for your own garden. And getting there is half the fun: the two-lane road that takes you from Highway 30 to the nursery's entrance winds through a stretch of bucolic countryside that would put anyone in a good mood.

Mike Smith, Maurice Horn, and Scott Christie, the trio of plantsmen who started Joy Creek in 1994, wanted to create a specialty nursery that offered the plants they loved but couldn't find in local nurseries. So they bought a 40-acre dairy farm in what was then a rural community and set about creating what they thought was going to be an exclusively mail-order plant business. Early on they decided to retain the natural landforms of ridge, valley, and forest-clad hills rather than create artificial terraces. The area, near the confluence of the Willamette and Columbia rivers, sits in a vortex of conflicting microclimates. Winds and rain blow in from the Pacific; warm, dry air flows down from the eastern high desert; and there's enough elevation to retain winter snows longer than nearby Portland does.

Clematis, penstemons, dianthus, hostas, and hydrangeas were among the plants Maurice, Scott, and Mike originally championed. They propagated the plants from seeds collected in the wild and sold the starts via mail order only. But demand grew as more and more people came to visit, and eventually Joy Creek opened a half-acre retail plant area and about 4 acres of display gardens. The nursery and the gardens have evolved over time, as the owners have developed an ever-more-sophisticated palette of plants adapted for modern gardens. They have also patented several hybrids of their own, such as a bright yellow helenium called 'Tijuana Brass', and expanded their landscape design and installation services.

Take your time when you visit Joy Creek because there is much to see and appreciate. Strolling through the display gardens around the 1920s-era wood-frame farmhouse is a real delight. Snugly enfolded within the natural contours of the landscape, the

Wandering through the display gardens at Joy Creek Nursery reveals surprises like this patch of Siberian iris near the edge of the property.

gardens and stock fields make good use of the hilly terrain and its mini-microclimates, opening up to reveal distant vistas that are like the borrowed scenery used in Japanese garden design. The mixed borders that line the shrub- and tree-shaded paths in one area are offset in another by dry borders of sun-loving lavender and drought-resistant perennials that prefer a hotter, drier Mediterranean climate.

Joy Creek plant specialties are scattered throughout. Turn a corner and you may find the white, double-petaled 'Arctic Queen' clematis scrambling up the branches of a dark evergreen shrub, or encounter the Joy Creek–patented *Miscanthus sinesis* 'Gold Breeze', a dramatic ornamental grass that holds its own in grand mixed borders or patio pots. As you leave the woodland gardens, with their specimen trees and giant old rhodies, you'll come to various patches where specialty genera like hardy fuchsias and hydrangeas are grown. Continue down the hill to the very edge of the property, where a patch of Siberian iris puts on a real show in May. Old-fashioned and short-lived, these iris are out of favor with many gardeners these days, but they're still cultivated at Joy Creek for no other reason than that the owners love the way they look. Now that's a good nursery for you.

ladd's addition gardens

Bounded by SE Hawthorne Boulevard, SE Division, SE 12th, and SE 20th Streets, Portland, OR 97214
laddsadditiongardens.com
Visit late May through July for rose gardens, April through
    September for Ladd Circle
Open daily, no set hours

$ Admission free
🚌 Public transportation
♿ You'll need to walk a few blocks to see all five gardens
🐕 Dogs on leash

Five uniquely shaped garden-parks in Portland's first planned community

When it comes to livability, Portland ranks high on the list. And a large part of what makes it so livable is its wonderful mix of neighborhoods. Ladd's Addition in southeast Portland is a neighborhood within a neighborhood, and it's absolutely unique in its look and layout. Now more than a hundred years old, Ladd's Addition was Portland's first planned community, and five gardens were part of its unusual design. The entire neighborhood is on the National Register of Historic Places.

The developer of Ladd's Addition was—who else?—William Sargent Ladd, an enterprising Vermonter who came west to cash in on the California gold rush but ended up instead in the brand-new "city" (trading post) of Portland, Oregon. Talk about being in the right place at the right time! Ladd started out selling liquor shipped by boat from San Francisco, moved into retail and farm produce, started a bank, partnered in steamship and railroad lines, and moved big-time into real estate. Twice elected mayor, Ladd knew everyone and everything that was going on in the pioneer settlement (known back then as Stumptown and with a population of 891). By the time he died, this indefatigable pioneer capitalist had an estate valued at ten million dollars.

In those early days, Portland's east side was mostly gently rolling farmland carved out of a primeval forest. In 1867, Ladd bought 162 acres of land there and started a dairy farm. By the time this dairy farm became Ladd's Addition, Ladd owned more than 6 square miles of Portland, most of it on the east side, including the acreage that would become Crystal Springs Rhododendron Garden.

A couple of events in 1891 triggered the sixty-five-year-old Ladd's decision to plat his dairy farm into a residential neighborhood. First, the rival cities of Portland (on the west side of the Willamette River) and Albina and East Portland (both on the east side) consolidated into one city called Portland. Second, the Hawthorne Bridge opened, making access to the east side easier. And soon a streetcar line would run along Hawthorne Boulevard, the northern boundary of Ladd's farm.

Thousands of old-fashioned hybrid roses are planted in the rose gardens in Ladd's Addition, a planned community in southeast Portland that's now more than a hundred years old.

Ladd's Addition is a fascinating piece of Portland's urban-planning history. Ladd drew up the plans himself. What influenced him to break from the strict rectilinear grid pattern that was then the norm and come up with a street pattern unlike anything ever seen in Portland—or indeed anywhere on the West Coast—will probably never be known. Although it's been accepted as fact that he was influenced by L'Enfant's plans for Washington, DC, there is nothing to support this claim. Perhaps he had a premonition of the City Beautiful movement that would gain a foothold at the Chicago World's Fair of 1893.

Ladd divided the rectangular acreage with two bisecting streets that formed an X. The four isosceles triangles thus formed converged at a circular center park (Ladd Circle). In the middle of each of the four quadrants he placed a smaller diamond-shaped park to act as a roundabout for through traffic; the four quadrants were further divided into smaller triangles, quadrilaterals, parallelograms, and trapezoids. When he submitted his final plat, it consisted of thirty-two blocks containing 716 lots with two through streets bisecting the neighborhood on lines at right angles to the general city street grid, two diagonal through streets, and sixteen shorter streets. The blocks were further split by service alleys (another unique feature in alleyless Portland) intended to promote the development of Ladd's Addition as an "upper status"

A unique example of urban planning, Ladd's Addition was designed more than a century ago with five gardens that remain a neighborhood treasure.

area (deliveries in the rear, please). The dizzyingly precise geometry of Ladd's street plan makes perfect sense if you view it from the air or on a map but makes it almost impossible to navigate at street level—until you get the hang of it.

The multimillionaire Ladd died in 1893, the same year a hard-hitting depression halted new construction. The streets of Ladd's Addition remained bare until 1907, when a mix of European white birches, little-leaf lindens, Norway maples, and American elms was planted. Today, these century-old trees form a sumptuous green canopy throughout the neighborhood. (The elms are inoculated every year against Dutch elm disease.) Streets were paved and sidewalks laid in 1908.

Now another important figure, also from New England, entered the story. Emanuel (Emil) Mische, the Harvard-educated horticulturist who'd worked for Olmsted Brothers before becoming Portland's superintendent of parks, developed a plan for the plantings in the still-bare gardens of Ladd's Addition. In 1910, Mische's plans began to be implemented. Camellias and perennials were planted in Ladd Circle (today filled with giant rhododendrons). But roses were on Mische's mind—three years later he would create the sunken rose garden at Peninsula Park—and roses were what he planted in the four diamond-shaped parks in Ladd's Addition. The four parks, known as Maple (north), Orange (south), Mulberry (east), and Cypress (west), showcase some three thousand old-fashioned hybrid roses in sixty different varieties. Ladd dedicated all five parks to the City of Portland, but today the rose gardens are maintained almost entirely by volunteers through the Friends of Ladd's Addition Gardens.

The homes on the narrow, leafy streets of Ladd's Addition present a compendium of residential architectural styles of the early twentieth century. Development began in the northern section, closest to the streetcar line on Hawthorne and the west side (downtown) business district, and moved south. The first large houses were built in the Craftsman and American Foursquare style, succeeded by Mission, Tudor, and Colonial Revival styles, and finally by the smaller bungalow style.

Ladd's original plan has never been altered, and his five garden-parks and oddly shaped blocks with their early-twentieth-century homes make Ladd's Addition a marvelous time capsule and a wonderful place to walk any time of year. Just remember to take a map with you when you go.

lan su chinese garden

239 NW Everett Street, Portland, OR 97209
lansugarden.org
Visit year-round

....

- 📞 (503) 228-8131
- 🕐 Open daily Apr–Oct 10am–6pm, Nov–Mar 10am–5pm
- 💲 Admission fee
- 🚌 Public transportation
- 🐕 No dogs

The most authentic classical Chinese garden outside of China

With more than thirty thousand plant species (one-eighth of the world's total) and a garden history that dates back at least three thousand years, it's no wonder that China has been called the Mother of Gardens. Plants native to China fill our gardens, yet there are only three examples of Chinese gardens in the entire United States (with a fourth under construction in Seattle). Portland is lucky to have not only the best but also the most authentic Chinese garden outside of China.

Visiting Lan Su Chinese Garden provides a fascinating glimpse into China's cultural, spiritual, and horticultural history. This is not a modern garden in any sense of the word. It's a classical Chinese garden, which means it replicates an urban garden style that came to prominence during the Ming dynasty (the same dynasty that built the Great Wall of China and produced all those delicate porcelain vases). During this period, 1368 to 1644, an educated class of scholars, poets, and government officials built walled house-and-garden compounds that were both retreats and private pleasure grounds. Suzhou, on the lower reaches of the Yangtze

Red lanterns reflected in the waters of Lake Zither add a magical glow to an evening at Lan Su Chinese Garden.

River in southeastern China, became famous for urban gardens of this type.

The impetus for building a classical Chinese garden in Portland started in 1985 when Portland city officials traveled to Suzhou—Portland's new sister city—and saw its fabled gardens for the first time. It took fifteen years of planning and fund raising, but civic-minded and garden-savvy Portlanders finally got their wish. In 1999, sixty-five craftspeople from Suzhou arrived in Portland to construct the garden, which covers one city block that was formerly a parking lot. The intricately detailed architectural components were made in China and shipped to Portland, along with five hundred tons of specially chosen rock. The garden opened in 2000 and has been a must-see attraction ever since.

A classical Chinese garden can be confusing to Western eyes because it's so different from a Western garden, where plants reign supreme. In a classical Chinese garden, fully two-thirds of the enclosed garden space consists of ornate pavilions and halls grouped around a lake and connected by winding paths and zig-zagging galleries. The serpentine walkways slow one's pace and illustrate the Chinese proverb, "By detours, access to secrets." Moving from one structure to the next, the visitor is presented with a sequence of carefully composed scenes that unroll and reveal themselves like a scroll of landscape paintings. The goal is not to imitate nature, as in the West, but to create an idealized miniature landscape using rocks, water, trees, and plants. The *qi*, or energy, inherent in these natural elements is meant to blend harmoniously with the architecture and flow through the garden. (Taking one of the daily guided tours will help you to better understand the complex world view that defines and illuminates this garden.)

Before you enter, you'll get tantalizing glimpses of the garden through its so-called leak windows. Set in the outer walls and throughout the inner garden, these geometrically shaped windows allow a view to leak through from one part of the garden to another. The large inscribed rock in the stone gateway, called the Crescent Cloud, is the first of many pieces of rockery placed throughout the garden. Limestone rocks like this one, mined for centuries from Lake Tai near Suzhou, are prized for their slender, asymmetrical shapes, their rough texture, and for the holes that allow *qi* to flow freely through them.

If you walk in a counterclockwise direction from the entrance, the first building you come to is Knowing the Fish Pavilion, a square pavilion overlooking Lake Zither. Next comes Reflections in Clear Ripples Lounge House, where the owner of such a garden would take guests to have tea, engage in a game of Chinese chess, play a musical instrument, or relax. The waterside Flowers Bathing in Spring Rain pavilion is notable for its carved ginkgo wood panels depicting the gardens of Suzhou. Celestial House of Permeating Fragrance serves as a sanctuary where the master of the house goes to write poems, practice calligraphy and painting, and listen to the rain while enjoying the fragrance of the winter blossoms in the courtyard. The small Half a Window Clustered in Green Hillside Square Pavilion offers a lookout toward the lake and surrounding architecture, and a view of the miniature landscape that frames the casement of the scholar's study.

The Tower of Cosmic Reflections, the only two-story building in the garden, serves as a teahouse. Tea has been a part of Chinese

life and culture for more than a thousand years. Introduced first as medicine, tea later became associated with Taoist philosophy as an expression of the oneness between human beings and the natural world. Monks used tea to stay awake during long meditation sessions. By the time teahouses became popular, during the Ming dynasty, tea was firmly established as a social beverage and serving tea had its own elaborate etiquette. The teahouse here is a perfect spot to sample authentic Chinese tea and teacakes while enjoying a view of the garden.

Next comes the Moon-Locking Pavilion, where visitors come on a clear moonlit night to see the moon's reflection locked in the embrace of the waterside pavilion's shadow. Painted Boat in Misty Rain, an unusual boat-shaped pavilion with willow, banana, and hibiscus on one side and lake-growing lotus on the other, has seats along the railing that make it conducive to a romantic rendezvous. Finally you come to the Hall of Brocade Clouds, the main building in the garden, where the host traditionally meets and entertains guests. It's called a four-sided hall because the beautifully carved lattice doors and windows provide views on all four sides.

As you wind your way through the garden, visiting the ornate pavilions and admiring the constantly changing views, you'll encounter a wonderfully diverse assortment of plants, including specimen trees, rare and unusual shrubs, and perennials, including magnolias, cymbidiums, camellias, rhododendrons, and bamboo. About 90 percent of the plants are indigenous to China, and most of them were donated to Lan Su by Oregon gardeners and nurseries. Each tree and flower in a classical Chinese garden has its own symbolic meaning. For example, the pine is the emblem of longevity and tenacity, as well as constancy in friendship; hollow-stemmed bamboo represents a wise and modest man who can be flexible in a storm without breaking; and spring-blooming plum trees are revered as the symbol of rebirth.

leach botanical garden

6704 SE 122nd Avenue, Portland, OR 97290
leachgarden.org
Visit spring through early summer

- 📞 (503) 823-9503
- 🕐 Open year-round, Tues–Sat 9am–4pm, Sun 1–4pm; closed major holidays
- 💲 Admission free
- 🚌 Public transportation
- ♿ Terraced trails are not suitable for wheelchairs or the infirm
- 🐕 No dogs

A hidden gem developed
from botanizing trips into
the Oregon wilderness

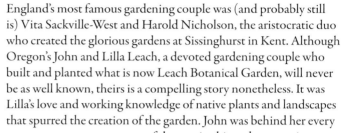

England's most famous gardening couple was (and probably still is) Vita Sackville-West and Harold Nicholson, the aristocratic duo who created the glorious gardens at Sissinghurst in Kent. Although Oregon's John and Lilla Leach, a devoted gardening couple who built and planted what is now Leach Botanical Garden, will never be as well known, theirs is a compelling story nonetheless. It was Lilla's love and working knowledge of native plants and landscapes that spurred the creation of the garden. John was behind her every step of the way in this endeavor, going with her to Oregon wilderness areas on plant-collecting expeditions with their two pack mules, Pansy and Violet.

The Leach Botanical Garden is a hidden gem nestled alongside Johnson Creek, about three blocks from the anonymous strip mall that is SE Foster Road. You'd never guess that this cultivated oasis was once a pig farm with a hidden bootlegger's still during Prohibition. The 4.5-acre parcel that John and Lilla bought in 1931 was part of a 320-acre donation land claim from the 1850s; today the garden has grown to encompass about 14 acres.

Walking in from the parking lot, what you see first is Sleepy Hollow, the romantic cottage-style manor house John and Lilla had built in 1936. With its gabled roof, shingled sides, and wrought-iron weathervane of the Headless Horseman (John's handiwork), the house dozes contentedly beneath giant conifers and the terraced gardens that John and Lilla spent the latter part of their lives creating. The house now serves as the visitor's center and gift shop, so you can go inside and have a look at the hand-pegged

The enchanted and enchanting stone cottage where Lilla and John Leach lived while their house was being built sits beside Johnson Creek.

oak floors and step out to the paved terrace. (Come here for one of the after-hours summer cocktail benefits and you'll really feel the magic of the place.) You can also see the truly gorgeous little stone cottage overlooking Johnson Creek where the lovebirds lived during the summers before their big house was completed.

Both John Leach and Lilla Irvin were native Oregonians whose ancestors came overland on the Oregon Trail. John became a druggist and drugstore owner. Lilla, whose grandparents were part of the communal Aurora Colony founded near Salem in 1856, was a strong-minded and very independent woman with a passion for botany. She graduated from the University of Oregon in 1908 and reputedly turned down John's early proposals of marriage until he assured her he could handle pack mules and all the hardships of botanizing trips into the Oregon wilderness. Their wedding was an outdoor ceremony held on September 13, 1913, at 12:13 p.m., with thirteen guests in attendance. They obviously didn't think 13 was an unlucky number.

As you explore the grounds, climbing up the terraced hillside and into the forest, you'll discover several different plant collections, some that focus on the flora of Oregon before European settlement, others that have claimed an ornamental or scientific niche in the garden. Johnson Creek, a free-flowing tributary of the Willamette River, divides the property and adds another layer of enchantment to it. (It also floods its banks almost every spring.)

The south-facing hillside beside the house collects enough warmth in this otherwise cool, forested canyon to support the alpinelike plants found in the Siskiyous, where the Leaches spent ten summers on plant-collection expeditions. This is where you'll find the historic collection of plants they discovered, including a species of kalmiopsis (a shrub in the heath family native to southwestern Oregon) now officially named *Kalmiopsis leachiana*. This kalmiopsis is one of five plants Lilla is credited with discovering. The others are *Iris innominata*, *Sedum moranii*, *Sophora leachiana*, and *Triteleia hendersonii* var. *leachiae*.

Other specialty collections include flora of the southeastern United States, an extensive fern collection, a camellia collection, and a new hardy fuchsia collection. Because it's a botanical garden, most of the plants are labeled. Delicate little alpine plants are at their best in the spring through early summer, so come then if you can.

Created by John and Lilla Leach on the hillside behind Sleepy Hollow, their house in southeast Portland, the rock garden at Leach Botanical Garden is planted with rare and delicate alpine specimens.

It's something of a miracle that this garden is here at all. The childless Leaches willed the garden and buildings to the City of Portland with the stipulation that if the city did not assume stewardship within ten years, everything would go to the YMCA. When the ten years were up in 1981, city bureaucrats who knew nothing about the garden were about to sign it over to the Y (which wanted to demolish the buildings) when the city parks commissioner decided to have a look. He was bowled over by what he found—as you will be—and today this living, loving legacy of Oregon plant and garden history is operated by Portland Parks and Recreation.

peninsula park
rose garden

700 N Rosa Parks Way, Portland, OR 97217
portlandonline.com/parks
Visit late May through July for peak bloom

- 📞 (503) 823-3620
- 🕐 Open daily 5am–midnight
- $ Admission free
- 🚌 Public transportation
- 🐕 Dogs on leash

The first public rose garden in Portland, on the urban east side

Can the City of Roses ever have too many roses? Apparently not. But while everyone knows about the International Rose Test Garden in Washington Park, many Portland residents and visitors don't have a clue that the Rose City has a second major rose garden in north Portland. Not just major, but historic. In fact, the rose garden in Peninsula Park predates the one in Washington Park and was the first public rose garden in Portland. It's now more than a hundred years old.

If rose lovers don't know about Peninsula Park, it might be because it's on the urban east side. But don't let its location deter you. Before or after your garden exploration, you can easily go for a spin or a stroll down nearby N Mississippi Boulevard or N Alberta Street, both of which offer restaurants and shopping.

Before 1909, when the city acquired the 16 acres that is now Peninsula Park, the area was the site of a roadhouse and a horse-racing track. But as in many U.S. cities at the time, Portland's civic leaders were influenced by the City Beautiful movement that sought to reshape and beautify urban centers by creating formal gardens and building public monuments. That's

Now more than a hundred years old, Peninsula Park Rose Garden in north Portland is a neighborhood jewel that evokes the past and serves as a contemporary gathering spot.

why the new Peninsula Park, designed by Oregon architects Ellis Lawrence and Ormond R. Bean and completed in 1913, included ornamental street lighting, an octagonal bandstand, a community center, a playground, and a sunken rose garden with a fountain in the center—all of which survive in the park today. The bandstand, a venue for concerts and patriotic speeches during World War I, is the only remaining structure of its kind in Portland. The rose garden portion of the park, which covers 2 acres, was designed by city landscape architect Emanuel (Emil) Mische, previously Portland superintendent of parks and former Olmsted Brothers employee.

Portland's official rose, the beautiful pink hybrid tea called 'Madame Caroline Testout', was cultivated in this garden and planted by the thousands along Portland's streets. In its early years, the rose garden was one of the must-see sights in the city, but its rosy pre-eminence changed in 1917 when Washington Park was chosen as the site of a new International Rose Test Garden and all the annual Rose Festival hullaballoo moved to the west side. The fact that the rose garden in Peninsula Park still exists and is as well maintained as it is tells you something about Portland's civic pride—and its continuing love of roses.

If you visit the garden in July, you'll be rewarded with the delicious scent of the flowering linden trees planted near the park's entrance on N Albina. Then, as you walk down into the garden, you'll see and smell the roses. Part of this garden's appeal is that it has not been structurally altered or modernized over the years, so it's like stepping down into a botanical time capsule. The rose beds, edged with boxwood, are laid out in formal geometric

patterns around the century-old fountain in the center and rise in brick-faced tiers around the sides. In 2013, to celebrate Peninsula Park's hundredth anniversary, all the beds in the center of the garden were planted with new roses. A balustrade encloses the garden at the upper park level, with big shade trees and park benches behind it. In the hundred years since this garden was planted, Portland has changed, garden design has changed, the climate has changed, and we have changed—but what hasn't changed is the pleasure of a rose.

A perfect place to wake up and smell the roses (and linden trees), Peninsula Park Rose Garden is Oregon's only sunken rose garden.

pittock mansion

3229 NW Pittock Drive, Portland, OR 97210
pittockmansion.org
Visit May through September for roses and border plantings,
 year-round for house and view

....

📞 (503) 823-3623
🕐 Grounds open daily dawn to dusk; house open daily
  Feb–Jun and Sep–Dec 11am–4pm, Jul–Aug 10am–5pm,
  closed Jan
💲 Admission to grounds free, fee for house visit
🐕 Dogs on leash in park, not permitted inside house

A grandiose relic with panoramic city views and landscaped grounds

There are gardens at Pittock Mansion—or flowers, anyway—but it's the view that steals everyone's attention. This grandiose relic of Portland's past sits on a ridge that's nearly 1,000 feet high and juts out like the prow of a ship from verdant Forest Park behind it. From this mansion-crowned summit, the highest point in northwest Portland, you can see almost the entire city spreading eastward toward the Cascades. When the weather is clear, five major Cascade peaks can be seen, including the summitless silhouette of Mount Saint Helens, which erupted in 1980, and iconic Mount Hood, the 11,250-foot peak called Wy'east by the ancient Multnomah tribe.

Henry Pittock, who took possession of this view when he moved into his new 16,000-square-foot mansion in 1914, had been one of the first white men to scale Mount Hood. That was in 1857, just four years after Henry arrived in Oregon as a penniless seventeen-year-old who'd trekked from Pittsburgh to Portland along the Oregon Trail. It must have given the seventy-eight-year-old Pittock, who'd amassed a fortune as publisher of the *Oregonian*, a touch of pride and nostalgia every time he looked out the windows of his new hilltop mansion and caught a glimpse of the glacier-capped peak he'd stood atop so many years earlier.

Completed in 1914, Pittock Mansion was the home of Henry Pittock, one of Portland's most powerful men, and his rose-loving wife, Georgiana.

From the parking lot (which used to be the tennis court), you can approach Pittock Mansion—and see the stupendous view—by one of two routes. If you head to the right, on the path beneath the south side of the house, you'll pass Gate Lodge, the former groundskeeper's quarters, and a modest rock garden that adds a bit of color and interest to this area. If you continue on the pathway you'll circle around the lawn in front of the house and be rewarded with the panoramic view. Your second option is to head from the parking lot straight toward the house, passing the gift shop set up in the former three-car garage. This route takes you past an entrance display garden to the porte cochere and entrance to the mansion. Continue on the path that winds around this side of the house and you'll come out on the same walkway that encircles the entire lawn.

The mansion was designed by San Francisco architect Edward T. Foulkes and took five years to build. Stylistically the structure is a French Renaissance Revival chateau with exterior walls of Italian Tenino sandstone. The heritage roses that edge both sides

Though the once-extensive gardens at Pittock Mansion have been scaled back, visitors can still enjoy panoramic views of Portland and Mount Hood from the grounds.

of the lawn are a tribute to Georgiana Burton Pittock, a rose lover and founding member of the Portland Rose Society, the first of its kind in the United States. Active in all kinds of charitable and civic organizations, this pioneer mother of five, who arrived in Portland from Iowa in 1860 by way of the Oregon Trail and married Henry Pittock when she was fifteen and he was twenty-six, established a competition for the judging of roses and organized the Rose Society's first rose show in 1889 as a benefit for her church. It became a yearly event and led to the first Rose Festival in 1907, a Portland tradition that continues to this day.

Georgiana died in 1915, just a year after moving into her new mansion; Henry died in 1919; and the last Pittock family member to live in the mansion, a grandson, sold the place and left in 1958. By that time, the house was a dilapidated wreck and the grounds were a mess. The house would have been torn down if a group of concerned citizens hadn't rallied to the cause and spearheaded a restoration effort that turned the gloomy ruin into a city landmark and a one-of-a-kind treasure. Pittock Mansion has been open to the public since 1965.

You can wander through the mansion on your own or join one of the forty-five-minute guided tours. Nearly a third of the mansion is taken up by a magnificent marble staircase and hallway constructed of Italian and domestic marbles. The Jacobean-style library, paneled with Honduran mahogany, has a quatrefoil design plaster ceiling and a fireplace of French Caen stone. Superlative plasterwork and marquetry floors are found in the small, circular Turkish smoking room, and Honduran mahogany was also used for the wainscoting and ceiling beams in the Edwardian-style dining room. The elliptical drawing room, with its elaborate plaster moldings and cornices, commands a 180-degree vista of the city and Mount Hood. On the second floor, a four-room master suite used by Henry and Georgiana is flanked by smaller suites once occupied by the couple's daughters and their husbands. The house was built with such up-to-the-minute conveniences as a central vacuum system, a walk-in refrigerator, and intercoms.

Much as I would like to see Portland Parks and Recreation turn this place into a major garden destination, that isn't likely to happen. So garden lovers will have to be content with the roses, the rock garden, the bright annuals, a bit of border planting, and a few rhododendrons and ornamental trees scattered about the long green carpet of lawn that unfurls toward that incomparable view.

portland japanese garden

611 SW Kingston Avenue, Washington Park, Portland, OR 97205
japanesegarden.com
Visit year-round, April through May for azaleas and cherry trees

....

- 📞 (503) 223-1321
- 🕐 Open daily year-round, Apr–Sep Mon noon–7pm, Tue–Sun 10am–7pm; Oct–Mar Mon noon–4pm, Tue–Sun 10am–4pm
- $ Admission fee
- 🚌 Public transportation
- ♿ Steep stairs make the Natural Garden unsuitable for wheelchairs or those with mobility issues; all other gardens are accessible
- 🐕 No dogs

World-class traditional Japanese garden set on a hillside

Built into a forested hillside in Washington Park above the International Rose Test Garden, the Portland Japanese Garden occupies a 5.5-acre site that was once home to the Washington Park Zoo. Designed by Professor Takuma Tono, a Japanese landscape master from Tokyo, the garden took four years to complete and was opened to the public in 1967. It is considered by many to be the most authentic Japanese garden outside of Japan, and to my mind it is one of the most beautiful gardens in the United States.

From May through September an open-sided bus is available to take visitors from the parking lot up to the entrance. More scenic is the gravel footpath that begins at the lovely Antique Gate—constructed of wood, stone, and clay tiles—and climbs up through the forest to the entrance.

Japanese gardens are typically flat, so Portland's is unique in the way it uses the terrain of its hillside setting. The contrast between the towering Douglas-firs that surround the garden (considered borrowed scenery) and the clipped and pruned pines, cherry trees, azaleas, and rhododendrons within it adds to its interest.

A walk through the immaculately tended grounds will introduce you to five examples of ancient Japanese gardening styles influenced by Shinto, Buddhist, and Taoist philosophies. Plants, stones (the "bones" of a Japanese garden), and water are used to create areas of serene calm and contemplative beauty. Secondary elements include pagodas, stone lanterns, water basins, arbors, and bridges. In this idealized, miniaturized, carefully controlled haven, even the trunks of the trees are exfoliated with wire brushes to remove moss and the mottled look of the bark.

The Moon Bridge in the Strolling Pond Garden at Portland Japanese Garden invites repose and reflection.

Inside the main gate, the path to your right passes through a wisteria arbor framing an antique five-tiered stone pagoda lantern and leads down a gentle incline past a bank of perfectly clipped azaleas to the Strolling Pond Garden, the largest garden on the site. During the Edo period (1603–1867), when this garden style was at its height, strolling pond gardens were attached to the estates of wealthy aristocrats and feudal lords and used for recreation. Portland's version consists of an upper and lower pond connected by a stream. The gracefully arched Moon Bridge crosses the north end of the upper pond and a zigzag bridge takes you through beds of iris to the koi-filled lower pond with its picturesque waterfall.

A smaller and more rustic tea garden, separated from the main path by a bamboo fence and entry gate, occupies the northwest corner of this area. The ceremonial teahouse within it was constructed in Japan (using pegs instead of nails) and reassembled here in 1968. This superbly crafted structure has inner walls of sliding paper doors (*shoji*) around a traditional room the size of four and a half tatami mats used for studying and practicing the tea ceremony.

The Natural Garden that covers the south hillside is the most contemporary of the five gardens. Here, stone steps wind down past shallow, meandering waterscapes and through trees and shrubs that create a wilder and more enveloping atmosphere. This garden focuses primarily on deciduous plants and is laid out to present seasonal change.

The path leads to the abstract, Zen-inspired Sand and Stone Garden with weathered stones rising from a bed of gravel raked to suggest the sea. This plantless gardening style, so unusual to Western eyes, is referred to as dry landscape and was developed in Japan in the later Kamakura period (1185–1333). This contemplative type of garden was typically part of a Zen monastery.

The Flat Garden to the north, behind the pavilion, shows how the aesthetic principles of the dry landscape garden have continued to develop over time. What you first see is a great "lake" of white gravel with two green "islands"—one round and one shaped like a gourd—floating within it. They are meant to resemble a sake cup and gourd bottle, symbols of pleasure and happiness. The stones, trees, and plantings around the perimeter of the gravel lake add spatial depth, seasonal beauty, and symbolism to the composition. The century-old Japanese laceleaf maple represents autumn,

the weeping cherry represents spring, black pines represent winter, and the cool "water" of the raked-gravel lake surrounding the two islands is an imaginary representation of summer. The garden is meant to be seen from a single viewpoint either from within the pavilion or from the veranda.

The large wooden pavilion is used for special events and provides a majestic view of Portland and Mount Hood from its eastern terrace.

Designed in five stages between 1963 and 1990, the Portland Japanese Garden is now poised for a major expansion that will bring this world-class garden into the twenty-first century. Renowned Japanese architect Kengo Kuma has been chosen to lead the project, which includes construction of new garden spaces, a cultural and education center, a gift store, and a teahouse that will serve the public.

The Sapporo Pagoda Lantern, with a stone-and-moss map representing the island of Hokkaido at its base, greets visitors near the entrance of Portland Japanese Garden.

salem
& vicinity

The flowers of showy gas plant (*Dictamnus albus*), like these in a patch at Dancing Oaks Nursery, give off a flammable, citrus-scented gas.

adelman peony garden

Display garden and showroom
at largest retail peony grower
in the Pacific Northwest

You'll encounter sights like this sea of 'Coral Sunset' peonies in full bloom as you stroll through the fields at Adelman Peony Garden.

5690 Brooklake Road NE, Salem, OR 97305
peonyparadise.com
Visit mid-May through the first week in June

....

📞 (503) 393-6185
🕐 Display gardens open daily late Apr to mid-Jun
$ Admission free
♿ Easy wheelchair access in flower-display shed, otherwise grass walkways
🐕 Dogs on leash

Carol Adelman grew up on a farm in the Willamette Valley, about a mile from where she now grows some of the most prized and prize-winning peonies on the West Coast. When she was a child, her father would take her across the road to look at a neighbor's enormous collection of peonies. She never forgot how beautiful they were, and in 1993, after years of growing apples and other crops, she and her husband, Jim, changed course and planted their first peonies. They are now the largest retail grower in the Northwest, shipping plants and cut flowers worldwide. Their peonies have won several best-of-show honors at the American Peony Society national conventions.

"When people think of peonies," Carol says, "they usually think of heritage varieties—the kind their grandmothers or great-grandmothers had." Women of earlier generations were generally so busy with time-consuming household chores, Adelman says, that they needed their flowers to be hardy and easy to grow. Peonies fit the bill.

Native to Asia, southern Europe, and western North America, peonies have a long and illustrious history going back as far as 1000 BCE in China, where they were used as medicine. By the eighth century they had become prized possessions in the imperial gardens of China and Japan. Though herbaceous varieties were cultivated in European gardens in the Middle Ages (more for their medicinal than ornamental value), the Chinese tree peony did not arrive in Europe until 1789. Hardy herbaceous varieties started arriving in the United States in the 1830s and it was these, not native species, that were planted in pioneer gardens. Literally hundreds of hybrids are available today, but they all have one common Chinese ancestor, *Paeonia lactiflora*.

During the approximately three-week bloom season at Adelman's, you'll be able to see and purchase three of the oldest heritage peonies in America—the fragrant double-whites 'Festiva Maxima' (1851) and 'Madame de Verneville' (1885) and the raspberry-red 'Felix Crousse' (1881)—as well as brand-new hybrids that are just coming onto the market. In all, Adelman grows and sells about 185 varieties of the three different types of peonies—bush, tree, and intersectional (a cross between bush and tree peonies). The colors, ranging from pure white to deep mahogany, with lots of pinks, reds, and some exquisite yellow varieties, are rich and true, thanks to Oregon's cloudy skies (because the color tends to bleach out with too much sun). Some varieties are deliciously fragrant.

Brooks Gardens

During the May-and-June blooming season, peony and iris aficionados can also visit Brooks Gardens, 4 miles northeast of Adelman Peony Garden. This family-owned and operated farm grows and sells more than 250 varieties of peonies and a thousand varieties of bearded iris. A 3-acre conifer arboretum and display garden showcases a collection of historic bearded iris and peonies. 6219 Topaz Street NE, Brooks, OR 97305. brooksgardens.com.

Carol has planted a pleasantly old-fashioned display garden next to the house, mixing the peonies with other companion flowers. You can also walk through the peony fields—there are grass walkways—where similar colors of different peony varieties are massed together for maximum effect. Catalogs are available and cut blooms are displayed in a big outbuilding. Bush and tree peonies are available in containers (or dormant bare-root divisions can be shipped in the fall).

cecil and molly smith rhododendron garden

5065 Ray Bell Road, St. Paul, OR 97137
rhodies.org
Visit anytime the garden is open in April and May

··

- 📞 (503) 771-8386
- 🕐 Generally open first weekend in Apr to third weekend in May, Sat–Sun 11am–4pm
- 💲 Admission fee
- ♿ Not all paths are wheelchair accessible
- 🐕 No dogs

Sloping 3-acre garden reflecting the springtime beauty of Willamette Valley woodlands

The Willamette Valley south of Newberg is among Oregon's most quietly scenic areas—once you get off I-5, that is—with country roads that wind past hop fields, filbert orchards, dairy farms, and the Willamette River. Oregon's historical roots run deep in this fertile part of the valley. The small town of St. Paul, named for the St. Paul Mission established by Archbishop François Norbert Blanchet in 1838, boasts the first brick building to be constructed in the Pacific Northwest (St. Paul Catholic Church at 20217 Christie Street, built in 1846) and the Pioneer Cemetery (east side

Clouds of springtime color greet visitors at Cecil and Molly Smith Rhododendron Garden near St. Paul, Oregon.

of Main Street), where Oregon's only veteran of the American Revolutionary War is buried. The entire center of St. Paul is listed on the National Register of Historic Places. The town is famed for its rodeo, one of the largest and oldest in the United States, which draws tens of thousands of visitors in early July. Lovers of rhododendrons might want to pay a visit earlier in the season to enjoy a little-known but very special garden.

Open only on weekends in April and May, the Cecil and Molly Smith Rhododendron Garden was the creation of a native Oregonian couple who loved Oregon natives. Their sloping 3-acre garden, first planted in 1951, reflects the springtime beauty of shady woodlands throughout the Willamette Valley. But that's only part of the botanical story you'll find here, for Cecil was something of a genius with the genus *Rhododendron*. One of Oregon's foremost rhododendron collectors, he helped sponsor plant-collecting trips to the Himalayas and experimented with hybridizing his favorite rhodies. By crossing *R. yakushimanum* and *R. bureavii,* he created the towering 'Cinnamon Bear' rhododendrons that are now the garden's signature plants. His other rhododendron crosses, the showy pink-fading-to-white 'Noyo Brave'(1963) and yellow-with-red-freckles 'Yellow Saucer' (1972), have become standards in the world of rhododendrons.

What I particularly like about this springtime garden, besides the rhododendrons, is its self-sustainability. Moss-covered logs and tree stumps have been utilized for their aesthetic appeal (some used as planters) rather than cleared away. The natural forest duff created by the canopy of Douglas-firs, paperbark maples, Japanese flowering cherries, and wild hazelnut bushes provides most of the garden's nutrients, so hardly any fertilizers are needed. Spending an hour here on a balmy spring day is a quietly magical and memorable experience.

Heirloom Roses

Roses, not rhodies, steal the show at Heirloom Roses, a premium rose nursery about 3 miles from the Cecil and Molly Smith Rhododendron Garden. Heirloom's 5-acre display garden, open year-round from dawn till dusk, is filled with hundreds of fragrant varieties that bloom late May through October, with peak bloom in June. In addition to Heirloom's Own, signature roses bred to be champions of color, fragrance, health, and form, you'll find trademarked designer specialties like David Austin English Roses, renowned for the strength and complexity of their fragrances, and English Legend Roses from the Harkness rose firm in Hertfordshire. Climbers, ramblers, floribundas, grandifloras, hybrid teas, shrubs, miniatures, and minifloras, you'll find them all at Heirloom. 24062 NE Riverside Drive, St. Paul, OR 97137. heirloomroses.com.

dancing oaks nursery

17900 Priem Road, Monmouth, OR 97361
dancingoaks.com
Visit April through September; spring for daffodils

📞 (503) 838-6058
🕐 Open Mar–Oct Tue–Sat 9am–5pm, Sun 10am–4pm
$ Admission free
🐕 Dogs on leash

Draped with vines and the branches of a weeping blue Atlas cedar, a rustic pergola forms a long, shady tunnel at Dancing Oaks Nursery.

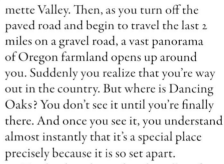

Nursery display gardens cushioned in the Coast Range foothills featuring an often surprising mixture of trees, shrubs, and perennials

Getting to Dancing Oaks is quite an experience. Leaving the main roads west of Monmouth, you pass orchards and small pockets of white oaks, the trees that once blanketed the Willamette Valley. Then, as you turn off the paved road and begin to travel the last 2 miles on a gravel road, a vast panorama of Oregon farmland opens up around you. Suddenly you realize that you're way out in the country. But where is Dancing Oaks? You don't see it until you're finally there. And once you see it, you understand almost instantly that it's a special place precisely because it is so set apart.

This land, cushioned in the rolling foothills of the Coast Range in the central Willamette Valley, is what pioneers dreamed of and trekked thousands of miles to homestead in the 1840s. Dancing Oaks occupies part of the farm where Fred Weisensee, one of the owners, grew up. His partner, Leonard Foltz, grew up in a similarly rural environment closer to Corvallis. They started Dancing Oaks in 1997 because they wanted to live in the country again and indulge their unabashed passion for plants.

That passion is evident as you wander through the nursery's display gardens, which convey a sense of curiosity and enthusiasm for all kinds of plant material. Spread over 2.5 acres and used as testing grounds for plant hardiness and performance, the different garden areas have an informal, interconnecting flow that presents an ever-changing and often surprising mixture of plants, trees, and shrubs. Local wildflowers share space with hardy perennials, new hybrids, ornamental trees, and exotic introductions collected on plant expeditions to Chile and South Africa. In the space of five minutes you can encounter thriving examples of a Chilean firetree (*Embothrium coccineum*), an evergreen ornamental with striking red flowers; the showy and long-lived (up to sixty years) gas plant (*Dictamnus albus*), whose flowers give off a flammable, citrus-scented gas; and a stand of gorgeously blue false indigo (*Baptisia australis*). Look, too, for ornamental grasses and bamboos, dry-shade euphorbias, hardy fuchsias, ferns, and even carnivorous plants (in the Water Garden).

Dancing Oaks has become known for its selection of small ornamental trees, including the striking and much-sought-after variegated ginkgo (*Ginkgo biloba* 'White Lightning'), its green leaves striped with cream-colored bands. If you come early in the spring, you can enjoy fields of blooming spring bulbs, including nearly two hundred different varieties of daffodils.

A long, rustic pergola, made from salvaged cedar and covered by a weeping blue Atlas cedar and a mantle of vines, is the most dramatic architectural component in the garden. The grounds are further enlivened by three water features, metal sculptures, hand-blown glass art, finely constructed wind chimes, and urns. At the end of your visit, you can even buy a dozen freshly laid eggs from Fred and Leonard's hard-working chickens.

Weeping giant sequoia, *Rosa rugosa* 'Hansa', and Armenian cranesbill (*Geranium psilostemon*) frame a view into one of the tranquil garden rooms at Dancing Oaks Nursery.

deepwood estate

Historic Queen Anne–style mansion with grounds partially designed by the Northwest's first female landscape architects

An air of quiet, old-fashioned elegance pervades Deepwood Estate, which was placed on the National Register of Historic Places in 1973. Completed in 1894, the house was built for a family that lived in it for only sixteen months. Dr. Luke A. Port, who'd purchased the 4-acre lot in Salem's Yew Park Addition a year earlier, hired William C. Knighton to design the house. It was the first residential commission for Knighton, who would later design the Oregon Supreme Court Building in Salem and the Governor Hotel in Portland. The house, built in an American version of the so-called Queen Anne style popular from about 1880 to 1910, has many distinctive features, including an asymmetrical façade with an angled, pedimented porch, bay windows, and balustrades. It was one of the first homes in Salem to have electricity and indoor plumbing, and its interior details include stained glass windows made by the Povey Brothers of Portland (so highly regarded they were called the Tiffany of the Northwest) and eastern golden oak woodwork.

It was a fine, showy, and expensive residence, but when his college-age son drowned, Dr. Port sold his new house to George and Willie Bingham in 1895. The Binghams—George was Salem's district attorney and later a prominent judge—lived in the house for twenty-eight years, adding an orchard, a grape arbor, and vegetable gardens. When the Binghams died, the house was sold in 1924 to Clifford Brown and his wife, Alice, who became the last and longest resident of Deepwood—she lived there until 1968—and was the person responsible for the charming gardens visitors enjoy today.

The gardens at Deepwood Estate were designed by Elizabeth Lord and Edith Schryver, the Northwest's first professional female

1116 Mission Street SE, Salem, OR 97302
historicdeepwoodestate.org
Visit April through May for erythroniums in the
  woodland garden

- ☎ (503) 363-1825
- ⏱ House open May–Sep Wed–Mon 9am–noon;
  Oct–Apr Wed, Thurs, Sat 11am–3pm; gardens open
  daily dawn to dusk; house can only be visited as part of
  a tour; tours begin on the hour
- $ Admission fee
- 🚌 Public transportation
- ♿ Parking is one block south at 12th and Lee;
- 🐕 Dogs not allowed in house; on leash in gardens

Seen here through
an ornamental fence
in the Scroll Garden,
the Queen Anne–style
house at Deepwood
Estate was among the
first homes in Salem
to have electricity and
indoor plumbing.

landscape architects. Lord (1887–1976), Salem-born daughter of
a governor of Oregon, and Schryver (1901–1984), from the Hudson Valley in New York, both attended the Lowthorpe School
of Landscape Architecture, Gardening, and Horticulture for
Women in Groton, Massachusetts. After graduating, Schryver
was hired by Ellen Shipman, one of America's first female landscape designers, and worked for five years in Shipman's New York
office. Lord and Schryver met in 1927, when they were both on a

European tour of famous gardens. Soon after, they formed a personal and professional partnership that lasted some forty years and saw the creation of more than 250 residential, civic, and institutional landscapes throughout the Northwest. Lord-Schryver is the only Oregon firm recognized in *Pioneers of American Landscape Design*, published by the National Park Service.

When the widowed Alice Brown commissioned the newly formed firm of Lord-Schryver in 1929 to design formal gardens around the house, they created a series of garden rooms (a concept used in great early-twentieth-century English gardens like Hidcote and Sissinghurst) and embellished them with architectural elements such as covered arches, arbors, pergolas, ornamental gates, fences, and brick walkways. Expanses of lawn were edged with flowering trees, shrubs, and herbaceous borders that provided a succession of color, form, and texture throughout the year. Now owned by the City of Salem, the graceful Lord-Schryver gardens at Deepwood are maintained and being restored by a team of volunteers.

The Entry Garden around the front steps of the house has remained virtually unchanged since 1894. The fall-blooming Japanese sasanqua camellia in front of the east bay windows of the house was planted during the Lord-Schryver period in the 1930s. To the south, the expansive Great Room Garden contains a wrought-iron gazebo from the 1905 Lewis and Clark Exposition held in Portland. The grape pergola, an original Lord-Schryver design, is planted with clematis, rose, and grape to ensure a succession of blooms from spring through fall. The Spring Garden next to it, defined by boxwood hedges and painted wooden fencing, is planted with peonies, poppies, and roses and contains an old quince tree from the orchard planted by the Binghams.

Bush's Pasture Park

Deepwood is the only example of a Lord-Schryver residential garden that is open to the public, but you can see another example of their collaborative work at neighboring Bush's Pasture Park, where Lord created historically accurate plantings around the Bush House, built in 1878, and Schryver oversaw the installation of the Tartar Rose Garden and plantings around the Bush Barn Art Center. The 90-acre park, once an orchard and pasture owned by prominent Salem pioneer Asahel Bush, was converted into a city park and community art center in the 1950s. 890 Mission Street, Salem, OR 97302.

The Running Brick Walk with its bright summer borders is one of the signature features of the gardens created at Deepwood Estate by Lord and Schryver, the first female landscape architects in the Northwest.

Lord-Schryver's Running Brick Walk passes under a holly arch and takes you to the Tea House Garden, an enclosed space that was planned as a moon garden where pastel-colored flowers would glow in the moonlight. To the right, a path leads to the ivy arbor with its ivy-framed windows and on to the Scroll Garden, which contains boxwoods designed with the S-shaped scroll pattern that was Elizabeth Schryver's signature trademark. From here, a path leads past the tournament-size tennis court built in 1926 to the Shade Garden with its lonely column from the ruins of the 1876 Oregon Statehouse (it burned down in 1935) and continues to the Secret Garden designed for Alice Brown in the 1960s on the west side of the house. Just outside the Deepwood property, along Mission Street, a block-long English border garden inspired by the designs of Gertrude Jekyll (who influenced the work of Lord-Schryver) was created in 1982.

At the western edge of the property, a nature trail winds through a woodland where Pringle Creek separates Deepwood from Bush's Pasture Park. When the woodland was restored and cleared of invasive blackberries, native Oregon fawn lilies (*Erythronium oregonum*) began to reappear. They now put on such a spectacular display from March through early April that Deepwood hosts an annual Erythronium Festival every spring.

the oregon garden

879 West Main Street, Silverton, OR 97381
oregongarden.org
Visit year-round, April and May for flowering shrubs and
    trees, June through August for annuals and perennials

- 📞 (503) 874-8100
- 🕐 Open daily May–Sep 9am–6pm, Oct–Apr 10am–4pm
- 💲 Admission fee
- 🐕 Dogs on leash

The Amazing Water Garden with its serpent rising from the water lilies is one of the many display gardens to be enjoyed at The Oregon Garden.

A series of specialty gardens and diverse landscapes showcasing plants and trees that grow in Oregon

The Oregon Garden is a botanical theme park of sorts, where visitors can explore a diverse collection of display gardens, specialty collections, created habitats, and original landscape features spread over 80 acres in the heart of the Willamette Valley. Inaugurated in 2000 and originally meant to serve as a kind of outdoor showroom for the multibillion-dollar Willamette Valley plant industry, the garden is now managed by a company that operates The Oregon Garden Resort, an on-site hotel and restaurant, but it remains a showcase and showplace for Oregon-grown plants and plants that can be grown in Oregon. The educational mission of the garden has grown significantly over the years, and so has the collection of outdoor sculptures that adorn the grounds. You'll enjoy this multifaceted garden more if you explore its many components on foot; a tram makes a circuit every half hour but doesn't let passengers off along the way. Pick up a map at the visitor center and don't be surprised if you end up spending two or three hours wandering around.

The Oregon Garden is unique in that it formed a partnership with the nearby city of Silverton to create a wetlands area using the city's treated wastewater, and it reuses that water to irrigate all of its gardens. The wetlands area, fringed with water-loving cattails, bulrushes, red alder, and red-twig dogwoods, is a haven for frogs and other wildlife. So is the Amazing Water Garden, an award-winning water-based display garden where a Loch Nessie-looking serpent rises from the water lilies. You'll encounter other water features, including splashing fountains, quiet ponds, and reflecting pools, elsewhere in the garden.

The Conifer Collection, flanked by a pair of weeping giant sequoias (*Sequoiadendron giganteum* 'Pendulum'), was the first specialty garden to be dedicated in 2000. It contains one of the nation's largest collections of dwarf and miniature conifers, many of them unique, all of them grown from sports or collected in the wild. Each of these cone-bearing trees has a real presence and personality.

With its topiary animals, in-ground hobbit house, tree fort, and colorful flowers, the Children's Garden is a great place to let

The Frank Lloyd Wright Usonian House at The Oregon Garden

If you're visiting The Oregon Garden and are interested in architecture, reserve in advance to visit the Gordon House, the only Frank Lloyd Wright–designed house in Oregon, and the only one in the Pacific Northwest open to the public. Designed by Wright in 1957 and moved in 2001 to a beautiful wooded site at The Oregon Garden from its original setting on the south side of the Willamette River near the Charbonneau District in Wilsonville, the house is a wonderful example of Wright's mid-century Usonian style, featuring an open floor plan, a carport, cantilevered roofs with broad overhangs, and floor-to-ceiling windows. The house can only be visited on a guided tour; call (503) 874-6006 to reserve.

your kids blow off some steam. And if you've brought Fido along (on a leash), let him check out the Pet-Friendly Garden, where you can pick up some ideas on how to landscape your own garden with plants that are safe and nontoxic to pets.

If you live in the Northwest and are wondering what to plant in your own garden, pay a visit to the Northwest Garden. It's filled with a lush assortment of plants and trees that thrive in this part of the world. I'd also suggest that you visit the Sensory Garden, loaded with plants that can be enjoyed for their special scents and textures. This area, located near the visitor center, includes a couple of nice architectural features, such as a wood trellis made of aromatic Port Orford cedar and a rain-curtain fountain.

Natural areas have been incorporated into the overall scheme of The Oregon Garden. The Lewis and Clark Garden, for instance, features many of the native plants Meriwether Lewis and William Clark documented on their historic journey to the Pacific Ocean more than two hundred years ago. Even more significant is the Native Oak Grove, a beautiful remnant of the mighty white-oak forest that once covered much of the Willamette Valley. The star here is the massive Signature Oak, 100 feet tall and four hundred years old. Located in the southern part of the garden, both of these areas are living museums with interpretive signage that highlights the significance of the plants and trees.

Designed for the physically challenged, the Sensory Garden features a rain wall and plants that can be enjoyed for their textures and scents.

schreiner's
iris gardens

Dazzling gardens and fields of
blooming iris on display at the
nation's largest retail grower of iris

3625 Quinaby Road NE, Salem, OR 97303
schreinersgardens.com
Visit last two weeks in May for peak blooms

....

- 📞 (800) 525-2367 or (503) 393-3232
- 🕐 Open May 10–Jun 9, dawn to dusk (check Web site to confirm yearly dates)
- $ Admission free
- 🐕 No dogs

Tens of thousands of iris and companion plants fill the brilliantly colored display beds at Schreiner's Iris Gardens.

The fertile Willamette Valley with its wet, mild winters and hot, dry summers offers ideal growing conditions for countless food and flower crops. In fact, nurseries in the valley are now so abundant that Oregon has become the nation's number one exporter of ornamental plant products. Come spring, some of the big flower producers open their grounds to visitors and show off their product in lavish display gardens and growing fields. This is what Schreiner's Iris Gardens, the nation's largest retail grower of iris, does from mid-May to early June. And it does it so well that over the past decades it's become a springtime tradition for Portlanders and valley residents to visit Schreiner's and enjoy the spectacle of five hundred named varieties of iris in bloom. It's a great way to discover eye-catching blossoms and order them on the spot for your own garden.

What makes this springtime ritual even more appealing is that Schreiner's is a hands-on family business. During the bloom season, especially on weekends, Schreiner's becomes like a big dawn-to-dusk family social. Chairs and picnic tables are set out on the lawn beneath the shade trees so visitors can relax, enjoy a picnic lunch after touring the 10 acres of display gardens, or just sit for a few minutes amid the sea of flowers. As with daffodils and tulips, the iris season doesn't last all that long, which makes you appreciate even more the care—and weeding—that has gone into creating this fabulous display.

For fabulous it is, with sixteen new introductions every year and a palette of colors that range from the inkiest of blacks to the purest of whites and just about every color in between: coppery bronzes, velvety purples, winey burgundies, azure blues, sunny yellows. (Pure red is the only color that iris hybridizers haven't been able to successfully achieve.) Some varieties are single colors, some are multihued. Size varies too, and the display beds combine dwarf, intermediate, and tall varieties, both bearded and beardless

(Japanese, Siberian, Louisiana). The iris beds are loaded with companion plants that add even more dazzling color.

The tall bearded iris that are the biggest sellers at Schreiner's are hybrids of two species: the bluish-lavender *Iris pallida*, native to Italy, the Tyrol, and the Adriatic, and the smaller, yellow-and-brown *I. variegata*, native to Hungary and the Balkans. The first hybrids appeared naturally on mountainsides where these two species grew together and were cross-pollinated by bees.

Named for Iris, the Greek goddess of the rainbow, and known as the rainbow flower because of its extraordinary range of colors, the iris has a long and fascinating cultural history. Iris root was used medicinally for centuries (and is still used today to make

orris root), and in many ancient civilizations the flowers accrued a royal symbolism. Herbaceous iris, also known as flags, were being cultivated in botanical gardens in Holland and England by the late sixteenth and early seventeenth centuries. Scientific classification and hybridization began in England in the early nineteenth century. The founding of the American Iris Society in 1920 led to further study, collection, propagation, hybridization, and naming of the many different iris species. At that time, however, iris were rarely available from American sources and had to be imported from England, France, or Germany.

Enter Francis X. Schreiner, a buyer for a department store in St. Paul, Minnesota. A chance meeting with John Wister, the first president of the American Iris Society, piqued Schreiner's initial interest and involvement with the family Iridaceae. By 1925 this German-American business traveler had collected more than five hundred varieties of iris and was growing them, with the help of his son, Robert, on an acre of ground in Minnesota. Eventually Francis X. decided to sell iris commercially and published his first catalog in 1928.

But freezing winters and the dust storms of the 1930s took a serious toll on the iris stock, and after much research into soil and growing conditions, Bob Schreiner moved the business to its present location in the central Willamette Valley. His two siblings, Connie and Gus, joined him a year later. As their business grew, especially during the iris boom of the 1970s, the original Schreiner iris farm expanded from 15 to 50 to 200 acres. It's now run by Liz, Ray, and Steve, the third generation of Schreiners to be in the business of iris.

Pull up a chair and enjoy the springtime spectacle of five hundred varieties of bearded, Japanese, Siberian, and Louisiana iris blooming at Schreiner's Iris Gardens in Salem, Oregon.

sebright gardens

7185 Lakeside Drive NE, Salem, OR 97305
sebrightgardens.com
Visit April to mid-June for blooms, but there is plenty to see
throughout the summer

📞 (503) 463-9615
🕐 Open Apr–Sep 10am–5pm, closed Tue–Wed in Apr and
Sep; check opening dates on Web site
$ Admission free
🐕 Dogs on leash

Hundreds of hostas, ferns, and epimediums are sold "under the big top" at Sebright Gardens.

Impressive display gardens showcasing hostas and other shade-loving plants

If you're looking for attractive and unusual herbaceous perennials to enliven the shadiest spots of your garden, this delightful nursery, owned and operated by self-avowed plant geek Tom Johnson and his partner, Kirk Hansen, is the place for you. Sebright specializes in hostas, ferns, and epimediums. The covered area where row upon row of these three stalwarts of the shade garden are neatly displayed is a bit mind boggling.

Who knew there were so many hostas? These hardy, easy-to-grow members of the asparagus family (Asparagacea) come in

Mid-America Garden

A partner garden to Sebright, and located adjacent to it, Mid-America Garden is devoted—and I mean *devoted*—to bearded iris. Founded some thirty years ago in Oklahoma City by Paul Black, a prize-winning iris hybridizer, Mid-America moved to the iris-friendly Willamette Valley in 1998. Black and Tom Johnson of Sebright Gardens introduce new hybrid varieties of bearded iris to their collection every year. Tall bearded iris, border bearded iris, tall miniature bearded iris, intermediate bearded iris, standard dwarf and miniature dwarf bearded iris—you can examine all of these and more in Mid-America Garden's colorful planting fields. beardedirisflowers.com.

an amazing variety of sizes, leaf shapes and textures, coloration, and flowering habits. That may explain why they have reputedly become the country's top-selling perennial. Most of the species that provide our modern plants were introduced from Japan (where they are used in cuisine) to Europe in the 1830s and made their way to U.S. gardens by the 1850s. You'll see dozens of varieties growing in Sebright's impressive display gardens, ranging in size from miniature (3 inches or less) to nearly giant (30 inches).

If you live west of the Cascades you're undoubtedly aware of sword ferns (*Polystichum munitum*), the hardiest and most ubiquitous evergreen fern in our coniferous forests and Northwest gardens. Sword ferns are bold and useful, but let's face it—they can be monotonous. If you want to expand your fern repertoire, Sebright sells about fifty different varieties of hardy garden ferns that tolerate all kinds of growing conditions, from shade to full sun. For alternatives to swords, have a look at the plumy soft-shield fern (*Polystichum setiferum* Plumosomultilobum Group); the evergreen lace fern (*Microlepia strigosa*) from Hawaii; or the beaded wood fern (*Dryopteris bissetiana*), whose glossy fronds look good in flower arrangements.

Epimediums, it seems, are the new darlings of the dry-shade garden. Collectors and plant people are rushing off to southern China, where most epimediums are found, to hunt for new species of these early-spring bloomers, and more hybrid varieties are appearing all the time. Many plants in this genus belonging to the barberry family (Berberidaceae) are reputed to be aphrodisiacs—especially the species known as horny goat weed (draw your own conclusions); other colorful common names for epimediums

include rowdy lamb herb, barrenwort, bishop's hat, and fairy wings. Deciduous or evergreen perennials with graceful branches and four-petaled flowers that range in color from white, pink, rose, and purple to yellow, orange, and red, epimediums require only two to three hours of sunlight a day, making them perfect buddy plants for hostas, ferns, and other shade lovers.

The display gardens at Sebright are a real delight and show off the amazing variety of plants that can be grown in the Pacific Northwest. There's a relaxed and pleasantly old-fashioned country ambience here that's matched by the friendliness of the helpful and hard-working owners.

eugene, central oregon & the oregon coast

A trail beside the Coast Fork of the
Willamette River at Mount Pisgah
Arboretum shows off the scenery
of the central Willamette Valley.

The Castle Crest Wildflower Garden is located along Rim Drive on Crater Lake, a seven-thousand-year-old volcanic caldera famed for its deep, clear, shimmering blue waters.

castle crest wildflower garden

East Rim Drive, Crater Lake National Park, Crater Lake, OR 97604
nps.gov/crla
Visit July and August

- 📞 (541) 594-3000
- 🕐 Park always open; garden blooms Jul–Aug
- 💲 Admission fee (to enter the national park)
- 🚌 In summer, buses leave from Crater Lake Lodge and make a loop around Rim Drive
- ♿ Parts of the trail require walking on flagstones through a wet meadow, unsuitable for those with limited mobility
- 🐕 No dogs

A short loop trail through forest and meadow above the deepest lake in North America spotlights native trees, plants, and wildflowers

Oregon's only national park preserves spectacularly beautiful Crater Lake, one of the wonders of the West. The lake, 26 miles in circumference and more than 1,900 feet deep, fills a caldera formed roughly seven thousand years ago when Mount Mazama blew its top in a series of volcanic eruptions and then collapsed. The deepest lake in North America, and the seventh deepest in the world, Crater Lake is remarkable for the clarity of its shimmering blue water.

Crater Lake National Park

Crater Lake National Park is open year-round, but because it receives an average of 14 feet of snowfall every year, July and August are the only reliably snowless months to see the park's alpine flora in action. The best way to view spectacular Crater Lake, cupped and shimmering beneath the 2,000-foot cliffs of its volcanic caldera, is by driving around it on the 33-mile Rim Drive. There are viewpoints and special areas along the way (including Castle Crest Wildflower Garden). If you want information on hiking trails and points of interest, stop in at the park headquarters, where you can also obtain tickets for boat rides on Crater Lake. Thanks to a refurbishment and upgrade in the 1990s, historic Crater Lake Lodge (usparklodging.com/craterlake) is once again the most inviting spot to stay in or near the park. If you don't stay at the lodge, at least stop in for a meal or a snack in the restaurant, just to enjoy the ambience.

Crater Lake is naturally the focal point of the park, but garden lovers visiting in July and August—the only time of the year when the park is free of snow—will want to add Castle Crest Wildflower Garden to their day's itinerary. A short, easy loop trail, at an elevation of 6,434 feet, takes about thirty minutes to complete and provides a marvelous introduction to the trees, plants, and flowers that are essential elements of this mountain's unique ecosystem.

The trail, laid out by Boy Scouts in 1929, first passes through a forest dominated by mountain hemlock and Shasta red fir, with a smaller component of subalpine fir and lodgepole pine. A multitude of flowering plants and wildflowers suited to moist soils and plenty of sunlight flourish in the wet meadow that is the highlight of this natural garden. Tiny mountain violets (*Viola lutea*), Gorman's buttercups (*Ranunculus gormanii*), pink alpine shooting stars (*Dodecatheon alpinum*), and white-flowered American bistort (*Polygonum bistortoides*) start the show while there's still snow on the ground.

A colorful hillside of Lewis's monkeyflower (*Mimulus lewisii*) blooms in July and August at the Castle Crest Wildflower Garden in Crater Lake National Park.

The color and complexion of the meadow, fed by streams and snowmelt, changes constantly over the summer months. Look for Pacific red elderberry (*Sambucus racemosa*), giant red Indian paintbrush (*Castilleja miniata*), Eastwood's willow (*Salix eastwoodiae*), Columbian monkshood (*Aconitum columbianum*), Pacific bleeding heart (*Dicentra formosa*), arrowleaf groundsel (*Senecio triangularis*), blue stickseed (*Hackelia micrantha*), Lewis's monkeyflower (*Mimulus lewisii*), and common pearly everlasting (*Anaphalis margaritacea*).

The dry slopes section of the garden was formed by pumice and loose rock ejected onto the slopes of Mount Mazama during its final eruption period. Pioneer grasses, spreading phlox, scarlet gilia, rabbitbrush goldenweed, and pussypaws are the most prominent plants that have adapted themselves to this thin, parched soil. Watch for rufous hummingbirds in this area, and the stocky gray American dipper that haunts the garden's gurgling, rock-strewn creek.

connie hansen garden

Small, richly textured coastal garden
hidden in a residential neighborhood

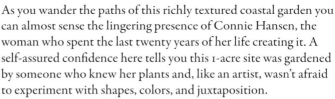

1931 NW 33rd Avenue, Lincoln City, Oregon 97367
conniehansengarden.com
Visit April through June for rhodies, azaleas, primulas, and
iris; July through September for perennials

....

📞 (541) 994-6338
🕐 Open daily year-round dawn to dusk; visitor center/gift
shop open Tue, Sat 10am–2pm
$ Admission by donation
♿ Grass-covered pathways may be difficult for wheelchairs
🐕 No dogs

Planted in the 1970s, a Japanese snowbell tree (*Styrax japonicus*) stands in front of a red-leafed Chinese stewartia (*Stewartia sinensis*) in the Connie Hansen Garden on the Oregon coast.

As you wander the paths of this richly textured coastal garden you can almost sense the lingering presence of Connie Hansen, the woman who spent the last twenty years of her life creating it. A self-assured confidence here tells you this 1-acre site was gardened by someone who knew her plants and, like an artist, wasn't afraid to experiment with shapes, colors, and juxtaposition.

The garden is hidden—enclosed might be a better word—within a residential neighborhood in Lincoln City. You could easily drive by and never be aware of it. Only a discreet sign and a small parking lot alert you to its presence. Though the garden is small, its artful design makes it seem much larger, with surprises to be found along its meandering paths and around every corner.

The property already had a bit of garden history when Connie Hansen bought it in 1973. The small Garden House that now serves as a visitor center and gift shop was the house and gallery of a local artist with the unfortunate name of Maud Wanker. It was she who started gardening on the site back in the 1950s. Fog-loving Sitka spruce (*Picea sitchensis*), old alders, and a tree-sized *Rhododendron* 'Cynthia' are legacies of the Wanker era.

Connie Hansen was a widow when she moved to Lincoln City, and her cherished garden in Walnut Creek, California, had just been demolished to make way for a BART station. She was ready to start a new life and a new garden, and this moist, sheltered site was perfect for growing her favorite plant, the iris. In late spring and early summer you will see an astonishing profusion of them, and companion primulas, growing in beds beside the creek that runs along the north side of the garden. This creek is spanned by three simple wooden bridges.

Connie Hansen's first plantings—Japanese snowbell (*Styrax japonicus*), Japanese maples, and *Magnolia* 'Alexandria'—are big

Cascade Head Trail

The area around Cascade Head, a giant headland about 10 miles north of Lincoln City, is so unique it has been designated a United Nations Biosphere Reserve. A rare example of a maritime prairie, the headland rises hundreds of feet above the Salmon River estuary and is home to native grasses and wildflowers as well as elk, deer, bald eagles, falcons, and great horned owls. The Nature Conservancy has created a remarkable 6-mile trail up, along the side, and over the top of Cascade Head all the way to the coastal town of Neskowin. The trail provides spectacular vistas of the Salmon River, the Coast Range, and the Pacific.

To reach the trailhead, turn west from U.S. 101 onto Three Rocks Road (just north of the Salmon River) and follow it about 2.5 miles to Knight County Park at the end. Park there and walk back to Savage Road, where you'll find a half-mile boardwalk trail that takes you to the trailhead. There's an initial thousand-foot elevation gain, after which the trail becomes relatively easy. This is a fragile ecosystem, so stay on the trail. No dogs or bikes are allowed.

trees now, and her collection of species and hybrid rhododendrons is fully mature. Hundreds of rhodies, from the tiniest varieties to the tree-sized *Rhododendron* 'Sir Charles Lemon' and *R.* 'Dame Nellie Melba', burst into bloom in April and May, complemented by spring bulbs, azaleas, and other flowering shrubs. The lush colors and interesting plant combinations are truly magical.

Irregularly shaped perennial beds created to house the hundreds of plants Connie grew from seeds were cut into what was originally lawn. Extended and expanded over the years, they add even more jewel-like splashes of color to the garden's palette, especially in summer and fall. Many of the plants that grow in these beds today are originals planted by Connie, but some have of necessity been replenished or replaced over the years. The volunteers who have overseen the garden since Connie Hansen's death in 1993 are dedicated to preserving her remarkable botanical legacy, but they also know that a garden is a living work of art that changes from year to year. They have extended the property and are creating new areas within it, such as the eye-catching heather berm, a small sunny hillock planted with masses of bronze, purple, and white heathers.

One of the great things about the Connie Hansen Garden is that there are always plants from the garden for sale, often rare or unusual varieties not commonly found in area nurseries. They're potted up and reasonably priced—a bonanza for collectors. The sale plants are outside the visitor center and you can buy them even if the visitor center is closed. (Put your money in one of the envelopes by the front entrance and slip it through the mail slot.) When the visitor center is open, you can buy seeds collected from the garden's special plants.

Private gardens in the United States rarely outlast their owners, but thankfully the special qualities of Connie Hansen's garden were recognized in her lifetime and have been preserved for lucky visitors today.

hendricks park

2198 Summit Avenue (Summit Avenue and Skyline Boulevard), Eugene, OR 97403
eugene-or.gov/facilities/Facility/Details/80
Visit year-round; April and May for rhodies

- 📞 (541) 582-4800 (Eugene Parks)
- 🕐 Open daily 6am–11pm
- $ Admission free
- ♿ Some steep hillside paths are unsuitable for wheelchairs
- 🐕 No dogs in Rhododendron Garden; on leash elsewhere

Historic city park on a hill with rhododendron garden, urban forest, and remnant oak savanna

A springtime stroll through Hendricks Park with the birds singing, the oak trees leafing out, and the rhododendrons blooming all around is a surefire antidote for the gray blahs of winter. Combine your visit to Hendricks Park with a ramble through nearby Mount Pisgah Arboretum and you have the makings of a pleasant day in the scenic southern Willamette Valley.

Eugene's oldest city park, 78-acre Hendricks Park was founded in 1906 on a hill about a mile from the University of Oregon campus. Half the land was donated by Thomas Hendricks, who served as Eugene's mayor and helped to establish the U of O. Hendricks wisely foresaw the value of preserving a portion of the area's landscape in its natural state for future generations to appreciate and enjoy. A mosaic of prairie, oak savanna, and oak woodland with Douglas-fir, the land acquired for the park was a microcosm of this hilly region's ancient landforms, wildlife habitats, and cultural history. Over the last century, however, much of the park has become a predominantly Douglas-fir forest that includes some two-hundred-year-old trees. The remnant oak knoll that has survived is considered so ecologically and historically valuable that its protection and restoration was a specific objective in the Hendricks Park Forest Management Plan created in 2000.

For thousands of years, oak woodland and savanna covered much of the southern Willamette Valley. It has been reduced to less than 7 percent of its historic range, making it among the most threatened ecosystems in North America. Approximately two hundred species

A dappled glade in the Rhododendron Garden at Hendricks Park invites a leisurely stroll even when the rhodies aren't in bloom.

Mount Pisgah Arboretum

About 9 miles southeast of Hendricks Park, Mount Pisgah rises 1,531 feet above the Coast and Middle forks of the Willamette River. Part of the Howard Buford Recreation Area, Lane County's largest park, Mount Pisgah Arboretum covers some 210 acres between the Coast Fork and the mountain's western slope. The diverse terrain includes riverside trails, paths through Douglas-fir and incense-cedar forests, and expansive views across remnants of the ancient white-oak savanna. Most of the arboretum has been left in its natural state, allowing visitors to enjoy the rough-edged beauty of native habitats. Rich in wildlife, the arboretum is home to threatened or endangered species of bats, Western pond turtles, and red-legged frogs, and its huge variety of migratory and resident songbirds, raptors, and waterfowl makes it one of the most popular birding spots in the region. 34901 Frank Parrish Road, Eugene, OR 97405. mountpisgaharboretum.com.

of birds, mammals, reptiles, and amphibians, including several rare species, use oak forest habitat. Although much of the oak habitat in the Willamette Valley has been replaced by agriculture and urban development, you can still see small pockets of the mighty white oaks in Hendricks Park, Mount Pisgah, and several locations along the 12-mile Ridgeline Trail system that connects Hendricks Park with other scenic buttes and foothills in south Eugene.

In Hendricks Park, you'll find many of these fine old white oak trees in the park's renowned Rhododendron Garden, established in 1951 by members of the quaintly named Eugene Men's Camellia and Rhododendron Club. More than six thousand unusual rhododendron species and hybrids, as well as many other interesting trees, shrubs, and perennial flowers, have been planted in this area since then. The floral show starts as early as February with the smoky purple *Rhododendron ririei,* peaks in April and May, and lasts into June with the fragrant white *R. auriculatum.* Interspersed with the rhodies and adding even more color to the woodland bouquet are yellow witch hazels and giant white magnolia blossoms. A different kind of beauty takes over when the rhododendrons fade and the dappled lawns and pathways invite summertime strolls.

The 12-acre Rhododendron Garden serves as a gateway to the rest of Hendricks Park. From here you can explore the Native Plant Garden, a living lexicon of plant species native to the southern Willamette Valley. Loaded with springtime delights such as trilliums and erythroniums, this garden was created in 2002 and reflects ongoing efforts to eradicate invasive species and restore the unique oak woodland ecosystem. The Native Plant Garden is a bridge between the Rhododendron Garden and the park's 60 acres of urban forest, which has been left relatively undisturbed except for hiking trails.

Remnants of the ancient oak savanna that once covered the Willamette Valley can still be seen at Mount Pisgah Arboretum near Eugene.

Owen Memorial Rose Garden

Rose lovers can easily combine a trip to Hendricks Park and Mount Pisgah Arboretum with a visit to Owen Memorial Rose Garden in Eugene. Located along the Willamette River near the Washington/Jefferson Street bridge, the 8.5-acre garden and riverfront park was established in 1951 and features more than forty-five hundred heritage and heirloom roses. The rose garden is also home to the Oregon Heritage Cherry Tree, thought to have been planted in 1847 from stock that came overland on the Oregon Trail. When it's covered in white blossoms in the spring, this ancient fruit tree outshines everything else in the garden. 1820 Roosevelt Boulevard, Eugene, OR 97402.

shore acres state park

89814 Cape Arago Highway, Coos Bay, Oregon 97420
shoreacres.net
Visit late February and March for spring bulbs; April to
mid-May for azaleas and rhododendrons; June through
September for roses, annuals, perennials

- 📞 (541) 888-2472
- 🕐 Open daily year-round 8am–sunset
- 💲 Admission fee (for state park)
- ♿ Beach inaccessible to those with limited mobility
- 🐕 No dogs

Beautifully maintained formal estate garden on the coast above a white-sand beach

This may be the only garden where you'll hear sea lions barking
as you sniff the roses. Though it's now a state park, Shore Acres
began life as the private estate of pioneer shipbuilder and lumberman Louis J. Simpson. As his fortunes rose, so did Simpson's social
ambitions. The enclosed observation building that now offers
visitors a protected spot to view the pounding waves of the Pacific
stands on the site of Simpson's two grandiose residences. The first
was destroyed by fire in 1921; its replacement was massive even by
today's McMansion standards: two stories high and 75 yards long.
Alas, after being the Gatsby of Oregon's central coast, Simpson lost
his fortune during the Depression, and his house with its 5-acre
formal garden fell into disrepair. The whole parcel was purchased
by the State of Oregon in 1942, and though the house couldn't be
salvaged, restoration work began on the gardens in the 1970s.

Thank heavens someone had the foresight to recreate this rare
and enchanting botanical relic of a bygone age. There is nothing

This aerial view of Shore Acres State Park shows the layout of Louis Simpson's formal gardens and the white-sand beach below.

Darlingtonia State Natural Site

What, you ask, is *Darlingtonia*, the plant protected at this small wayside site just off whizzing Highway 101? Well, *Darlingtonia californica* (a.k.a. cobra lily or California pitcher plant) is a unique and increasingly endangered plant indigenous to boggy areas in northern California and southwestern Oregon. And the darling *Darlingtonia* just happens to be carnivorous. It's not a man-eater, but it does trap and digest hapless insects that are lured in by the nectar in its yellow-and-red flowers and are then trapped by stiff hairs and slide down the tube to their doom. A boardwalk allows you to view *Darlingtonia* in its natural habitat—an eerily beautiful sight. It looks as though hundreds of bright-green eyeless cobras are rising from the bog. Highway 101, 5 miles north of Florence, Oregon.

South Slough National Estuarine Research Reserve

In 1972 the South Slough inlet of the Coos River became the first federally protected estuary in the United States. Once you see it, you'll understand why these 5,000 acres of tidal flats, vast marshes, and meandering channels are so important to the health of the coastal ecosystem. Stop in at the Interpretive Center for a map and take the Railroad Trail and then the Sloughside Trail to see the characteristic estuarine habitats. It's an easy hike, about a mile each way, and the pristine coastal scenery is absolutely glorious. 61907 Seven Devils Road, Charleston, OR 97420. southsloughestuary.org.

like Shore Acres anywhere else on the Oregon coast—for the very good reason that the weather conditions make seaside gardening on this scale a difficult proposition.

After driving through dense coastal forest to reach Shore Acres, you will find it something of a surprise to step into this expansive and beautifully maintained formal garden with its decorative palm trees. You enter through a portico (information and gift shop to one side) that frames the garden's long central axis with its brick paving and charming central fountain. Quadrants of green lawn edged with boxwood contain smaller boxwood parterres filled with spring-blooming azaleas and rhododendrons, August-blooming dahlias, and more than six hundred rose bushes—a miraculous sight along the Oregon coast—at their best in June and July. To the east sits the former caretaker's cottage and a gazebo with border plantings of red and white astilbe. At the southern end of the formal garden, steps lead down to a picturesque water garden filled with water lilies and edged with acanthus. On warm sunny days this scenic spot, with dragonflies zooming over the water lilies and tadpoles swimming beneath them, is a favorite place for painters to set up their easels.

The lovely water garden at Shore Acres State Park is a favorite spot for painters to set up their easels.

Beyond the gate just west of the water garden you enter the coastal woodlands that serve as a buffer between the sea and the gardens. A fairly easy path leads down to Simpson's Beach, a beautiful crescent of white sand in a protected cove between towering cliffs. If you continue on the path beyond the beach you'll see the offshore island that is home to seabirds and those barking sea lions.

washington

seattle
& vicinity

Blossoming cherry trees along Azalea Way are a famous sight in Seattle's Washington Park Arboretum.

bellevue botanical garden

12001 Main Street, Bellevue, WA 98005
bellevuebotanical.org
Visit year-round; June through September for
    perennial garden

....

- 📞 (425) 452-2750
- 🕐 Gardens open daily dawn to dusk, visitor center daily
    9am–4pm
- 💲 Admission free
- 🚌 Public transportation
- 🐕 No dogs

Eye-opening surprise in the midst of residential neighborhoods and office parks

In just a couple of decades on either side of the turn of the
twenty-first century, Bellevue, Washington, grew from a small,
low-key suburb of Seattle to a high-rise city for high-tech companies like Microsoft. The change came so rapidly and altered the
landscape so drastically that the creation in 1992 of a botanical
garden that preserves a portion of Bellevue's old terrain can be
seen as a fortuitous event. The scope and variety of the land and
display gardens found on these 53 acres near downtown Bellevue
comes as an eye-opening surprise and provides a welcome respite
from the increasingly enclosed residential neighborhoods and
office parks around it.

Bold colors and dramatic year-round displays characterize the Perennial Border Garden at Bellevue Botanical Garden.

Stop in first at the new visitor center, opened in 2014, and pick up a map. From here you can head off to explore specific display gardens or follow trails and pathways that loop through the entire garden. (Allow about seventy-five minutes if you want to see everything.)

The low-slung house in the gardens was formerly the home of Cal and Harriet Shorts, whose bequest of the house and surrounding gardens led to the establishment of the Bellevue Botanical Garden. Designed in 1957 by noted Northwest architect Paul Kirk (who also designed, three years later, the beautiful guesthouse at Bloedel Reserve), the house exemplifies Kirk's mid-century blending of Asian and Northwest styles to create a kind of regional International style that is quietly attuned to the landscape.

A trail at the southeast corner of the house leads downhill to the Tateuchi Viewing Pavilion overlooking the Rhododendron Glen and the lush Ground Cover Garden, where a profusion of ground covers grows beneath maples and alongside a stream. The main path continues through the Rhododendron Glen at the edge of a second-growth forest. This original portion of the Shorts's garden is planted with fifty different varieties of rhododendron, a colorful delight from spring through early summer, as well as summer-blooming hydrangeas, winter-blooming Oriental paper-bush (*Edgeworthia chrysantha*) with its fragrant yellow blossoms, and a premier collection of some 750 hardy ferns.

From the Rhododendron Glen, the path brings you to the wooden entrance gate of the Yao Garden, a traditional Japanese garden planted with delicate Japanese maples, azaleas, rhododendrons, and viburnums. This small contemplative garden honors Bellevue's relationship with Yao, its sister city in Japan, and uses Japanese stone lanterns as focal points.

A path off the main trail from the Rhododendron Glen loops south through the Native Discovery Garden, a landscape where native plants—all of them ecologically sound and low maintenance—illustrate how a garden can be adapted to the climate and conditions of the Pacific Northwest. Adjacent to a natural wetland, this area features a bronze sculpture by David Maritz titled "Owl's Glare," showing an owl in flight.

From here, another branch off the main trail leads through the woods to an area called The Ravine Experience. As you cross the suspension bridge that spans a deep, natural ravine, you get a bird's-eye view of the area's original topography, native understory, wildlife, and conifers.

If you return to the main trail, now called the Lost Meadow Trail, and head north, you'll pass a beautiful stand of mature alders and wend your way through a 10-acre area of woodlands, meadows, and wetlands now being restored and enhanced to create native plant communities. Back in the 1930s, this reclaimed meadow area was cleared for farming.

The Lost Meadow Trail joins the Tateuchi Loop Trail, which will bring you to the remarkable Perennial Border Garden planted in tiers along a sloping hillside framed by deciduous trees and shrubs. Renowned for its bold colors and dramatic year-round displays, this award-winning garden is maintained by the Northwest Perennial Alliance.

The trail winds around to the Waterwise Garden beside the Shorts's residence. This alluring landscape with its diverse array of plants illustrates how Northwest gardeners can create healthier home gardens that conserve water, lower chemical use, reduce run-off, recycle waste, and preserve habitat, all without sacrificing beauty.

The Fuchsia Garden adjacent to the Waterwise Garden offers a dazzling display of perennial fuchsias that bloom from early summer through fall. There are some one hundred different varieties of winter-hardy fuchsias that can be grown in the Pacific Northwest, attracting hummingbirds and providing an amazing variety of flower forms and colors.

The Alpine Garden is another showcase garden you won't want to miss. Granite outcrops with gravelly margins recreate an alpine environment with tiny wildflowers and mountain hemlock adapted to the harsh conditions found high in the mountains.

A springtime swath of daffodils brightens the grounds behind the Mid-Century Modern house of Cal and Harriet Shorts, now part of Bellevue Botanical Garden.

bloedel reserve

7571 Dolphin Drive, Bainbridge Island, WA 98110
bloedelreserve.org
Visit year-round; April through June for spring bulbs,
   rhododendrons, camellias

- 📞 (206) 842-7631
- 🕐 Open year-round Tue–Sun 10am–4pm; Jun–Aug
  Thur–Sun until 7pm
- $ Admission fee
- ♿ Wheelchairs available, some paths not wheelchair
  accessible
- 🚌 Unless you live on Bainbridge Island, you'll need to take
  a ferry to get there
- 🐕 No dogs

One of the country's great gardens, artfully woven into a forested maritime landscape

Bloedel Reserve is the Pacific Northwest version of a grand
English or European estate, where guests are met at a gatehouse
and ushered into a world of impeccably maintained grounds. It's
one of the great gardens of the United States, but let's get something straight right off the bat: you won't find showy beds of
ornamental flowers or bright perennial borders, as you would, say,
at The Butchart Gardens. The glory of Bloedel Reserve is the way
Northwest native and nonnative plants, shrubs, and trees have
been skillfully combined to create a series of gardens that are artfully woven into a forested, maritime landscape.

    That's not to say you won't see flowers or color—far from it.
In the spring, the woods and meadows are lushly carpeted with
naturalized bulbs, banks of rhododendrons and camellias put
on a spectacular show, and the unique Moss Garden glows with
an almost unearthly green luminescence. In the summer, along
the sun-dappled forest trails, you'll encounter blue-flowered

Flanked by majestic English elms, the Bloedel residence sits in a setting reminiscent of an English landscape park.

hydrangeas, and in the fall, the leaves of Japanese maples and clumps of cyclamen add vivid splashes. These gardens unfold and reveal their beauties in a natural seasonal progression that never feels forced.

It takes a fortune to create and maintain an estate garden of this caliber, and Prentice Bloedel's fortune came from his father's timber company, where he worked until his retirement in 1950 at age fifty. The 150 acres he then bought on Bainbridge Island were covered with a second- and third-growth forest of Douglas-fir and western red cedar. (The land had been logged a century earlier.) Bloedel and his wife, Virginia, lived on the property from 1951 until 1986 in a French chateau-style house that had been built by the previous owner in 1931. About 70 acres of the estate were left as undisturbed forest, and the remaining 80 acres—now cared for by ten full-time gardeners—were shaped into the series of gardens the public enjoys today. Although Prentice Bloedel consulted and worked with some of the top landscape architects of the day, the overall vision for the gardens was his alone. (His sister-in-law, Eulalie Wagner, was also a gardener and started her own garden at Lakewold, in the Tacoma/South Sound area.)

Pick up a map when you arrive because there is no signage along the winding trails, and, if you're able, follow the route that gives you the full tour. It begins at the Meadow where the Bloedels once pastured their herd of sheep, skirts around the Bird Marsh, and continues into a woodland with towering, moss-draped conifers, ferns, salal, and spring wildflowers. Within the forest, a trestle bridge crosses a stream and an artfully constructed boardwalk traverses a bog that's home to native carnivorous cobra lilies (*Darlingtonia californica*) and giant yellow skunk cabbage (*Lysichiton americanus*). The path emerges into a parklike setting with a pond and attendant weeping willow surrounded by lush green lawns and fringed by giant cedars. The Bloedel residence, open to the public, sits at the end of this domesticated landscape. The house, flanked by two majestic English elms, is more a period curiosity than a piece of notable architecture, but you'll want to go in to see the furnished living room, dining room, and library on the first floor. Interestingly, the area behind the house, with its sweeping view of Port Madison Bay, was of little interest to the Bloedels and they never did much with it.

The Waterfall Overlook just north of the house leads down to a picturesque waterfall area planted with flowering shrubs and spring ephemerals. Continuing north, you pass a beautiful grove of Himalayan birches and come to Christmas Pond. This area, presented as a Christmas gift from Prentice to his wife in 1970, features a romantic little bridge over a stream planted with pink candelabra primroses, Virginia Bloedel's favorite flower.

Dozens of rhododendron species and thousands of spring-blooming bulbs and wildflowers enliven The Glen, and the rare coral root orchid—a once-hardy native that's becoming increasingly rare—can be seen growing on decaying logs along the Orchid Trail.

The architectural highlight of Bloedel Reserve is the guesthouse designed by Paul Kirk in 1960. A synthesis of a Japanese teahouse and a Northwest Native American longhouse, the structure sits within a small but masterful Japanese garden designed by Fujitaro Kubota (creator of Kubota Garden). The nearby Moss Garden is another highlight. Prentice Bloedel tried to start this

Native mosses form a soft green carpet in the Moss Garden at Bloedel Reserve.

garden by planting plugs of Irish moss. The Irish moss triggered the emergence of eleven native mosses that now cover the earth like a green velvet carpet.

The final segment of the tour brings you to the Reflection Pool, a tranquil spring-fed pool enclosed within an English yew hedge, and the Camellia Walk, a woodland path lined with enormous camellias that leads you back to the gatehouse. At the end of your visit, I can almost guarantee you'll agree with Prentice Bloedel, who described Bloedel Reserve as "a place where people find refreshment and tranquility in the presence of natural beauty."

Visiting Bloedel Reserve is an easy and enjoyable adventure that requires a scenic forty-minute ferry ride across Puget Sound from downtown Seattle. (There is another ferry from Edmonds, north of Seattle.) Washington state ferries (wsdot.com/ferries) run all day and into the evening, so you can combine your garden visit with breakfast, lunch, or dinner in Winslow, the main town on Bainbridge Island.

dunn gardens

Graceful estate garden landscaped
by Olmsted Brothers on a bluff
overlooking Puget Sound

Flanked by old stone urns, this little stairway beside the Tennis Court Lawn at Dunn Gardens evokes the grace and charm of Olmsted Brothers' original design.

13533 Northshire Road NW, Seattle, WA 98177
dunngardens.org
Visit April through June; October for fall foliage

- 📞 (206) 362-0933
- 🕐 Open Apr–Jul and Sep–Oct for guided tours by reservation at 1pm Thurs, 10am and 1pm Fri, and 10am Sat; closed Aug
- $ Admission fee
- 🚌 Public transportation
- No children under twelve
- No dogs

When Arthur Dunn, wealthy owner of Pier 71 in Seattle, bought several acres of logged-off land on a bluff overlooking Puget Sound to be used as a summer retreat for his family, he hired the most famous landscape design firm in America to create the garden. In 1915 Olmsted Brothers started work on Dunn's "country place"—today's Dunn Gardens. The gardens have matured and changed over the ensuing century, but the essential Olmsted aesthetic remains intact. The basic components of an Olmsted garden will be recognizable and understandable as you walk through this wonderfully preserved example.

At its simplest, an Olmsted design creates sweeping green lawns and surrounds them with naturalistic groupings of trees, flowering borders, shrubs, and ground covers, always enhancing views, natural water features, and rock outcrops. The artfulness of an Olmsted design is its apparent artlessness—nothing looks forced or unnatural. In their plantings, Olmsted Brothers favored reds, purples, and whites. Yellow was severely frowned upon.

At the time the garden was created, only a few Douglas-firs were left on the property. Many of the deciduous trees the Olmsteds chose for the new garden were to be shipped from Ohio by train. The train got stuck in a blizzard, however, and the trees never made it west, so local trees were used instead. Their age now gives them a stately grace, but over the decades the trees have closed off the view of Puget Sound and the Olympic Mountains that Dunn found so appealing. Some trees were damaged in the ice storm of 2012.

In the 1940s, after Arthur Dunn's death, the estate was divided among family members and today consists of three separate properties with a connecting path that winds through four major sections of the garden.

Between 1948 and 1991, the eastern portion of the estate, once the site of the "motor garage" and kitchen garden, was enhanced and developed into a woodland garden by Edward R. Dunn, Arthur's son. Dunn turned the garage into a house (today's visitor center), added a rock-edged pond and water garden, and planted a rich mixture of rhododendrons, dogwoods, and maples beneath the canopy of Douglas-fir, chestnuts, and maples. This area is known for its splendid seasonal effects. In the springtime, an abundance of forest-loving trilliums and erythroniums grace the paths, and the lawns are covered with thousands of crocus. In the summer, a perennial flower border adds an edge of color, and the deciduous trees turn burnished shades of orange and red in the fall.

The Ravine Trail winds westward through a stand of large conifers to the Great Lawn, a lush green carpet surrounded by a dense tree canopy that was a central feature of the original Olmsted-designed estate. The Croquet Lawn, bordered by a berm of winter heather and perennial flowers, is another seasonal and textural delight in this historic garden. For a more contemporary take on garden design, have a look at the Curators' Garden behind the visitor center. There, co-curators Charles Price and Glen Withey have created a small garden of their own using a bright, brilliant palette of plant color decidedly different from the muted tones favored by Olmsted Brothers. There's even yellow.

elisabeth carey miller botanical garden

Tiered botanical garden with a Puget Sound view, created by a renowned plantswoman

The Elisabeth Carey Miller Botanical Garden is a fabled place, in part because it is so difficult to get into. Only five hundred people are allowed in per year, and the five hundred "early bird" slots that become available in September (for the following season) always vanish in a couple of hours, as do the slots that become available in February. It's as challenging as trying to procure a seat at the Bayreuth Festival, but worth the effort if you're a dedicated plantsperson or garden aficionado.

The garden was Elisabeth (Betty) Miller's private domain and plant laboratory. It has a somewhat rarified feel to it, in part because of its tony surroundings in The Highlands, a century-old gated community on Puget Sound in north Seattle. Once past the gatekeeper, you follow an immaculately groomed road through a quiet and quintessential Pacific Northwest maritime landscape to the house where Betty lived with her husband, Pendleton. It's not a manse. In fact, it's rather modest, in that well-mannered, well-built, and unpretentious style of the late 1940s. But it's the rear of the house you'll see first, as you walk up from the parking lot below. The site, with its west-facing view across Puget Sound to Bainbridge Island, slopes down in tiers, much like a garden on the Mediterranean. And it's on these west-facing slopes, landscaped

Address provided when you make a reservation
millergarden.org
Visit May through September

....

📞 (206) 362-8612
🕐 Open May–Sep by reservation only
$ Donation requested
🏷 The garden can only be visited on a tour; tours fill up quickly and must be booked in advance for following year; you can reserve early (in Sep) for a fee, or in Feb
🐕 No dogs

Betty Miller's important collection of alpine plants was preserved by replanting it in beds around a new stone stairway.

with many of the four thousand or so plants in the Miller collection, that the magic of this garden becomes apparent.

Pendleton Miller was a Yale-educated lawyer, but it was Betty who wore the plants in the family. Born in Montana, she studied at the University of Washington and eventually became known as one of the most knowledgeable plantswomen in the country. When it came to cultivating plants, she was dedicated and demanding, always searching out new species, testing them in her garden, and introducing them to the public. Hybrids were not of much interest to her; it was species that she collected and grew, no matter how finicky and difficult. She obtained seeds and starts from sources around the world, but—like most plant collectors—found Asia to be a particularly rich source of attractive and unusual plant material. She was the first person in the United States to cultivate golden Japanese forest grass (*Hakonechloa macra* 'Aureola'), now a garden staple.

About two-thirds of this approximately 4-acre garden is in shade, and discovering attractive shade-tolerant plants was one of her lifelong passions. In the Upper Woodland and other shady areas, for instance, she planted dozens of forms of trillium with flowers that are white, beige, purple, and even a luscious black. Species rhododendrons add rich bursts of woodland color in the spring, and Japanese maples and other *Acer* species add a vibrant autumn glow. Her attention to detail is apparent everywhere you look.

The Miller Garden, like any other garden, has inevitably changed over the years. Trees and shrubs have matured, some plants have spread or died, and new plants have been introduced. But the basic focus of Betty's botanical attention remains unchanged. As you descend from the Upper Woodland down to the terraces behind the house, the scope and variety of this collection becomes apparent.

She was interested in ground covers for their aesthetic appeal and because they could be used to help minimize weeds. Epimediums, with their charming spiderlike flowers, interesting foliage, and ability to grow in dry-shade conditions, were another interest. Some two hundred forms of epimediums are planted in the Miller Garden, and the curatorial staff is evaluating many of the new species that have become known and available since the opening of China. And what would a shady garden be without ferns? There are more than 240 fern species and cultivars here, including old and rare ferns. Another woodland plant Betty collected and cultivated was hepatica. The garden contains more than a hundred selections of this lovely woodland plant, many of them brilliantly colored cultivars from Japan.

Betty's collection of alpine plants has changed the most, in large part because more and more shade was being cast on the original alpine beds from maturing trees. To remedy this situation and preserve the collection, a new stone stairway was constructed with new beds for the sun-loving alpines on either side.

Betty Miller didn't keep her botanical knowledge to herself. She was active in dozens of local and national gardening organizations, introduced many new plants to gardeners, and was instrumental in establishing the Center for Urban Horticulture at the University of Washington Botanic Gardens. She selected the plantings for Seattle's Freeway Park, which opened in 1976, and for traffic islands throughout the city. She and her husband were major philanthropists, and endowed the Elisabeth C. Miller Botanical Library at the Center for Urban Horticulture. The library, as one might expect from a woman whose garden is a Northwest treasure, contains one of the largest and finest collections of plant and garden books in the nation. You might not be able to get into the Elisabeth Carey Miller Botanical Garden, but you can always get into the botanical library that bears her name.

Columns created by the artists Little and Lewis provide a colorfully dramatic entryway to the Evergreen Arboretum and Gardens.

evergreen arboretum and gardens

145 Alverson Boulevard, Everett, WA 98201
evergreenarborteum.com
Visit year-round; spring and summer for flowering shrubs and perennials

- ☎ (425) 257-8597
- ◷ Open daily dawn to dusk
- $ Admission free
- 🚌 Public transportation
- 🐕 Dogs on leash

Imaginative mix of trees, plants, and outdoor sculptures that serves as a shining example for community parks everywhere

The Evergreen Arboretum and Gardens sets a shining example for community parks and gardens everywhere. An imaginative mix of trees, plants, and well-placed outdoor sculptures, it has the coherence and sophistication you'd expect to find in a well-maintained private garden. But community is the key element that has made Evergreen such a success, for it takes the ongoing efforts of a dedicated board and volunteers working together with state, city, and local governments and businesses to keep a garden of this caliber going and growing.

The arboretum and gardens have evolved considerably since 1963, when the Everett Parks Department first donated 8 acres of land to the Everett Garden Club for a new arboretum. A few years later, the Parks Department took the land back, gave it to the newly enlarged Legion Memorial Golf Course, and moved the arboretum to a smaller 3.5-acre site. (The first tree ever planted, a pin oak, still resides on the tenth hole of the golf course.) In the 1970s it was decided that the new site should include themed and display gardens as a way to educate the public about plant and landscaping options that work well in Pacific Northwest urban residential settings. The recently installed Small Urban Tree Walk is a good example of how the garden incorporates education into its landscaping. A winding pedestrian pathway that links Legion Park to the arboretum and gardens, the walk is planted with attractive trees that won't reach more than 35 feet tall and can be grown beneath power lines in an urban setting.

The entrance to the arboretum and gardens is signaled by striking blue concrete columns made by the popular Bainbridge Island–based artists George Little and David Lewis. Adjacent to the entrance area is the Snohomish County Master Gardener Demonstration Bed, installed in the mid-1990s and loaded

with a colorful selection of easy-to-care-for plants chosen and maintained by the Snohomish County chapter of Washington State University Master Gardeners. Take a look at the smooth, light-colored pavements that lead you deeper into the gardens. They're made from pervious crushed glass and a binding agent that lets the surface absorb water.

The Conifer Garden, the first garden to be planted in 1979 at the new site, contains a beautiful collection of cone-bearing trees in the cypress, yew, and pine families. They all have different forms—upright, weeping, or prostrate—and range in color from green to blue to yellow. From here, the path leads you up an incline to the Viewing Mound, a garden overlook created in 2005 on excavated fill. The focal point here is Pam Hom's fountain titled "Fibonacci," a finned metal dome that directs water down in a spiral pattern. The lower flanks of the mound were redesigned in 2006 as a rock garden with an assortment of low-growing, drought-resistant alpine plants.

The plants along the Northwest Native Trail that links the Viewing Mound to the open-air pavilion were selected to demonstrate the variety of low-maintenance, disease-resistant native plants that can easily be grown in a Northwest garden. From here, the path leads you over to the west side of the garden, shaded by tall Douglas-firs. Here you'll find the environmentally friendly Rain Garden. At first glance it may look like nothing more than a shallow depression lined with rocks and fringed by native woodland plants and ferns. But this garden, a collaborative effort of the Master Gardeners and the Department of Public Works, is carefully designed to collect, absorb, and filter storm water runoff from asphalt and other nonpermeable city surfaces, thus reducing the volume of pollutants entering sewers and, ultimately, Puget Sound. This area is also home to the Woodland Garden and Fernery and the Japanese Maple Grove, a collection of twenty-five outstanding cultivars that vary in leaf shape and growth habit, and range in color from dark green to burgundy and hot pink.

The Evergreen Arboretum and Gardens is an ongoing adventure, with new projects planned for the future. It represents the very best of collaborative community garden partnerships, and once you've seen it, I'm pretty sure you'll agree that it fulfills its stated mission "to spread understanding and enjoyment related to the plant world by providing an easily accessible public garden dedicated to study, relaxation, and inspiration."

"Fibonacci," an intriguing metal fountain by artist Pam Hom, is one of the many pieces of outdoor sculpture at Evergreen Arboretum and Gardens.

heronswood

A much-loved and freshly resurrected garden filled with rare and exotic plants

7530 NE 288th Street, Kingston, WA 98346
heronswood.com
Visit on open days April through September

A tall hedge of
hornbeam encloses
a small pond at
Heronswood, a
fabled garden on
the Kitsap Peninsula
west of Seattle.

📞 (360) 297-7410
🕐 Open three times per year (for spring, summer, and fall
plant sales) or by reservation for groups of ten or more
$ Admission free for sales; fee for garden
🐕 No dogs

Few gardens in the Pacific Northwest have prompted as much angst, drama, ecstasy, and despair as Heronswood. The story of how this fabled garden on the Kitsap Peninsula fell victim to corporate mismanagement and nearly vanished, only to be resurrected by a local Native American tribe, has all the makings of a prime-time soap opera.

Founded in 1987 by legendary plantsman and explorer Dan Hinkley and his partner, architect Robert L. Jones, Heronswood quickly developed into a mecca for plant enthusiasts thanks to the abundance of rare and tantalizing plants offered for sale and to the expertly designed and maintained display garden. Occupying a densely forested 15-acre site about 25 miles northwest of Seattle, the garden grew into a dazzling botanical showcase with some ten thousand plant species, many of them grown from seed collected by the indefatigable Hinkley during his plant-hunting expeditions to Asia. Heronswood was more than just a pretty garden—it was a plant laboratory with an emphasis on responsible collection and evaluation to ensure that newly introduced species would not become invasive. Plant lovers unable to visit the garden during the plant sales could order from a Heronswood catalog that listed more than twenty-four hundred plants.

Small wonder that Heronswood gained international renown. And small wonder, too, that a giant seed company cast its corporate eyes in the direction of Heronswood. Gardens are about growing plants, and corporations are about growing money, and this corporation was about growing money from growing plants that it hadn't grown itself. It wanted to acquire and sell Hinkley's seed stock and plant material to a larger market. And who wouldn't be flattered and excited at the prospect of seeing their business expand and reaping a financial reward for years of hard work? It's the American dream, after all.

Heronswood was at its zenith when, in 2000, Hinkley and Jones sold it to the W. Atlee Burpee Company, based in Pennsylvania. Fans were apprehensive, but Hinkley and Jones remained at the helm and for a while all went on as usual. Then, in 2006, Burpee abruptly shuttered the place and transferred the stock to Pennsylvania, saying that the Heronswood nursery was not profitable. They backed up their decision with the preposterous claim that gardeners are "predominantly on the East Coast." The ensuing uproar within the gardening world was deafening, but I'm sure it didn't hurt Burpee's bottom line.

For the next six years the once-great garden at Heronswood was minimally maintained while Burpee unsuccessfully sought another buyer for the property. For a while it looked like Heronswood might end up as condos and a golf course, but fortunately a Pacific Northwest Native American tribe, the Port Gamble S'Klallam, purchased the property at a sealed-bid auction in June 2012. Committed to restoring the garden to its former glory, the tribe hired renowned gardener Nancy Heckler as general manager. Hinkley and Jones both serve on the restoration steering committee.

So now Heronswood is growing again, and the garden's most celebrated features live on: the extensive woodland garden, with its plethora of rare plants and water feature created by local artists George Little and David Lewis; the long, curving Blue and Yellow Border; the mixed borders surrounding the house; and the elegant potager, with its sculpted hornbeam arches. Although visitors now have to pay admission to see the garden during the three yearly plant sales, the sales can be attended free of charge and feature the cream of the Northwest's specialty nurseries—reason alone to plan your visit accordingly.

There may be no second acts in American lives, as F. Scott Fitzgerald famously remarked, but fortunately there are sometimes second acts in American gardens. Heronswood is one of them.

Visitors can enjoy the restored gardens at Heronswood during the plant sales held three times a year.

kruckeberg botanic garden

20312 15th Avenue NW, Shoreline, WA 98177
kruckeberg.org
Visit year-round; April and May for spring bulbs and
    flowering trees and shrubs

- 📞 (206) 546-1281
- 🕐 Open year-round Fri–Sun 10am–5pm
- $ Admission by donation
- ♿ Lower garden area may be difficult for wheelchairs
- 🐕 Dogs on leash

Rare and native flora assembled in a wooded setting by a botany professor and an artist

It never ceases to amaze me how many beautiful and fascinating gardens are hidden away in otherwise nondescript neighborhoods throughout the Pacific Northwest. Kruckeberg Botanic Garden is one of them. This small and appealing public garden was the home and botanic laboratory of Dr. Arthur Kruckeberg, a professor of botany at the University of Washington, and his wife, Mareen, an artist and self-taught horticulturist. They bought the 4-acre property in 1958 when it was a farm, and spent the next half century amassing a collection of rare and native flora. Today some two thousand species are represented here, everything from champion trees (meaning they are the largest of their species in the state or region) to tiny ground covers. The plants are labeled to make identification easy.

This is not a fussy or overly manicured garden, which is another reason it's so likeable. There's a lived-in quality to it, as if the Kruckebergs had just taken off their gloves and gone home

Outdoor sculptures complement the arboreal delights found at Kruckeberg Botanic Garden in north Seattle.

after a day of gardening. But it's also very focused, because all the plants here, no matter how exotic, do well in the cool, moist climate of Puget Sound. The trick (as every gardener knows) is in the placement, which must provide optimum growing conditions for the plant and also show off its distinctive features.

A variety of choice trees, shrubs, and dry-shade plants (lots of autumn cyclamen in August and September) border the wide paved path that leads from the entrance gate. Here you'll see examples of low-growing Japanese white pine (*Pinus parviflora*), the deciduous dawn redwood (*Metasequoia glyptostroboides*) from China, and tall stewartia (*Stewartia monadelpha*) with its striking cinnamon-brown bark. The pathway leads to MsK Rare and Native Plant Nursery, which can easily distract you from continuing farther into the garden. Come back after you've seen the many rare delights in the lower garden—some of the plants you'll encounter are for sale at the nursery.

Dr. Kruckeberg collected seeds and cuttings from colleagues and plant enthusiasts around the world. Mareen, the artistic eye of the pair, was instrumental in deciding where the seedlings or cuttings were planted. The Kruckebergs used the Douglas-firs and other native plants on the property as background for their constantly expanding collection.

There's no particular way to explore the garden. Follow the path and let your eye guide you to the plants you find most intriguing. The trees show off an impressive range of bark textures, growth habits, leaf and needle shapes, and colors. Among the interesting personalities you'll meet at this international gathering of coniferous and deciduous trees and woodland shrubs are the Japanese striped-bark maple (*Acer capillipes*), the Japanese larch (*Larix kaempferi*) with its delicate cones, the trident maple (*Acer buergerianum*) from eastern China, and the rather forbidding-looking Spanish fir (*Abies pinsapo*) with its stiff, needle-sharp branches and upright cone clusters. A magnificent giant sequoia, 90 feet tall and grown from a small cutting planted by Dr. Kruckeberg in 1958, is the oldest tree in the collection.

The garden is enhanced by large outdoor sculptures and rustic benches. Future projects include the development of a new Bog Garden (love that skunk cabbage!) and a California-Oregon bioregional garden.

The MsK Rare and Native Plant Nursery located behind the Kruckeberg's converted 1904 farmhouse is reason enough to pay a visit to this garden. It's one of best nurseries in the region for unusual and hard-to-find woodland plants, all of them propagated from seeds and cuttings taken from plants in the Kruckeberg collection. You'll find native plants for sun or shade, alpine rarities from the Siskiyous and Cascades, ferns, trilliums, bog plants, and more. The nursery was Mareen Kruckeberg's idea, and plant sales help defray some of the garden's operating costs. This is not a mail-order operation; you have to shop on-site.

kubota garden

Living work of art developed by a top
Japanese gardener on land he owned

A river of flowing springtime color graces this corner of Seattle's Kubota Garden.

9817 55th Avenue S, Seattle, WA 98178
kubotagarden.org
Visit year-round; March through June for azaleas and rhododendrons

- 📞 (206) 684-4584
- 🕐 Open daily year-round
- $ Admission free
- ♿ Wheelchair accessible as far as Tom Kubota Stroll Garden
- 🐕 Dogs on leash

All Japanese gardens share the same aesthetic principles developed hundreds of years ago, yet each one is unique in terms of plant material and the way the garden has been shaped to fit a particular terrain. The Seattle Japanese Garden, for example, is a formal strolling garden with exactingly created miniature landscapes meant to be viewed from several points along a path. Kubota Garden, on the other hand, is larger and less restrained, with smaller gardens within it and areas that look almost wild (though nothing is ever completely wild in a Japanese garden). Kubota offers more surprises and secret places, with its hills and valleys, streams, and waterfall.

One other major difference between the two gardens: the Seattle Japanese Garden was created for a specific site in the University of Washington Arboretum, while Kubota Garden was created on a site that was originally the home, business office, and plant nursery for one of Seattle's top Japanese gardeners and garden designers. The property expanded over the years and evolved into a living work of art. Today it is a public park and a historic landmark within the city of Seattle.

An immigrant from the Japanese island of Shikoku, Fujitaro Kubota was a self-taught gardener who came to the United States in 1907 and worked for the railroad before he founded the Kubota Gardening Company in 1923. Four years later he bought 5 acres of clear-cut swampland in Seattle's Mount Rainier area to indulge his passion for gardening in the Japanese manner. He established his garden and nursery business there and eventually owned 20 acres. His other public gardens in the Seattle area include the gardens on the campus of Seattle University and the Japanese Garden at Bloedel Reserve on Bainbridge Island. During World War II, Mr. Kubota and his family, along with thousands of other Japanese-Americans, were interned at Camp Minidoka in Idaho. A year before his death at age ninety-four, Mr. Kubota was presented with the Fifth Class Order of the Sacred Treasure by the Japanese government in recognition of his achievements and for introducing and building respect for Japanese gardening in the United States.

Kubota used Mapes Creek, which runs through the property, to create the necklace of ponds that are a special feature of the garden today. New features have been added to the garden in recent years, such as the entry gate with its sliding bronze door, designed and installed by Gerard Tsutakawa in 2004, and the Stone Garden and massive bronze temple bell that you see upon first entering.

At the Overlook, a living green window provides a tantalizing glimpse into the gardens below. If you follow the main path, you'll come to the Spring Pond, originally used for irrigation, and the Japanese Garden, the most traditional part of the garden. The rocks here are twelve-thousand-year-old local relics of the last Ice Age. West of the Japanese Garden, Mapes Creek runs through what is now designated the Natural Area, where original nursery plantings of bamboo, yew, birch, and other plants have been left to mature. The creek is spanned by the red Heart Bridge, similar to traditional bridges on the Japanese island of Shikoku.

Farther to the northwest, a trail leads up the miniature Mountainside, a special area built in 1962 to celebrate the Seattle World's Fair and commemorated with a memorial stone (placed here when Mr. Kubota was eighty-three years old) that tells the history of the garden in Japanese. A waterfall cascades down the Mountainside over rocks brought from North Bend, east of Seattle. From the Lookout you'll have a comprehensive view of the garden below.

The arched Moon Bridge to the east (meant to symbolize the difficulty of living a good life because it is difficult to walk up and down) leads to the Tom Kubota Stroll Garden created by Fujitaro's son Tom in 1999. This expansive area features lawns, rocks from the High Cascades, and an assortment of magnificent trees, including an enormous weeping Atlas cedar, weeping Norway spruces, and a grove of cornelian cherry trees (*Cornus mas*). Continuing south, you'll come to the Kubota Terrace with more open lawns and late-summer-blooming plants.

meerkerk rhododendron gardens

3531 Meerkerk Lane, Greenbank, WA 98253
meerkerkgardens.org
Visit year-round; April to mid-May for peak rhododendron
    blooms; June through September for perennials

- 📞 (360) 678-1912 or (360) 222-0121
- 🕐 Open daily May–Sep 9am–dusk; Oct–Apr 9am–4pm
- $ Admission fee
- 🚌 Unless you live on Whidbey Island, you'll have to take a ferry to get there
- 🐕 Dogs on leash

Clouds of springtime color in a tranquil woodland setting on Whidbey Island

Tucked between the Olympic Peninsula and the ever-busy I-5 corridor of western Washington, Whidbey Island is one of the longest islands (35 miles) in the United States and forms the northern boundary of Puget Sound. Part of the island sits in the rain shadow of the Olympic Mountains to the west, giving it something of a split personality when it comes to climate, rainfall, and vegetation. The southern and wettest part of Whidbey has conifers (notably Douglas-fir), deciduous trees (alder and bigleaf maple), and understory plants that are similar to those on the mainland. On the northern part of the island, however, you'll see Oregon white oak (also known as Garry oak), Pacific madrone, and Sitka spruce—as well as the lovely native rhododendron,

The new gatehouse at Meerkerk Gardens was modeled after a similar building at Highgrove, Prince Charles's estate in Gloucestershire, England.

Rhododendron macrophyllum. The driest and calmest part of the island lies in the center, between these two microclimates, and it's here, around Whidbey Island's waistline, that you'll find Meerkerk Rhododendron Gardens.

Hidden within this 53-acre forest preserve is a 10-acre secret garden that showcases hundreds of hybrid and species rhododendrons. Many of these rhodies are now more than sixty years old, some of them are giants, and all of them are spectacularly beautiful in April and May, when they add clouds of color to their tranquil woodland setting.

Certain plants, like styles of clothing and architecture, typify an era. You might call the Meerkerk rhodies Mid-Century Modern, for many of them represent the species and hybrids that were known, collected, and propagated during the 1960s. Since then, of course, the number of hybrid rhododendrons has expanded enormously, but it's not often that you see mature plants of this stature.

Rhododendrons became the passion and pastime of Max and Ann Meerkerk, who moved to Whidbey Island in 1961. The couple had a colorful history. Descended from Prussian nobility and forced to flee Germany, Max was a much-married international traveler who lived in Asia before World War II. Ann was born Ann Wright in Minneapolis in 1916, studied art at Ohio University, and became a ceramist. Fleeing the Midwest, she moved to New York, opened a ceramics shop in Greenwich Village, and lived the life of a creative free spirit. Max and Ann met and married in 1950 when Ann was thirty-two and Max was sixty-two. Ann was his fifth wife.

They raised Weimaraners and took all fifty-five dogs with them when they moved west in the 1950s. At some point they traveled to England and visited Exbury, the Rothschild estate in the New Forest, famed for its collection of rhododendrons, azaleas, camellias, and rare trees and shrubs. The woodland gardens at Exbury provided the inspiration for the Meerkerks' secret garden on Whidbey Island. Max bought 13 acres of land in 1961 and started to plant Chinese varieties of rhododendron. Artistic Ann selected colors, developed groupings, and added companion plants to

complement the new rhodies. To protect their garden, Max bought the 40 acres of land that surrounded it.

After Max's death in 1969, Ann continued to develop and work on the garden. She had also become a weaver (or a fiber artist in today's parlance), raising her own sheep, having them sheared, dyeing their wool, spinning it on the antique spinning wheels she collected, and weaving it on one of her twenty-five looms. Before her death in 1979, she bequeathed the 53 acres to the Seattle Rhododendron Society to care for as a "peaceful woodland garden with an emphasis on rhododendrons and companion plants."

And that's what you'll find at Meerkerk, which you enter through a charming new gatehouse modeled after a Neo-Gothic building at Highgrove, Prince Charles's estate in Gloucestershire, and constructed of limestone and yellow Port Orford cedar. The not-for-profit organization that runs Meerkerk has worked hard to expand the garden's all-season interest, and there's plenty to enjoy year-round, both in the 10-acre garden and the 43 acres of surrounding woodland with its 5 miles of nature trails.

But April and May are definitely the most magical months to visit Meerkerk. That's when thousands of daffodils, bluebells, auriculas, foxgloves, and foxtail lilies carpet the beds beneath blossoming cherry trees, dogwoods, magnolias, and early rhododendrons. Some five hundred hybrids and about three hundred rhododendron species are found at Meerkerk, which also acts as a research facility for creating new hybrid varieties. Ann and Max preferred late-blooming crosses, so you'll find rhodies in bloom almost year-round. On my last visit there, on an afternoon in mid-May, I was amazed at the number of honeybees I saw and delighted to hear their loud humming—a once-familiar sound of spring that has become less frequent because of hive collapse.

Much as I love the robust, big-leaved, Mid-Century Modern rhodies at Meerkerk, I am even fonder of the garden's examples of *Rhododendron macrophyllum*. Leggy, with delicate pink flower clusters that are smaller and less showy than any of the hybrids, these native rhododendrons serve as a reminder of the shy, and now threatened, woodland beauties that have adorned maritime forests in the Pacific Northwest since time immemorial.

Once the secret garden of a Prussian former nobleman and an American artist, Meerkerk Gardens showcases a colorful collection of Mid-Century Modern rhododendrons.

roozengaarde

15867 Beaver Marsh Road, Mount Vernon, WA 98273
tulips.com
Visit mid-April through early May; check Web site to find out
    when tulips are in bloom

- (360) 424-8531 or (800) 732-3266
- Display garden and gift shop open 9am–7pm during
  Skagit Valley Tulip Festival; gift shop year-round Mon–
  Sat 9am–6pm, Sun 11am–4pm
- $ Admission fee during Tulip Festival
- Easier access and parking on weekdays; roads are
  jammed on weekends during Tulip Festival
- No dogs

Tulip display garden and fields of the largest bulb producer in the United States

A tulip-loving friend of mine was gazing in wonder at one of RoozenGaarde's vast tulip fields shimmering red and yellow in the April sun. "Who needs Holland?" she asked.

Well, RoozenGaarde needs Holland because that's where all their tulip hybridizing is done. And family ties with Holland are strong, since the Roozen family is of Dutch origin and has been active in the Dutch tulip business since the 1700s. But since 1950 their tulip fields have all been in the Skagit Valley, about an hour north of Seattle. With its soft, moist maritime air, this pan-cake-flat valley is definitely reminiscent of Holland, except that on clear days you can see the North Cascades looming up to the east.

It's here that William Roozen, a salesman for a Dutch bulb company, settled in 1947, worked alongside local farmers and bulb growers, and eventually purchased the Washington Bulb Company. He had 5 acres of land for growing tulips. By the 1980s, when his daughter Bernadette Roozen Miller started RoozenGaarde (the garden, gift shop, and online sales outlet of Washington Bulb

Company), the Roozen family had turned their business of growing tulips, daffodils, and irises into the largest in the world, with more than 1,000 acres of fields and 15 acres of greenhouses. I think you can safely assume you've cornered the tulip market when your company's online domain name is tulips.com.

It's interesting to note that the first speculative bubble in recorded history centered on the tulip. The tulip's popularity and cultivation in the Netherlands started around 1593 and tulips soon became coveted status symbols. Competition to grow the most beautiful tulip was fierce, and people were willing to pay extraordinary sums for a single bulb. Batches of some rare bulbs had a higher price than a house. Despite attempts to limit the speculation, the tulip craze grew crazier as people sold land, houses, and valuable objects to invest in the bulbs. The term tulipomania refers to this period when prices for bulbs skyrocketed to astronomically high levels. When the speculative market for tulips collapsed, fortunes were lost overnight. Sound familiar?

If you're fond of the genus *Tulipa,* you'll want to head to Roozen-Gaarde's display garden and tulip fields in the Skagit Valley when the tulips are in bloom. It's a sight you'll never forget, and it draws—like Keukenhof and the big Interflora tulip show in Holland—hundreds of thousands of visitors every year. But take note: when it comes to visiting tulip fields, timing is everything. Be sure to check the RoozenGaarde Web site before making your trip to Mount Vernon, where the display garden and most of the tulip fields are located.

You know tulips are big business in this part of the world when you start encountering highway signs marked "Tulip Route" and begin to see the size of the tulip fields. The spring-bulb business plays a major role in the local and state economy, with millions of bulbs being grown, harvested, and shipped every year.

The vast tulip fields of RoozenGaarde and other local bulb growers draw hundreds of thousands of visitors to the Skagit Valley every spring.

Skagit Valley Tulip Festival

RoozenGaarde is one of the official sponsors of the Skagit Valley Tulip Festival, which celebrates . . . you guessed it, the tulip. Held in April, the festival, with its roster of events, draws thousands of visitors to the tulip fields and the towns of Mount Vernon and La Conner. Local wineries, breweries, farms, gardens, and restaurants all take part. tulipfestival.org.

RoozenGaarde's compact 3.5-acre show garden is well-designed and contains an interesting mix of shrubs and trees in addition to more than a quarter million spring-blooming tulip, daffodil, hyacinth, and muscari (grape hyacinth) bulbs. The theme and design varies year to year, and always includes the new tulip varieties being introduced. As you stroll through the gardens you can select from more than ninety tulip varieties and order them on-site for fall delivery. You can also buy gorgeous fresh-cut tulips that will last for up to a week.

When you visit the display gardens, pick up a map of the tulip fields and ask which fields are in best bloom (you can also check online). The field might be right across the street from the show garden, or a couple miles down the road. They all have parking lots and are easy to access. After a gray Pacific Northwest winter, your senses will definitely perk up when you see the colorful tulip fields stretching off into the distance. Flowers can brighten moods, and when you're surrounded by as many flowers as this, and so much color, you can be forgiven if you feel a little giddy.

seattle japanese garden

University of Washington Arboretum, 1075 Lake Washington Boulevard E, Seattle, WA 98112
seattle.gov/parks/parkspaces/gardens.htm
Visit April through June for maximum color; September
through October for fall foliage

- 📞 (206) 684-4725
- 🕐 Open mid-Feb–Apr Tues–Sun 10am–4pm;
  May–mid-Sep daily 10am–7pm; mid-Sep–Oct daily
  10am–5pm; Nov–mid-Nov Tues–Sun 10am–4pm
- $ Admission fee
- 🚌 Public transportation
- ♿ Stepping-stones, stone bridges, and uneven terrain
  make some parts of the garden difficult for wheelchairs
- 🐕 No dogs

A long-established traditional Japanese garden

The Japanese influence on Pacific Northwest horticulture has
been enormous in terms of both plant material and garden design.
Flowering Japanese cherry trees, evergreen Japanese azaleas, Japanese maples, and Japanese iris, to name just a few, have become
so familiar in our gardens and parks that we tend to take them for
granted. But seeing these plants in a Western-style garden is a very
different experience from seeing them in a formal Japanese garden,
where philosophy and symbolism inform every inch of the overall
design. And luckily, thanks to our cultural ties to Japan, we have
the best examples of Japanese gardens outside of Japan right here
in the Pacific Northwest.

Brilliant splashes of autumn color enliven the tranquil landscapes that unfold on a stroll through the Seattle Japanese Garden.

The Seattle Japanese Garden is one of two superlative Japanese gardens in Seattle (Kubota Garden is the other). Designed and constructed under the supervision of world-famous Japanese garden designer Juki Iida, the garden fits like a jewel into its 3.5-acre setting within the University of Washington Arboretum. Part of that jewel-like quality comes from the lake that forms the garden's centerpiece, enlivening its miniaturized landscape by reflecting the sky, clouds, and trees. Iida used the Japanese concept of borrowed scenery when he created this garden, utilizing the arboretum's forested hillsides to enhance and extend the visual reach of the smaller formal garden contained within them. In 1958, when

work began, the site was a marshy tract that had been exposed by the lowering of Lake Washington when the ship canal was built in 1917. Opened in 1960, the garden has now had more than fifty years to mature and is the oldest formal Japanese garden in the Pacific Northwest.

Nothing is left to chance in a Japanese garden. Even those elements that are meant to look spontaneous or natural have been carefully considered and placed within the overall design. This is a strolling garden with several meticulously created miniaturized landscapes within it. It is meant to be seen one landscape at

Blue wisteria and yellow Japanese iris form a springtime picture in the Seattle Japanese Garden.

a time, like a scroll of painted landscapes that unrolls and reveals new vistas as the visitor follows the winding path from one viewpoint to the next. In addition to a gorgeous selection of trees and shrubs, you'll encounter all the elements used in formal Japanese garden design—water, rocks and sand, bridges, stone lanterns, and water basins.

The stresses of the outer world are left behind as you pass through the entrance gate and enter the tranquil confines of the garden. A venerable Japanese cutleaf maple (*Acer palmatum* var. *dissectum*) and a beautiful paperbark maple (*A. griseum*) with shaggy, mahogany-colored bark stand near a dry stone stream and a flat-topped snow lantern. Conifers, maples, and rhododendrons cover the mountainside from which two streams emerge to form the lake. Continue on the main path with its sculpted azaleas to the three ginkgo trees (*Ginkgo biloba*) that are indigenous to Japan, Korea, and China. Ginkgos are among the oldest trees in existence and are considered living fossils of the dinosaur age.

Two traditional Japanese bridges span the lake. One is a simple earth-covered bridge and the other is a plank bridge. The pines on the island in the center of the lake are meant to represent Japanese cranes, but real blue herons are the birds you'll most likely see along the shore. They fly over from Lake Washington and help keep the koi (Japanese carp) population in check.

A blue wisteria (usually blooming in May) covers the outlet from the lake and serves as an entrance to the Walled Village, the name given to a higher area at the north end of the lake that provides a view of the entire garden. The two-hundred-year-old carved granite lantern on top of the knoll was a gift from Kobe, Seattle's sister city, in 1957.

A cherry orchard with a traditional shelter for resting and viewing the scene occupies the west side of the lake. On this side are the Moon-Viewing Platform, used for late-summer ceremonies honoring the rising of the full moon, and the Tea Garden, where tea ceremonies are performed (these must be booked in advance). The teahouse is a small post-and-lintel structure with a copper-shingle roof. Just south of it, a waterfall cascades over an impressive 8-ton boulder.

Above the teahouse, an eleven-tiered stone pagoda represents an ancient monastery in the mountains of Japan. Another stone bridge at the southern end of the lake leads back to the entry gate.

south seattle community college arboretum and seattle chinese garden

6000 Sixteenth Avenue SW, Seattle, WA 98106
southseattle.edu/arboretum; seattlechinesegarden.org
Visit April through October

- 📞 (206) 934-5219
- 🕐 Arboretum open daily dawn to dusk; Chinese garden Apr–Oct Wed–Sun noon–5:30pm
- $ Admission free for arboretum; fee for Chinese garden
- 🚌 Public transportation
- 🏚 No restrooms, as the Chinese garden is only partially finished
- 🐕 Dogs on leash in arboretum; not permitted in Chinese garden

Ridgetop arboretum and adjacent Sichuan-style Chinese Garden (under construction) with a dramatic view of Seattle

The collection of dwarf conifers in the rock garden at South Seattle Community College is among the nation's best.

If you love trees, you'll enjoy visiting this arboretum and the new Seattle Chinese Garden adjacent to it. The two are not affiliated except by location on a site overlooking downtown Seattle, Elliott Bay, and the West Duwamish Greenbelt.

The 5-acre arboretum was established in 1978 when students in the Landscape Horticulture Program at South Seattle Community College petitioned for an arboretum to serve as their living laboratory, and then designed and built it. Most of the plants on the Washington Certified Professional Horticulturist exam can be found in this arboretum, and it's used for courses in plant identification, arboriculture, pruning, irrigation, garden renovation, plant problem diagnostics, landscape management, and landscape construction. Basically it's an outdoor classroom that happens to be a pleasant and attractive place to stroll even if you know nada about trees. Pesticide-free since 2008, the arboretum was designated a National Wildlife Federation Urban Wildlife Sanctuary in 2012.

The arboretum is arranged around a winding path that leads to vignette gardens and planted areas showcasing particular tree species, some of them quite rare in the Seattle area. Head west from the entry garden and you'll come to the Coenosium Rock Garden, which contains one of the most significant collections of dwarf conifers in the United States. Among the rare and colorful beauties you'll find here are Korean silver fir (*Abies koreana*) with its attractive bluish-purple cones; Berrima gold incense cedar (*Calocedrus decurrens* 'Berrima Gold'), a native of Oregon, California, and Nevada that turns an intense gold color in the winter; a variety of Arizona cypress (*Cupressus arizonica* var. *glabra* 'Blue Ice') with reddish-brown peeling bark and blue-gray foliage; temple or needle juniper (*Juniperus rigida*), a graceful, weeping conifer from China, Russia, Japan, and North Korea; and tiger-tail spruce (*Picea torano*) from Japan, with its rigid and fiercely sharp needles arranged radially around the branches.

The path continues to the Milton Sutton Conifer Garden. This constantly growing collection includes some notable needlies such as a contorted white pine (*Pinus strobus* 'Torulosa') with weirdly twisted blue-gray needles; plume Japanese cedar (*Cryptomeria japonica* 'Elegans'), a Japanese native with soft, fluffy foliage that turns purple-brown in winter; and dwarf Serbian spruce (*Picea omorika* 'Nana'), a diminutive ornamental from Yugoslavia. The northwestern corner of the arboretum is taken up with the Acer Garden and the Sequoia Grove, both of them in open, natural settings.

The northeastern corner of the arboretum is the home of the Seattle Chinese Garden, where a 5-acre Sichuan-style garden planned by a team of garden designers in Seattle's sister city of Chongqing is under construction. The ridgetop site between Puget Sound and the Duwamish River, within sight of the Olympic and Cascade mountains and aligned with the Space Needle, is loaded with good feng shui. The garden is worth visiting even in its incomplete state to see the structures that have already been built and to envision what the future garden will look like when it's completed (sometime around 2018). It's not often that you can see a major garden as it's being constructed—especially a garden as exotic as this one. The only other Chinese gardens in the Pacific Northwest—Lan Su Chinese Garden in Portland, Oregon, and Dr. Sun Yat-Sen Classical Chinese Garden in Vancouver, British Columbia—are both urban, Ming-era scholars' gardens built by craftsmen from Suzhou, China. The Seattle Chinese Garden will feature elements common to all Chinese gardens, but it occupies a far more open and dramatic site and has garden areas outside as well as inside the buildings.

Designed by a team of Chinese garden designers from Chongqing and completed in 2010, the Knowing Spring Courtyard serves as the impressive entry to the Seattle Chinese Garden.

Stop in at the visitor center for some historical and geographical background before visiting the garden's major structure, the impressive Knowing Spring Courtyard. Completed in 2010, the courtyard will serve as the entry to the garden. Every aspect of its exterior and interior design exemplifies the ancient Chinese garden principles of yin and yang (harmony in the balance of paired opposites). Yin elements (soft, dark, feminine), represented by plants and water, are balanced by the yang elements of rock and architecture. Twelve intricate lattice windows, called leak windows because they allow views of the outside world to leak in, adorn the north and east walls.

Rocks, symbols of the mountains and valleys of the earth, are integral to Chinese garden design. The ancient, pitted limestone rocks used in Portland's and Vancouver's Chinese gardens come from Lake Tai near Suzhou. The tall, slender stones used here—called bamboo shoot rocks because they resemble shoots of bamboo—come from Zhejiang Province and the mountains outside Chongqing. The hardness of the stones is offset by the softness of the plantings: bamboo, grasses, and shrubs. Step through the main gate and turn right to reach the Pine and Plum Pavilion, the second structure to be built. From here you can see the entire garden site, which will include a lotus pond, a lake, a southern courtyard, and a teahouse.

volunteer park conservatory

1402 E Galer Street, Seattle, WA 98112
volunteerparkconservatory.org
Visit year-round

- 📞 (206) 684-4743
- 🕐 Open Tue–Sun 10am–4pm
- 💲 Admission by donation
- 🚌 Public transportation
- 🚻 No restrooms
- 🐕 No dogs

Century-old glass conservatory with an exceptional collection of artfully displayed tropical plants

Now more than a hundred years old, the Volunteer Park Conservatory is a prefab building that was shipped to Seattle from Massachusetts in 1912 and assembled on the site.

Give yourself lots of ooh-and-ah time when you visit the Volunteer Park Conservatory because this century-old glasshouse will wow you with its fascinating assortment of rare and exotic plants. It's the finest conservatory collection I've ever seen, in part because everything is so artfully displayed. It's a place that makes you feel like a kid discovering weird new wonders. The last time I was there, a man excitedly asked if I'd seen the black bat flower (*Tacca chantrieri*) in the next room and got tongue-tied as he tried to describe its intricate form.

You'd never guess from looking at this elegant building that it was shipped as a prefab kit from Brookline, Massachusetts, and assembled on-site in 1912. Although modeled after the mammoth Crystal Palace erected in London in 1851, the scale of this conservatory is intimate and unintimidating. Out front are seasonal beds of old-fashioned favorites like fragrant heliotrope, hollyhocks, and fuchsias. But once you step inside, it's a different world.

In addition to its many species of palm trees, the central Palm House where you enter showcases a collection of tropical orchids offset by the brilliant red shields of anthuriums from Hawaii and Costa Rica, multicolored crotons, and tall, tender ginger and banana plants from Asia. The Seasonal Display House to the right presents an ever-changing show of color and fragrance and is especially fetching in the spring when it's loaded with blooming bulbs, lilies, cyclamen, azaleas, and hydrangeas placed within permanent plantings of African sansevierias and giant yuccas from Mexico. Beyond is the dry, thorny realm of the Cactus House, where the variety of shapes, thorns, and growing habits is amazing, as are the flowers the cacti produce in the spring. The saguaro cactus in the center is an endangered species. Many succulents also grow in this room, including the oldest plant in the conservatory, a jade tree *(Crassula ovata)* grown from a small cutting planted in 1916.

The first room to the left of the Palm House is the Fern House. This warm, humid environment supports many species of ferns—delicate maidenhairs are everywhere—as well as primitive cycads from the dinosaur age. The boggy planters around the pool are home to carnivorous plants like the tiny Venus flytrap *(Dionaea muscipula)* and exotics such as bird-of-paradise *(Strelitzia reginae)* and brugmansias with long, pendulous, translucent trumpets. The final room is the Bromeliad House with its silvery epiphytic

A collection of thorny and prickly desert plants holds sway in the Cactus House at Volunteer Park Conservatory.

tillandsias, staghorn ferns, and spectacular spring-blooming epiphyllum hybrids.

The Volunteer Park Conservatory counts two rare corpse lilies *(Amorphophallus titanum)* among its many treasures. Native to the rainforests of Sumatra, this smelly giant boasts the largest single flower in the world (in the wild growing to 9 feet tall and 3 feet across) and blooms every seven to ten years. When it does, the conservatory becomes like a sideshow at the fair with curious visitors lining up to file past for a look and a (quick) sniff.

In 2011 this historic conservatory operated by Seattle Parks and Recreation nearly closed for lack of funding. If Seattleites ever allow that to happen, it will be an incalculable loss for plant lovers and a shameful day for the city.

Other Highlights of Volunteer Park

Century-old Volunteer Park is one of the gems of Seattle's park system and well worth exploring. In the early 1900s, civic leaders had the good sense to hire Olmsted Brothers, America's pre-eminent landscape design firm, to draw up a plan that set aside portions of Seattle's uniquely beautiful terrain as places for relaxation and recreation. The Olmsted Interpretive Exhibit on the observation deck in the Volunteer Park Water Tower chronicles the Olmsted legacy in creating Seattle's parks. Climb the stairway in the hundred-year-old Romanesque-style brick water tower, located in the southeast corner of the park near the reservoir, for commanding views of the city and Puget Sound. Open daily 11am–dusk.

Another highlight of Volunteer Park is the Seattle Asian Art Museum. Housed in a classic 1933 Art Moderne building, this small museum features rotating exhibits and displays a permanent collection of ancient Chinese pottery, Japanese kimonos, and other Asian treasures. Across from it stands Isamu Noguchi's 1968 outdoor sculpture called "Black Sun," a circular form created from Brazilian granite. seattleartmuseum.org.

And then there is the Volunteer Park Dahlia Garden. Dahlias are native to Mexico, Central America, and Colombia, but under the right conditions they also thrive in the cool Pacific Northwest—as you'll see when you visit the colorful dahlia garden just east of the conservatory. The Puget Sound Dahlia Association maintains this display garden of summer-blooming tuberous dahlias with their long stems and amazing variety of show-off flowers.

washington park arboretum

2300 Arboretum Drive E, Seattle, WA 98112
arboretumfoundation.org
Visit year-round

....

- 📞 (206) 325-4510
- 🕐 Arboretum open daily dawn to dusk; Graham Visitors Center open daily 10am–4pm except holidays
- $ Admission free
- 🚌 Public transportation
- 🐕 Dogs on leash

Urban treasure trove on Lake Washington

It took more than forty years of tenacious planning, scheming, and beneficial influence peddling to get this renowned arboretum off the ground—or into the ground, I should say.

In 1903, John C. Olmsted of the Olmsted Brothers landscape architecture firm submitted a design for a Seattle park system that included a botanical garden and arboretum. The arboretum remained an unfulfilled dream for three decades. Finally, in 1934, university administrators, city commissioners, and influential citizens worked out a plan to locate the arboretum in Washington Park on land that would be owned by the city but with plant collections that would be the property and responsibility of the university. Green-minded civic groups and individuals stepped up to defray the costs of designing and planting the arboretum. This was accomplished during the bleakest years of the Depression.

Since its official founding in 1935, the arboretum has weathered funding crises, neighborhood controversies (primarily over fencing and traffic), and storms that have toppled trees and frozen shrubs. But it has survived—and survived beautifully. Walking trails crisscross the varied terrain of woodland, wetland, and gardens, taking visitors to acclaimed collections of azaleas, rhododendrons, oaks, conifers, camellias, Japanese maples, and hollies. The Seattle Japanese Garden occupies the southwestern portion of the arboretum but is separate from it.

If you haven't visited the arboretum before, you can view a map of the grounds on the arboretum's Web site or stop in at the Graham Visitors Center for trail maps.

The arboretum is full of seasonal highlights, and something of special interest is always waiting to be discovered. The Joseph

Azalea Way, planted in the 1930s at the Washington Park Arboretum, is one of Seattle's springtime highlights.

A. Witt Winter Garden, a delight from late November through March, is a short walk from the visitors center via the Hillside Trail and features a central lawn encircled by tall cedars and firs and a tremendous assortment of smaller trees, shrubs, and perennials. The berry-bearing hollies are also at their peak from November through February.

Visit the Camellia Grove in March and April and you'll find a wide array of species and cultivar camellias in full bloom. The magnolias, with their large, fragrant flowers, bloom between March and May; showstoppers include *Magnolia dawsoniana* and *M. campbellii* in March, and *M. wilsonii* in May. There's also a 9-acre spring-blooming Rhododendron Glen, established in 1938 with the donation of an important collection of three hundred rhododendrons representing twenty-three species indigenous to the Himalayas, and another collection of hybrid rhodies donated in 1939.

But the arboretum's must-see springtime spectacle is, without a doubt, Azalea Way. Laid out on the site of the park's old horse-racing track, it's bordered by hundreds of Japanese cherry trees, eastern dogwoods, and understory azaleas. WPA workmen put in more than ten thousand hours of hand labor to complete Azalea Way.

In early summer, fragrant linden trees perfume the air. Later in the season, if you're seeking a bit of shade on a hot summer day (yes, that does occasionally happen in Seattle), head over to the Woodland Garden between the two ponds, or relax under the

Pacific Connections, the newest garden at the Washington Park Arboretum, features an entry garden with plants from New Zealand.

crabapple trees in the meadow behind the apiary. In the fall, it's lovely to wander through the arboretum's oaks section, where squirrels and acorns abound, and the Japanese maple collection, which reaches its peak color in September and October. (One garden contains Asiatic maples and another is devoted solely to the Japanese maple, *Acer palmatum,* and its many unique cultivars.) September through mid-October is also the time when the deciduous, mountain-growing larches turn a brilliant golden yellow before dropping their needles.

For a refreshing waterside stroll in any season, walk north along Arboretum Drive East, cross the road, and follow the gravel trail along the shoreline to the large wetland area that's a favorite spot for birders. The Pinetum with its assortment of evergreen and deciduous conifers is another year-round pleasure; the giant dawn redwood (*Metasequoia glyptostroboides*) along Arboretum Creek, and the coast redwood (*Sequoia sempervirens*) and giant sequoia or Sierra redwood (*Sequoiadendron giganteum*) near the Lynn Street entrance to the Pinetum are all more than seventy years old and 80 feet tall.

The newest area in the arboretum, called Pacific Connections, is a 12-acre site that contains meadows, gardens, and forests planted with an intriguing assortment of plants from five countries or regions connected by the Pacific Ocean: Cascadia (a.k.a. the Pacific Northwest), Australia, China, Chile, and New Zealand.

But all this only hints at the riches you'll find in this wonderfully explorable urban treasure trove.

UW Medicinal Herb Garden

A short drive from Washington Park Arboretum, the little-known but fascinating UW Medicinal Herb Garden was established as a research drug garden in 1911 and is among the largest public gardens of its kind in the world. Divided into seven sections covering 2.5 acres, the garden contains nearly a thousand labeled plant species used worldwide in historic and modern times for treating a wide array of ailments. In addition to familiar Pacific Northwest species you'll find plants like flannelbush with its bright yellow-gold flowers, Welsh onion, wild tobacco, wormwood, sneezeweed, and marsh mallows as tall as a human. Two statues of the Hindu monkey-god Hanuman, replicas of those found at the seventeenth-century botanical garden in Padua, Italy, preside over Cascara Circle, the garden's formal entrance. Stevens Way, UW campus, southwest of the Chemistry Building.

woodland park
rose garden

Elegant, old-fashioned, pesticide-
free rose garden from the 1920s

750 N 50th Street, Seattle, WA 98103
zoo.org/rose-garden
Visit late May to August when the roses are in bloom

....

- 📞 (206) 684-4075
- 🕐 Open daily year-round
- $ Admission free; fee to park in zoo lots during zoo hours
- 🚌 Public transportation
- 🐕 Dogs on leash

Dedicated in 1924, the Woodland Park Rose Garden harks back to an era when civic-minded rose lovers were scattering their rose seeds from Oregon to British Columbia. And why not? It's very difficult to dislike a rose. They are the most symbolic and celebrated of flowers, and have been for centuries. They smell good. And they grow beautifully in the mild climate of the Pacific Northwest. The early rose boosters were so successful that roses are now the most familiar garden plant in the Pacific Northwest. From May to August they star in festivals and spread their fragrance in gardens large and small.

A joint project of the Lion's Club and the Seattle Rose Society, this 2.5-acre rose garden adjacent to the Woodland Park Zoo is dedicated to the simple proposition that the genus *Rosa* in all its myriad forms is the most beautiful and inspirational flower known to humankind and deserves to be seen and appreciated by everyone, free of charge. Designed by Howard E. Andrews, the showcase garden is laid out in a cruciform shape within a half oval, with a few formal garden features to add architectural interest. The giant evergreen topiaries standing sentinel along the edges add to the quasi-English look that was popular at the time. A circular fountain bubbles at the intersection of the garden's two axes and a semi-circular bas-relief wall fountain burbles at the north end. A rectangular lily pond sits between the two fountains, with a gazebo (used for lots of weddings) anchoring the east end, and a pergola at the south end.

But this garden is really about the roses. Floribunda, grandiflora, hybrid tea, hybrid musk, miniature, polyantha, rugosa, David Austin, climber, shrub, tree—you'll encounter all of them as you wander past and around the nearly ninety rose beds. If you want to identify individual roses by name, pick up a map and identification key near the entrance. Though Woodland ceased to be a certified All-America Rose Selections test garden in 2010, you can

The fountain at the center of Woodland Park Rose Garden adds architectural interest to this old Seattle rose garden.

Seattle Sensory Garden

The Woodland Park Rose Garden is expanding its reach with the addition of an entirely new garden. The Seattle Sensory Garden, in which plants and other design elements are selected to provide year-round experiences for seeing, smelling, hearing, touching, and tasting for people of all ages and abilities, will flank the north and east sides of the 1924 rose garden. seattlesensorygarden.com.

still see All-America Rose Selections and new rose hybrids before they become available to the public.

A descendant of one of the very first roses brought to the Pacific Northwest lives in the garden, but you have to be something of a sleuth to find it. Louisa Boren Denny, one of Seattle's founding mothers, came west on the Oregon Trail, bringing with her some seeds from a sweet briar rose (*Rosa rubiginosa*) collected from a friend's garden in Illinois. In 1852 she planted the seeds at her log cabin on Elliott Bay, where it became well established. Every time Mrs. Denny moved, she took her rose with her, and it lived for decades. A few years ago, gardeners at the Woodland Park Rose Garden discovered at the park department nursery a very old sweet briar rose said to have been started from a cutting taken from the original Denny rose. They planted it in bed 48 at the north end of the garden. To find it, direct your steps to the bas-relief fountain, follow the main gravel path in front of it a few steps to the west, and look for the flowerbed above a low rock retaining wall. The rose, with very thorny canes, is close to the front of the bed with no tag or label. None of the other roses in the area have the very thorny canes of the sweet briar.

This elegant and enjoyable rose garden is unique in that it is 100 percent organic and pesticide-free—no easy feat, as every rose grower who has tried to deal with aphids, leafcutters, cankers, botrytis, mildew, and mold knows. It's been accomplished in this garden by using only rose varieties that are able to adapt to the natural soil, light, and rainfall conditions. Instead of poisonous pesticides, beneficial nematodes (ladybugs, for example) help fight aphids and other insect pests. Composting the soil and choosing the right plants reduces the need for chemical fertilizers and extra watering. It's a win-win for the environment, and, judging by the healthy vigor of the plants, for the roses, too.

Surrounded by fragrant roses, the gazebo at Woodland Park Rose Garden is a popular site for weddings.

tacoma & vicinity

A sculpture in the Teahouse at Lakewold evokes the neoclassical style favored by landscape designer Thomas Church.

chase garden

16015 264th Street E, Orting, WA 98360
chasegarden.org
Visit April through June

....

📞 (360) 893-6739
🕐 Open Apr–Oct Fri–Sun 10am–3pm
$ Admission fee
♿ Some areas of woodland path not suitable for wheelchairs
🐕 No dogs

Modernist Northwest garden with a Japanese influence and a spectacular view of Mount Rainier

She liked narrow paths, he liked wide ones. He liked straight lines, she liked curves. So it goes when any couple works together to create a garden. There's a yin and yang involved that ideally results in a garden aesthetically pleasing to both.

The co-creators of Chase Garden were Ione and Emmott Chase, two local lovebirds who worked side by side to turn a logged-out plateau overlooking the Orting Valley into a garden that exemplifies the new trend in Northwest house and garden design that appeared in the 1950s. Simple without being simplistic, Chase Garden combines elements of traditional Japanese design with the more naturalistic look of a Northwest woodland garden.

The garden is a perfect setting for the Mid-Century Modern house with its clean lines, broad overhangs, and use of natural materials, especially wood. It may look almost commonplace to contemporary eyes accustomed to suburban ranch-style houses, but the Chases' home was in the vanguard of the era's new residential vernacular, which opened up rooms and used sliding glass doors and picture windows to let in light and, in this case, take advantage of a spectacular view of Mount Rainier. Architect Walter Johnson designed the structure, but the Chases did much of the construction work themselves. Ione, who worked as hard as her husband on both house and garden, built the fireplace using local river rocks.

Emmott's job with Puget Sound Power and Light gave him access to the heavy equipment the pair needed to contour the 12 acres of land they purchased in 1943 (for four hundred dollars), build the garden beds, and haul up rocks and boulders they found in nearby rivers and streams to use as focal points in the garden. His job also took them to company construction sites where they found and collected native plants such as the bear grass (*Xerophyllum tenax*) they salvaged from Stampede Pass and transplanted to a meadow in their garden. Today, of course, these practices would be considered environmentally unsound and perhaps unlawful.

Before she married Emmott, her high school sweetheart, Ione briefly left the Orting Valley where they had grown up and

A mix of low-growing heathers, ground covers, and wildflowers provides sweeps of springtime color in the meadows at Chase Garden.

went to California to learn pattern making. One might say that the garden, with its seamlike paths and curvilinear plantings, is another reflection of her talent for planning, shaping, and stitching together the different parts of a garment. Her skills with needle and thread also came in handy when she sewed together hundreds of clumps of white heather to plant in the eye-catching heather banks that blossom in the spring along with thousands of white snowdrops and white-flowered *Hepatica nobilis.* A keen plantswoman and a practical gardener, Ione knew what worked and what didn't. To be a gardener, she said, you have to have patience—and plant enough of something to make an effect.

Another one of her best and simplest "effects" is the juniper hedge that runs along the perimeter of the sharply sloping property. It defines the lawn behind the house, helps to prevent erosion, acts as a windbreak, and sets the stage for the view of Mount Rainier. And it's drought resistant, which was an important (and forward-thinking) factor when it came to planning and planting the garden because the Chases left Orting during the dry months of August and September and went to their lakeside cabin in British Columbia. That's why the Chase Garden is not big on the showy summer blooms that many garden visitors expect. The Garden Conservancy, which has owned the garden since 2010, has

The areas near the entrance to the Chases' Mid-Century Modern house have the calm, sculpted look of a Japanese garden.

Mount Rainier National Park

If you're visiting Chase Garden you might want to combine it with a trip to Mount Rainier National Park, about 48 miles southeast of Orting, Washington. The king of the Cascade Range, majestic Mount Rainier rises some 14,410 feet above sea level and is the most glaciated peak in the contiguous United States. Six major rivers have their headwaters on this volcanic giant whose lower slopes, ringed by ancient forest and wildflower meadows, abound with wildlife. Established by Congress in 1899, the park encompasses some 368 square miles, nearly all of it designated as wilderness, has more than 260 miles of maintained trails, and offers a wealth of scenic and recreational opportunities. nps.gov/mora.

added a new Summer Color Garden, but that's not what Chase Garden is really about.

The goal of gardening, Ione Chase said, was to create beauty in a natural setting, and over half a century that is what she and Emmott did, using plants that blended into the landscape but provided form, texture, and a variety of spring blooms. The open areas closest to the house have a Japanese quality, with banks and mounds of low-lying heathers, shrubs, and ground covers set off by curving gravel paths and carefully placed rocks. Complementing these sculpted areas is a natural conifer woodland of Douglas-firs and mountain hemlock interspersed with introduced deciduous trees such as dawn redwood (*Metasequoia glyptostroboides*), ginkgo, and a katsura (*Cercidiphyllum magnificum*) with its distinctive autumn smell of burnt sugar or cotton candy. The understory is planted with an attractive mixture of native ferns, trilliums, mosses, vanilla leaf, Solomon's seal, and kinnikinnick.

When she was in her nineties and using a cane, Ione would walk out to survey the garden she and Emmott had begun fifty years earlier, pointing out what had yet to be done. She lived to be ninety-seven, and Emmott lived to be ninety-nine. It was their wish to open their garden to the public and to protect it from commercial development. With those goals in mind, they transferred ownership to the Garden Conservancy, and in 2010 the Chase Garden became the conservancy's fourth preservation project in the United States, thus ensuring the future of this simple, elegant example of Mid-Century Modern garden design.

lake wilderness arboretum

22520 SE 248th Street, Maple Valley, WA 98038
lakewildernessarboretum.org
Visit April and May for flowering rhododendrons,
   trees, and shrubs

....

- ☎ (425) 413-2572
- ⏰ Open daily dawn to dusk
- $ Admission free
- 🐕 Dogs on leash

Salvage arboretum on a former landing strip next to Lake Wilderness Park

It's amazing what you can do with an old landing strip. When they found out that King County was going to remove the old airstrip that had once served Lake Wilderness, a group of Master Gardeners and concerned residents banded together and got permission to create a public garden and arboretum on the 10-acre site.

What makes Lake Wilderness Arboretum so special is that it rescues old gardens that have lost their owners and moves them phlox, stock, and marrow to new digs at the arboretum. Imagine the plant material that would be lost or destroyed if these dedicated volunteers didn't organize bulldozers and flatbeds to move it all.

The first material to be donated is now the Steuber Rhododendron Collection. Collected over a thirty-year period by the donor, these rhodies are at their peak in late spring, with trilliums, hepaticas, and epimediums as their bloom-mates. In late May and early June the Smith/Mossman Western Azalea Garden bursts into bloom and scents the air. This is among the largest collections of deciduous western azaleas (*Rhododendron occidentale*) in the world. The Legacy Garden features plants from the gardens of

A totem pole marks the entrance to the Tribal Life Trail showcasing native plants used by Native Americans for millennia.

Loie Benedict and Marjorie Baird, two noted plantswomen of the Pacific Northwest.

In addition to the outstanding collections rescued from endangered gardens are other display areas to enjoy. One of the best is the Hydrangea Garden, a compendium of every kind of hydrangea you can think of (oak leaf, lace cap, mop top, climbing, variegated), in bloom from summer to fall. The vast Daylily Collection is another summer favorite, as is the Perennial Garden, which contains one of the largest collections of hardy fuchsias in the world and attracts droves of fierce little hummingbirds. The newest garden area, called the Tribal Life Trail, is a Master Gardener project that showcases native plants and provides information on how they were used by Native Americans.

In addition to the display gardens, the arboretum includes 26 acres of protected second-growth forest with a system of marked trails. There's also a very enticing nursery, where you'll find unusual and reasonably priced plants and be able to talk with the enthusiastic volunteer gardeners who make this community-minded place so appealing. The arboretum abuts 117-acre Lake Wilderness Park, a great recreational spot with swimming, boating, forest and shoreline hiking trails, and picnic tables.

lakewold

12317 Gravelly Lake Drive SW, Lakewood, WA 98499
lakewoldgardens.org
Visit year-round; March through May for peak
rhododendron bloom

....

- 📞 (253) 584-4106 or (888) 858-4106
- 🕐 Open Apr–Sep Wed–Sun 10am–4pm, Wed in Aug
  until 8pm; Oct–Mar Sat–Sun 10am–4pm; closed
  major holidays
- $ Admission fee
- ♿ Some areas are not easily wheelchair accessible
- 🐕 No dogs

**Romantic lakeside estate garden
created by a renowned plantswoman
and a famed landscape designer**

You might call Lakewold the sister estate of Bloedel Reserve, for
Eulalie Merrill Wagner, Lakewold's owner, was the sister of Virginia Merrill Bloedel. Raised in privileged surroundings, with
a family fortune based on timber, the Seattle sisters attended
finishing schools and married wealthy, socially prominent men.
Eulalie became an ardent, self-taught plant enthusiast interested
in garden design, but Virginia was perfectly content to let her
husband, Prentice Bloedel, do the gardening. Unlike her brother-
in-law, who was apparently more of a planner than a planter,
Eulalie was a vigorous, hands-on gardener. Docents at Lakewold
remember seeing her in the 1970s dressed in an Ultrasuede pants
suit and gardening gloves, trowel in hand, working in her garden.

Eulalie and her husband, Corydon Wagner, bought the 10-acre
estate on Gravelly Lake in 1938, when the area—now filled with
expensive homes—was still considered country. Previous owners
had built a house, done some landscaping, and used the property
since 1910 as a lakeside retreat. Eulalie wanted to live in something
more refined than the big Craftsman-style house, so it was torn

down and replaced by a Georgian-style mansion that epitomizes the gracious homes built by the rich in postwar, pre-McMansion America. Her sister's house at Bloedel Reserve is remarkably similar.

Eulalie was an engaged and accomplished plantswoman, but with 10 acres to landscape she needed someone to help her with the big picture. In 1950 she hired noted landscape architect Thomas Church to visit Lakewold and help her with its overall design. Church, educated at UC Berkeley and based in San Francisco, was famous for his neoclassical European-style garden designs. Working together and sometimes disagreeing, Eulalie and "Tommy" Church created the showcase gardens visitors see today. Church, who promoted the idea of gardens as outdoor rooms, provided a framework for Eulalie to work within.

Pick up a map of the gardens at the visitor center and begin your tour by strolling down the Circle Drive. Edged with some

The Shade Garden at Lakewold blossoms beneath the trunks of an ancient Douglas-fir near the neoclassical boxwood parterres.

nine hundred artfully massed rhododendrons underplanted with bunchberry (*Cornus canadensis*), Oregon clover (*Oxalis oregana*), Oregon grape (*Mahonia aquifolium*) and epimediums galore, the drive curves around a lawn graced by a Chinese empress tree (*Paulownia tomentosa*) and provides a suitably impressive introduction to the estate. The house itself is not always open for visitors, but don't be disappointed if you can't get in. Eulalie's favorite room, the Sun Room, has a wonderful garden outlook, but the rest of the house has a stiff, semi-formal look. The cast-iron verandah behind the house, with its cascading vines of blue and white wisteria, is the only part of the original Craftsman-style house that was retained. Just beyond the verandah is the Knot Garden, a kind of Elizabethan conceit planted with ribbons of fragrant, evergreen herbs around a carved stone well. Tucked into a corner beside the house, the shady and secluded Library Courtyard is planted with marginally hardy species such as *Rhododendron* 'Fragrantissimum' and flowering jasmine vine.

The beautifully patterned Brick Walk on the other side of the house serves as an invitation to enter Eulalie's romantic and gracefully elegant garden. Passing Mount Fuji cherry trees, geometrically patterned boxwood parterres, and Church's signature quatrefoil-shaped swimming pool (designed with inner ledges where guests could sit and lap martinis before doing their laps), the path leads to the fanciful lattice-roofed Teahouse framed by Pacific dogwoods (*Cornus nuttalli*). In the springtime, when the trees are in flower, this walk is shimmeringly beautiful.

A path leads from the Teahouse to the Shade Garden, where three kinds of trillium (*Trillium ovatum, T. sessile,* and *T. grandiflorum*) are planted with pink dogtooth violets (*Erythronium dens-canis*), Himalayan blue poppies (*Meconopsis betonicifolia*), and a Japanese maple (*Acer palmatum* 'Goshiki Shidare') beneath an enormous, multitrunked, centuries-old Douglas-fir.

Most of Lakewold's notable collection of Japanese maples are found in the Woodland Garden along the fern-fringed banks of a man-made stream and pond. Other notable trees in this leafy haven include Persian ironwood (*Parrotia persica)* and a Chilean firetree (*Embothrium coccineum*) with brilliant red blossoms in May and June. The path leads past a collection of native Oregon white oaks (*Quercus garryana,* also called Garry oaks) to Picnic Point, where Eulalie would serve tea to her grandchildren—using her finest silver tea service, of course.

A bevy of alpine cushion plants and miniature species bulbs decorates the Rock Garden, its paths flanked by tissuelike matilija poppies (*Romneya coulteri*) and Pacific Coast iris. In early spring, the fragrance of *Magnolia sieboldii* scents the air and a large patch of avalanche lily (*Erythronium montanum*) blooms at the bottom of the path.

Roses and a succession of late-spring and summer-flowering perennials, including hyacinths, peonies, alliums, hardy geraniums, and fall-blooming asters, make their home in the beds on the south side of the house. On your way out, step into the Hardy Fern Garden and have a look at Lakewold's newest garden room. It wasn't planned by Church or planted by Eulalie (the Hardy Fern Society built it), but it has a charm of its own. The Garden Shop, built into the original 1918 Carriage House, sells a tempting array of plants that are grown at Lakewold and can be difficult to obtain at local nurseries.

Lakewold and its wonderful gardens probably would have been demolished or redeveloped if Eulalie Wagner had not donated the entire estate to a nonprofit organization, The Friends of Lakewold, with the stipulation that an endowment fund be raised to ensure the continuing care of the gardens. "As we become more and more city creatures," she wrote at the time, "living in man-made surroundings, perhaps gardens will become even more precious to us, letting us remember that we began in the garden." The gardens she spent more than forty years of her life planning, planting, and perfecting opened to the public in 1989 and offer visitors a memorable introduction to a memorable woman.

Thomas Church's signature quatrefoil-shaped pool serves as a focal point on one side of Lakewold's Brick Walk.

pacific rim bonsai collection

Outdoor museum of exquisite beauty at the Weyerhaeuser world headquarters

33663 Weyerhaeuser Way S, Federal Way, WA 98003
weyerhaeuser.com/bonsai
Visit April through October

....

📞 (800) 525-5440 ext. 5206
🕐 Open Tue–Sun 10am–4pm
$ Admission free
🚍 Public transportation
👁 This is an outdoor museum and children must be supervised at all times
🐕 No dogs

At the Pacific Rim Bonsai Collection, dozens of exquisite examples of bonsai from the United States and Asia are displayed in an outdoor museum setting.

The Pacific Rim Bonsai Collection is not a garden in the way we generally think of gardens. It is, more accurately, an outdoor museum of living art. It is also the only museum of its kind and caliber in the Pacific Northwest, and the exquisite beauty of every bonsai on display may alter your appreciation for this ancient art form. Not everyone who loves plants is into bonsai (pronounced "bonesigh"), and there are many misperceptions about what it is and how it is created. In China, where bonsai originated, trees were being grown in pots as early as the second century. Penjing, the Chinese word for bonsai, means "potted scene" and refers to the Chinese tradition of adding dramatically shaped stones to a pot or tray to create a miniature scene. This esoteric hobby of nobles and scholars spread to Korea and Japan sometime between the eighth and thirteenth centuries. In Japan, the art of growing miniature potted trees was modified, aesthetically codified, and became bonsai.

At its simplest, a bonsai is a dwarfed, artistically shaped tree grown in a container and meant to evoke a certain mood or feeling. In other words, each plant is a living sculpture. A successful bonsai is trained to conform to certain traditional shapes and aesthetic standards. The mature examples in the Pacific Rim Bonsai Collection have been shaped and tended for decades, sometimes generations. Each one has a very definite personality or presence.

Weyerhaeuser opened this collection to the public in 1989 in conjunction with the Washington state centennial. It's a handsome place, serene and inviting, on the grounds of the company's world headquarters. The courtyard buildings at the entrance were designed by Seattle architect Robert Hoshide to reflect architectural elements from both Asian and North American Pacific Rim countries. The simplicity of Japanese design is combined with the

distinctive building materials (cedar siding and shingles, clear fir doors) of the Pacific Northwest.

The first building you enter is a conservatory showcasing tropical bonsai that need special care, but the rest of the permanent collection is displayed outdoors on a 1-acre site designed by landscape architect Thomas Berger. It has park and garden elements (benches and special landscape features), but it is really a museum in which outstanding examples of bonsai from Canada, China, Japan, Korea, Taiwan, and the United States are dramatically posed against freestanding walls that form open galleries connected by gravel paths. The size, age, and complexity of the bonsai—about sixty are on display at any given time—will take your breath away. You'll definitely have your favorites, and if you're familiar with the art of bonsai, you will spot a few celebrity trees that have been featured in books and magazines. First and foremost, however, you will realize that each one of these trees is a complex and amazingly precise work of art.

The trees used for bonsai are grown from nursery stock or taken from the wild. Any kind of tree can be used to create bonsai, but most of them are hardy, long-lived varieties with small leaves or needles and attractive bark. Spruce, pine, juniper, zelkova, pomegranate, and certain oaks and maples are the most common. The tree is grown in a simple, shallow ceramic container (literally translated,

This Japanese 'Mount Fuji' beech, native to the foothills around Mount Fuji, was propagated in 1953, and its bonsai training was begun in 1958.

the Japanese word bonsai means "a planting in a shallow container"). Over time, the tree is trained by careful shaping and pruning to grow into a particular style, such as formal upright, informal upright, slant, semi- and full cascade, forest planting, twin trunk, raft, landscape planting, clump, and literati. (You will see all these styles as you explore the collection.) All parts of the ideal bonsai—trunk, branches, twigs, leaves, flowers, fruits, buds, roots—must be in perfect scale with the size of the tree, and the trunk must give the illusion of maturity. To qualify as a bonsai, the miniature tree must be both a representation of nature and a creative expression. It's an art that requires Zenlike patience and precision.

Bonsai prefer an outdoor environment appropriate to their species, but even cold-hardy plants require protection in below-freezing weather because their roots may be exposed within their containers. (To give the appearance of age, the upper third of the root structure of a mature bonsai is often exposed.) Every plant remains on display throughout the winter but enclosed within a small glass greenhouse with an open front. When the temperature dips below freezing, a heater is placed inside each greenhouse and a glass front is affixed to it. The effect is dramatic in its own winterized way because each greenhouse becomes like a protective shrine guarding the precious living artwork within.

You can easily combine your trip to the Pacific Rim Bonsai Collection with a visit to the Rhododendron Species Botanical Garden directly adjacent to it. You'll need at least two hours to see both.

point defiance park

5400 N Pearl Street, Tacoma, WA 98407
metroparkstacoma.org/point-defiance-park/
Visit May through September for gardens, year-round for
    other attractions

📞 (253) 305-1000
🕐 Open daily dawn to dusk
$ Admission free
🚌 Public transportation
🐕 Dogs on leash in gardens; off-leash dog playground
    in park

Eight formal gardens in a large urban park with a commanding view of South Puget Sound

Much loved by locals, Point Defiance Park is not very well known outside the Tacoma area except as the place where you catch the ferry to Vashon Island. But if you're exploring gardens in this part of the Pacific Northwest, Point Defiance is worth a visit. One of the largest urban parks in the United States, encompassing 702 acres, the park is a family-friendly place with lots of scenic, recreational, and historic attractions—including eight formal gardens and a rare stand of old-growth trees.

The park is located at the tip of a peninsula that juts out into South Puget Sound. Because of its high cliffs and prominent location, it became a military reservation in the 1840s but was never used for military operations. President Grover Cleveland authorized its use as a public park in 1888, and by 1890, streetcars were bringing visitors to enjoy a variety of (now-vanished) waterside diversions.

The Rose Garden, among the oldest in the West, was established in 1895 by Ebenezer Roberts, a rose-loving Welshman who had become the city's superintendent of parks in 1888. (Roberts's home, an attractive Craftsman-cum-chalet structure behind the rose garden, now serves as the Point Defiance Visitor Center.) Covering about an acre, the Rose Garden is decidedly old-fashioned, and the kitschy addition of a wishing well may make you wince, but the beds are loaded with beautiful and fragrant varieties, and for generations of visitors this has been the focal point of the park.

The adjacent Dahlia Trial Garden, one of the largest official trial gardens in North America, contains plants grown from tubers sent by dahlia growers in the United States, Canada, England, New Zealand, and Australia. Each year, the dahlias are scored by official judges of the American Dahlia Society, and high scorers are included in the annual classification book, given names, and offered to the public. Blooms begin in July, but August is the best time to view the dahlias in full bloom.

The colorful Fuchsia Garden contains 125 different varieties of hardy deciduous fuchsias, and the Herb Garden showcases more than 150 perennial plants that thrive in the Puget Sound area. The Iris Garden is divided into five beds: one for tall bearded iris, two

At its best in August, the Dahlia Trial Garden in Point Defiance Park is among the largest dahlia gardens in North America.

for various median irises, and one for beardless iris (Siberian and Pacific Coast iris).

Azaleas, rhododendrons, Japanese cherry trees, crabapples, and large and small pines make the Japanese Garden a springtime pleasure, but this garden, established in 1963, is undergoing a transformation that will take several years to complete. The Northwest Native Garden, located just before the park exit, is also undergoing revitalization, but you can still wander the paths that wind past a waterfall, a pond, and a striking wooden gazebo designed by noted landscape architect Thomas Church. More impressive is the Rhododendron Garden, nestled within an old-growth forest.

Pleasant as the gardens are, you may find other areas of the park more engaging. Five Mile Drive winds through 400 acres

The Northwest Native Garden is one of eight display gardens in Point Defiance Park.

of old-growth forest preserved at the park's northern tip. (On Sundays, when the drive is closed to traffic, it makes a great bike or hiking trail.) Skirting through 450-year-old Douglas-firs and along cliffs that are 250 feet high, the drive has several scenic turnouts where you can stop to enjoy panoramic views of Vashon Island, Gig Harbor, and the Tacoma Narrows Bridge. These are prime wildlife-viewing areas where you might spot a bald eagle diving down from a snag to snatch a salmon, or see harbor seals basking and barking on offshore rocks. Owen Beach, on the east side of the point, is another favorite spot for strolling, picnicking, or just hanging out to enjoy the pleasures of the South Sound.

You might wonder how Point Defiance got its name. In 1836 Congress authorized the United States Exploring Expedition (sometimes called the U.S. Ex. Ex.) to explore and survey the Pacific Ocean and surrounding lands. When the expedition reached Puget Sound in the early 1840s to map its bays and estuaries, commanding officer Lieutenant Charles Wilkes purportedly noted that with a fort on the peninsula that is today's park, and another at Gig Harbor across the Tacoma Narrows, the United States could "defy the world."

Other Highlights of Point Defiance Park

Located on the west side of Point Defiance Park, Fort Nisqually Living History Museum is an award-winning restoration of a Hudson Bay Company trading post. The British-owned Hudson Bay Company maintained a series of trading forts that stretched from Fort Vancouver as far north as present-day Alaska. Fort Nisqually was the first nonnative settlement on Puget Sound. Today, staff and volunteers in period costume demonstrate what life was like in the 1850s. fortnisqually.org.

The most popular attractions in Point Defiance Park are the zoo and the aquarium. Both have been around for decades and gone through many changes, most notably the enlargement and upgrading of animal habitats. The zoo now features an Asian Forest Sanctuary; a popular "Cats of the Canopy" exhibit; Rocky Shores, featuring marine animals; Arctic Tundra with reindeer, Arctic foxes, and muskox; and Red Wolf Woods. The aquarium is divided into North Pacific and South Pacific areas. The plantings in and around the zoo are unusually well done. pdza.org.

powellswood

430 S Dash Point Road, Federal Way, WA 98003
powellswood.org
Visit April through August

- 📞 (253) 529-1620
- 🕐 Open Apr–Oct Tue–Sat 10am–3pm
- $ Admission fee
- ♿ Trails in woodland not wheelchair accessible
- 🐕 No dogs

Inspiring woodland and garden-in-progress newly risen from a barren wasteland

What treasures do the suburbs hide? And what nightmares do they conceal?

One suburban treasure is PowellsWood, a colorful new public garden and woodland above Redondo Beach in the Marine Hills neighborhood of South Puget Sound. The nightmare is what was done to these 40 acres before Monte Powell bought them in 1993 and started his restoration efforts.

First, of course, the land was logged. Then Cold Creek, the spring-fed, salmon-filled stream that ran through the property to Puget Sound, was drilled for local water use and eventually disappeared because the aquifer was pumped dry. After that, the owner of the property used part of it as a dump. A century's worth of environmental degradation turned what had been a verdant woodland into a barren wasteland. The only reason the entire ravine had not been sold off for development was that it had once been the Cold Creek watershed.

A visit to PowellsWood today shows you what can be done to restore and revitalize a piece of land that has had the life sucked out of it. It's now a lovely and even inspiring place to stroll and enjoy. It has to be mentioned, however, that PowellsWood is definitely a garden-in-progress. A major ice storm in 2012 took out

Hardy bananas and a colorful array of bedding plants give the upper gardens at PowellsWood an almost tropical look.

several specimen trees and changed the initial garden design overnight. The overall shape of the gardens is complete but the plant material in many of the beds is being rethought and replanted with less emphasis on annuals and more on perennials. Warmer temperatures resulting from climate change have also changed the kinds of plants that are being used.

The first gardens you see, around the visitor center and patio, were redesigned after the ice storm by landscaper Rick Serazin, who used hardy bananas and spiky, feathery, brilliantly colored plants in shades of red, yellow, chocolate, and lime-green to create a kind of "tropical lite" look. It's more showy than distinguished, but the plan is to gradually replant these bright summer borders with more interesting perennials that will provide shape, texture, and color throughout the year.

From the upper entrance gardens a wide swath of lawn flows down to the lush and lovely gardens below. More traditional in character, these lower gardens are primarily banked perennial borders that were first planted in 1997, along with Japanese cherries, European hornbeams, and large woody rhododendrons salvaged from building sites. High hedges of Portugal laurel, yew, and cypress create a sense of privacy and enclosure throughout the 3-acre display garden, shielding it from Dash Point Road and muffling traffic noise.

What you'll hear instead is a softly gurgling stream flowing over rocks to a lily-filled pond. The manmade stream, its margins planted with sedges and moisture-loving plants like gunnera, works as a cleaning and filtration system for rainwater runoff that eventually flows into Puget Sound.

It's hard to believe now, but this welcoming green oasis was a junk-filled brownfield back in 1993. To get the soil back into some semblance of health, Monte laid down tons of mulches and planted and plowed in green manure. Restoring and reinvigorating the soil is an ongoing process at PowellsWood—and it's done without herbicides or pesticides (though iron sulfate is used as slug bait). If the gardens all look relatively fresh and new, that's because they are.

The gardens in the lower valley lead into a 37-acre wedge of successional Doug-fir forest that stretches north to Puget Sound. This is the wood of PowellsWood. A Woodland Garden at the edge of the forest is planted with shade-tolerant ferns, mayapples, hellebores, epimediums, hydrangeas, and native vancouveria. You can look into the forest from a viewing platform or head down into it to hike along the trails.

For Monte Powell, who played in this forest as a boy and lives here today, cleaning up, clearing out, and creating a new PowellsWood has been an ongoing mission. A project of this scope requires vision, determination, financial resources, and a commitment to environmental stewardship. In the end, it's not only about giving something back to the community, it's also about giving something back to nature.

The lush and lovely lower gardens and pond at PowellsWood were created on an old dump site where nothing grew.

rhododendron species botanical garden

World-class collection in a
mature Douglas-fir forest at the
Weyerhaeuser world headquarters

33663 Weyerhaeuser Way S, Federal Way, WA 98003
rhodygarden.org
Visit year-round; March through June for rhododendron
    bloom; June for blue poppies

....

📞 (253) 838-4646
🕐 Open Tue–Sun 10am–4pm
$ Admission fee
🚌 Public transportation
🐕 No dogs

Over the last half century or so, hybrid rhododendrons have
become staples in Pacific Northwest gardens. Their popularity is
understandable, for rhododendrons come in an enormous variety
of shapes, sizes, and flower colors, and they thrive in the moist,
mild climate and slightly acid soil west of the Cascades.

But great as some of these hybrids are, it's the wild rhododendron species—the ones you'll rarely find at plant nurseries—that
truly capture the imagination of rhodie lovers and plant collectors. And that's why the Rhododendron Species Botanical Garden
(RSBG) is so special. About seven hundred of the approximately
one thousand known species in the genus *Rhododendron* are cultivated here. It's the finest collection of its kind in the world and
serves as a living museum to help conserve these beautiful, diverse,
and endangered plants. With much of their native habitat shrink-
ing or disappearing entirely, many of these wild species are threatened with extinction.

Rhododendrons are native to the temperate regions of Asia,
North America, and Europe, and the tropical regions of southeast
Asia and northern Australia. They grow at altitudes ranging from
sea level to 19,000 feet and are found in alpine conditions, coniferous and broad-leaved woodlands, temperate rainforests, and tropical jungles. Wild rhododendrons, as you'll see on your visit to the
RSBG, come in all shapes and sizes, from prostrate alpine creepers
to moderate-size shrubs to giant trees that can reach 100 feet or
more in the wild. Leaf shapes vary from tiny needles to 3-foot
platters, and flowers may be white, red, pink, yellow, blue, purple,
magenta, orange, or shades and mixtures of all of these colors.

The RSBG has been under the lovingly enthusiastic cura-
torship of Steve Hootman for more than two decades. Spread
over 22 acres in a mature Douglas-fir forest, this magical garden
invites year-round exploration. Adding even more oomph to the

Wild beauties like
this *Rhododendron
pingianum* from
Sichuan, China,
make their home at
the Rhododendron
Species Botanical
Garden.

rhododendrons, which bloom from January to October (with peak bloom from mid-April to mid-May), is the rich assortment of companion plants, theme gardens, and a new conservatory.

The main path from the garden entrance loops through the entire garden, but there are numerous side paths to explore in this rhodie wonderland. The rhododendrons are planted by section and subsection, and it's useful to pick up a copy of the guidebook if you want to identify specific plants. Some of the most notable rhodies and companion plants are labeled and included on a self-guided tour.

The Upper Woodland Garden, the first area past the entrance courtyard, features many rhododendron species with thickly indumented leaf undersurfaces. In rhodiespeak that means the bottoms of their leaves are covered with furry hairs or scales. In this area you'll also find two June-blooming magnolias: the pink flowers of *Magnolia sargentiana* var. *robusta* from China are among the largest of any magnolia in the world, while the giant leaves beneath the creamy white flowers of *M. hypoleuca* from Japan can grow up to 1.5 feet long. Look, too, for the early-spring-blooming *Paeonia mairei*, a rare, shade-loving, woodland species of peony from the wild forests of China. *Rhododendron cinnabarinum*, with its blue-green leaves and pendulous, tubular flowers, is native to the Himalayas.

The path continues past the Lower Woodland to the Big-Leaf Rhododendron Garden. Most of the big-leaved rhododendrons found here come from temperate rainforests in the Sino-Himalaya, where they grow to be very large trees with leaves up to 3 feet long. Continue past the long sweep of ostrich fern (*Matteuccia struthiopteris*) and look for the labeled *Rhododendron rex* on both sides of the path. *Rhododendron rex*, with its thick buff-to-gray indumentum on the undersides of shiny, deep-green leaves, can grow to *T. rex* size, attaining heights of 45 feet in its native China.

Soon, on your left, you'll see the garden's famous Meconopsis Meadow. This is the best display of Himalayan blue poppies (*Meconopsis betonicifolia*) in North America. And if you visit in June and see them in bloom, you'll never forget the sight. Towering over the poppies is a stand of giant Himalayan lily (*Cardiocrinum giganteum*) with stalks that grow to be almost 14 feet tall and fragrant flowers that open in late summer.

Farther on, fallen logs and overturned tree roots planted with ferns and woodland plants were used to create the Victorian

A field of rare Himalayan blue poppies is one of the botanical attractions at the Rhododendron Species Botanical Garden in Federal Way, Washington.

Stumpery, an English Victorian-era garden design that romanticizes nature by creating a "wild scene." Nearby is the Pond Garden, with its lush assortment of water-loving plants, and the Alpine Garden with its collection of low-growing, high-altitude plants from the mountains of Asia.

As you walk up toward the gazebo, you'll pass *Rhododendron russatum*, a dwarf alpine rhododendron from mountainous regions of China. Growing around the gazebo is *R. yakushimanum*, a rare species found only on the very top of an ancient volcano on Yaku Island, Japan.

Follow the sign to the Rutherford Conservatory. Built in 2010, this 5,000-square-foot conservatory showcases tropical rhododendrons (often called vireya rhododendrons) and some of the rare plants that grow with them in the remote mountains and cloud forests of Borneo, New Guinea, Vietnam, and other regions of southeastern Asia.

Most of the rhodies grown in the RSBG are not available in regular retail nurseries, so rhodie lovers will definitely want to browse the Garden Shop Nursery, where many of these rare and wonderful plants are for sale. Sales help to support the Rhododendron Species Foundation, a nonprofit organization dedicated to education, research, and conservation of rhododendron species.

You can easily combine your visit to the Rhododendron Species Botanical Garden with a visit to the Pacific Rim Bonsai Collection. These two superlative gardens share a common entrance courtyard on the Weyerhaeuser campus in Federal Way.

soos creek botanical garden

29308 132nd Avenue SE, Auburn, WA 98092
sooscreekbotanicalgarden.org
Visit year-round; spring and summer for peak flowering

- ☎ (253) 639-0949
- ◷ Open Wed–Sat 10am–3pm
- $ Admission free
- 🐕 No dogs

Diverse plantings—inspired by great gardens of the world as well as local history—sloping down to a rushing stream

By the 1890s, the rich bottomlands around Soos Creek had all been claimed, and Norwegian immigrants like Ole and Andrew Oie began buying and clearing parcels of the Soos Creek Plateau for their farms. Much of the plateau was owned by the Northern Pacific Railroad, and most of the people who settled on it were Scandinavians—primarily Norwegians, Swedes, and Finns. Between 1891 and 1905, Ole and Andrew bought, cleared, and farmed 200 acres. A century later, in 2011, a portion of this Norwegian immigrant farm became a noteworthy addition to the gardens of the Pacific Northwest when it opened to the public as Soos Creek Botanical Garden.

The 22-acre garden was created over five decades by Maurice Skagen, a descendant of the original farmers, and his partner, James Daly. In 1963, when Maurice first began acquiring plants, the land was still covered with remnants of native trees (Douglas-firs, western red cedars, hemlocks, vine and bigleaf maples) and with native perennials such as trilliums and skunk cabbage. To this

The Heritage Garden at Soos Creek Botanical Garden is filled with the kind of old-fashioned plants—peonies, irises, and climbing roses—that were typically shared among friends and families of earlier generations.

mixture Maurice added a large selection of conifers, azaleas, rhododendrons, and other evergreen shrubs. Visits to Sissinghurst (Vita Sackville-West's garden in Kent) and other great gardens of England and Japan expanded his vision for the garden and the plants that he wanted to grow in it. New additions included tree peonies from Kyoto and mountain ash varieties native to England. The botanical collection grew over the following decades as plants were acquired from friends, other gardens, and Pacific Northwest specialty nurseries. Today, this unique Northwest stroll garden, which changes character as it slopes down toward the rushing waters of Soos Creek, offers visitors an opportunity to enjoy a wonderful variety of plants and plant life in several different settings.

If you want to give yourself a good self-guided tour, pick up a garden map at the Soos Creek Heritage Center near the garden entrance. After your visit you may want to return to the center to learn more about the farming life of the early Scandinavian settlers on the 35-square-mile Soos Creek Plateau. A new rain garden near the entrance directs water runoff from the parking area to a small pond set among a grove of alders.

Presided over by an old-growth Douglas-fir, with a backdrop of ornamental trees and a yellow-blossomed 'Elizabeth' magnolia, the Heritage Flower Garden west of the house was inspired by the flower garden of Maurice's aunt, which was always full of shared plants like the old-fashioned peonies, irises, heathers, and climbing roses found here.

The path continues to the Elizabeth Fenzl Garden Room, an enclosed retreat featuring tree peonies, hardy fuchsias, climbing hydrangeas, azaleas, and an old 'Nelly Moser' clematis that scrambles up a Rainier cherry tree. (The idea to let roses and flowering vines climb up into the trees came from Sissinghurst.) Some of the unusual shrubs and trees in this area include *Eucriphia* (native to Chile and Australia), Persian ironwood (*Parrotia persica*), eastern white pine (*Pinus strobus*), Pacific dogwood (*Cornus nuttallii*), an umbrella pine (*Sciadopitys verticillata*), and a mature catalpa.

Beyond the large vegetable demonstration garden and the aviary, with its clucking and cooing contingent of doves, Asian pheasants, peafowl, cockatiels, and chickens, you'll arrive at the Pond Garden, laden with water lilies and edged with water-loving gunnera and umbrella plant (*Darmera peltata*).

From the pond, which sits at the top of the plateau, the garden begins its gradual descent down to Soos Creek. A long, gently sloping central lawn is defined on both sides by colorful mixed borders inspired by the English garden designer Gertrude Jekyll. A 15-foot-high banana tree (well wrapped every winter) stands at the top of the north border, and a snakebark maple with its striking striped bark sits partway down the south border. Deciduous azaleas, a wingthorn rose (*Rosa sericea*), a tamarisk tree, a golden ninebark (*Physocarpus*), and Moroccan broom (*Cytisus battandieri*) add to the kaleidoscope of color, form, and texture in the two borders.

At the bottom of the lawn, along the paths leading through a grove of giant western red cedars, you'll find an array of woodland and shade-tolerant plants, shrubs, and trees, including evergreen kalmias with their distinctive, June-blooming flower clusters, pieris, Solomon's seal, rhododendrons, magnolias, viburnums, and camellias. Of special interest is the blue Aptos sequoia in the northeast area of the cedar grove. The path to Soos Creek, the lowest point in the garden, takes you through the Ravine Garden, which mixes ferns and other native plants with rhododendrons, hardy geraniums, and Japanese maples. The sound of rushing water fills the air.

Finally, you come to the Oie Native Woodland, devoted to the ferns and wildflowers that thrived here along the margins of fast-moving Soos Creek before settlers, farms, or a botanical garden. Bleeding heart, trillium, twinflower, fringe cup, licorice fern, and sword fern all make their home here. The silver dollar plants (*Lunaria annua*) that sparkle in the summer sun in the Leonard and Olive Skagen Woods were seeded by those hard-working Norwegian immigrants who first settled Soos Creek.

The long, gently sloping lawn at Soos Creek Botanical Garden has richly planted borders that were inspired by the gardens of early-twentieth-century garden designer Gertrude Jekyll.

w. w. seymour botanical conservatory and wright park

316 South G Street, Tacoma, WA 98405
metroparkstacoma.org/wright-park/
Visit year-round

....

📞 (253) 591-5330
🕐 Open Tue–Sun 10am–4:30pm
$ Admission free
🚌 Public transportation
🐕 No dogs in conservatory, on leash in park

Century-old tropical-plant conservatory in historic, tree-filled city park

In 1906, a wealthy businessman named William Wolcott Seymour donated ten thousand dollars (equivalent to about two hundred thousand dollars today) to the city of Tacoma "to be used as deemed most advisable in beautifying the city." Born in St. Albans, Vermont, Seymour had made a fortune in the Pacific Northwest trading in timber and utilities and wanted to give something back to the city where he had prospered.

The city decided to use Seymour's money to build a tropical-plant conservatory in a public park created on land gifted to the city by Charles B. Wright, another civic-minded citizen, twenty

Now more than a
century old, the W. W.
Seymour Botanical
Conservatory in
Tacoma's Wright
Park is one of only
three Victorian-style
conservatories on
the West Coast.

years earlier. Now, more than a century later, the W. W. Seymour
Botanical Conservatory and Wright Park remain important focal
points in Tacoma's historic core. If you're in the vicinity, you can
spend a pleasant hour or two visiting both of them.

The conservatory, with its twelve-sided central dome, opened
to the public in 1908. It's one of only three Victorian-style glass
conservatories on the West Coast and is listed on the National
Register of Historic Places. Today, with travel to tropical locales
so easy and images of tropical plants instantly accessible on the
Internet, it's difficult to imagine the impact the tropical plants in
the conservatory had on early visitors. It was the first time many
of them had seen exotic flora—orchids, birds of paradise, citrus
trees—that came from a world far beyond the Pacific Northwest.
You won't find the richness and horticultural panache of Seattle's
Volunteer Park Conservatory here, but you will find brilliant
seasonal floral displays, more than two hundred orchids, and collections of vireyas (tropical rhododendrons) from southeast Asia,

clivias and agapanthus native to southern Africa, epiphyllums from Central America, plus cacti, ferns, palms, figs, bromeliads, and many other rare, unusual, and endangered plants. With some three hundred to five hundred blooming plants on display year-round, this is a pleasant place to come for an eye-warming splash of color when the weather turns dark and drear.

Wright Park, where the Seymour Conservatory is located, was born in 1886 when 20 acres were donated to the city of Tacoma for use as a public park. The idea for a public park had been floating around since at least 1873, when Frederick Law Olmsted, the most influential landscape architect in the United States, was asked to submit a park plan for Tacoma. Olmsted's naturalistic design, with its curvilinear streets and preservation of natural landscape features, didn't sit well with Tacomans, who liked their blocks square and their parks predictable. They rejected Olmsted's plan and dismissed the man who had created New York's Central Park. In 1890 they hired Edward O. Schwagerl to design Wright Park. By then, the idea of natural-looking park spaces had

The many delights found in green, graceful Wright Park in Tacoma's historic core include some of the largest specimen trees in Washington State.

become more acceptable, in part because of the rural cemeteries that were being created in cities back East. Schwagerl had helped design just such a cemetery in Portland (River View Cemetery, 1880). In Tacoma, Schwagerl drew up plans for Wright Park and Point Defiance Park before moving on to become Seattle's superintendent of parks. (Ironically, Schwagerl's plan for a park system in Seattle was rejected in favor of a plan submitted by Olmsted Brothers, the landscape design firm run by two sons of Frederick Law Olmsted.)

Part of what makes this graceful old park so appealing is its trees. More than 350 varieties of trees from the United States and Europe were planted when the park was first created. Some are still standing, but many were destroyed in the legendary Columbus Day Storm of 1962. Thirty of the existing trees are state champions (meaning they are the largest specimens in the state). Maps that show all the trees in the park by number are available in the Seymour Conservatory; a Champion Trees self-guided tour that highlights twelve of the champions can be borrowed from the conservatory (deposit required). Most of the park's trees have name labels on them; the twelve in the champions tour have special champion labels.

Statues collected in Europe in 1891 by Tacoma resident Colonel Clinton P. Ferry and donated to the park include the Greek maidens (known locally as "Fannie and Annie") flanking the park's entrance on Division Avenue, and two white stone Brussels lions located at the 6th Street entrance. And you have to love a park—at least I do—that includes a 1913 bust of Norwegian playwright Henrik Ibsen among its memorials.

Stone paths cut and laid by hand crisscross the remarkable alpine landscape at Ohme Gardens.

central, eastern & southern washington

fort vancouver heritage garden

Re-creation of the oldest kitchen
garden in the Pacific Northwest

Fort Vancouver National Historic Site, 612 East Reserve Street, Vancouver, WA 98661
nps.gov/fova
Visit May through September

The first plants to be cultivated in the Pacific Northwest were started from seeds shipped to the British Hudson's Bay Company at Fort Vancouver.

📞 (360) 816-6230
🕐 Visitor center open Mon–Sat 9am–5pm, Sun 10am–5pm; fort open noon–5pm; closed January 1, November 25, December 24, 25, 31
$ Admission free
🚌 Public transportation
🐕 No dogs

Here's a horticultural history question for you: What does the nineteenth-century craze for beaver hats in New York and Europe have to do with the creation of the first garden in the Pacific Northwest?

For the answer, we have to time-travel back to 1825 and poke around the grounds of Fort Vancouver. Back then, the Pacific Northwest was called the Oregon Country and was claimed by both the United States (which extended as far west as Ohio) and England. Furs were a hot commodity—water-repellent beaver hats were all the rage—and big fur-trading companies from both countries were eager to cash in. In 1825, the British-owned Hudson's Bay Company (HBC) built Fort Vancouver as headquarters for the company's twenty-three auxiliary forts in their Columbia Department (present-day Oregon, Washington, and British Columbia). Located on the north bank of the Columbia River about 90 miles east of the Pacific Ocean, Fort Vancouver was a large organization with lots of men who needed to be fed.

Keep in mind that no garden of any scale had ever been successfully planted in the Pacific Northwest before this time. The Spanish had made an attempt at Nootka Sound (in today's British Columbia), and at least one Native American tribe cultivated a now-extinct form of tobacco, but there had never been anything that could be called a garden. The Europeans and Americans who came west at that early date had no idea what would grow or when to plant.

Old Apple Tree Park

You can't leave Fort Vancouver without paying your respects to the oldest apple tree in the Pacific Northwest. Planted in 1826, this hoary elder is one of only three survivors from Fort Vancouver's historic HBC period (the other two are Douglas-firs at the east end of the Parade Ground). Modern development has almost entirely obliterated the fort's original orchard, so to reach the tree you have to follow an interpretive walkway planted with a panoply of Northwest native trees, herbs, and shrubs across the freeway to Old Apple Tree Park.

There, in a sliver of grass between a freeway ramp and the train tracks, stands the Old Apple Tree. You can't help but feel sorry for the old guy, isolated within a chain-link enclosure, kept alive by the ministrations of the Park Service, and never free from the awful din of the freeway and the clanking of freight cars. But he's still producing apples, and his genetic material lives on in some of the trees planted in 1962 in an interpretive orchard closer to the re-created fort.

That changed when Dr. John McLoughlin, the dynamic chief factor (superintendent of trade) of Fort Vancouver, had his workers plant about 3 acres with peas, beans, and potatoes. From then on, the fort's garden grew steadily. In 1826, Aemilius Simpson, who arrived with the HBC, introduced cultivated apples to the Pacific Northwest. The Royal Horticultural Society sent seeds from England to Fort Vancouver to ascertain what would grow in this new land. Some of the RHS seeds were brought by Scottish botanist David Douglas, who had first arrived in the Oregon Country in 1823 on a collecting expedition for the RHS. (The most famous of the approximately fifty Northwest native trees and shrubs and one hundred herbaceous plants Douglas introduced to England is the Douglas-fir, named in his honor.)

By 1833 an HBC employee named William Bruce had become the region's first professional gardener, tending a 7-acre kitchen garden that produced dozens of crops and was the largest garden west of the Mississippi and north of California. Dahlias from Hawaii grew in the thriving garden, and a visitor described seeing citrus trees in the orchard. Fort Vancouver's garden set the stage for the agricultural explosion that would soon transform the ancient oak savannas and forested valleys west of the Cascades into some of the richest and most productive farmland in the world.

That's a big build-up and I don't want to mislead you by suggesting the garden you see at Fort Vancouver National Historic Site today is anything like the garden of Dr. John McLoughlin's day. It's not. The fort, with its towering wooden palisades and corner towers, is a re-creation of the original. The garden is also a re-creation, greatly reduced in size and moved from its original location to the front entrance of the fort. But for anyone interested in the history of Pacific Northwest gardens, it's still worth visiting.

The original garden was divided into eleven beds, planted with vegetables, herbs, grains, and flowers, with strawberry-lined walkways and a summerhouse covered with grape vines. The vegetables in the re-created garden—including British soldier beans (also known as red-eye beans), runner beans, citron, yellow pear tomatoes, squash, and corn—are heirlooms, as are the herbs and grains (oats and buckwheat). Flowers include nicotiana, dianthus, coreopsis, and dahlias. To modern eyes, this is not a decorative garden so much as it is a practical one, but its well-ordered simplicity still evokes an important chapter in horticultural history.

After visiting the garden, pay the small fee and step inside the tall wooden stockade of reconstructed Fort Vancouver for a look at the Carpenter's Shop, the Fur Warehouse, the Indian Trade Shop and Dispensary, and the Bakehouse. The white-frame Chief Factor's Residence, where Dr. John McLoughlin lived until the area came under U.S. control in 1846, is the most civilized of the fort's buildings.

hulda klager lilac gardens

115 South Pekin Road, Woodland, WA 98674
lilacgardens.com
Visit during Lilac Days, when lilacs are at their peak, usually
from the third weekend in April to Mother's Day; check
Web site for yearly dates

- 📞 (360) 225-8996
- 🕐 Open most days 10am–4pm, but check Web site
- 💲 Admission fee
- ♿ Historic house is not wheelchair accessible
- 🐕 No dogs

Historic lilac garden created by famed hybridizer

Some plants are imprinted in our consciousness at a very early age.
We may be too young to know what they are, but they make a deep
and unforgettable impression. For me, it was lilacs. An enormous
hedge of old-fashioned *Syringa vulgaris* bloomed with lavish abandon in our yard every May and scented the entire neighborhood.
For about six weeks starting in mid-April, that same sweetly irresist-
ible fragrance draws thousands of lilac lovers to the Hulda Klager
Lilac Gardens, a pioneer farm with a white Victorian farmhouse
and hundreds of dwarf, shrub, and tree-sized lilacs. Although it's
now hemmed in on one side by a housing development and at the
rear by a protective dike with a railroad track atop it, the house and
4-acre gardens still manage to evoke a sense of old-fashioned country charm and have been designated a state historic landmark.

The biggest surprise here—if you think all lilacs are the pale
purple *Syringa vulgaris* that has been a staple in American gardens
for more than two hundred years—is the range of color. In addition to purple, you'll find white, blue, pink, lavender, and magenta

The Hulda Klager Lilac Gardens are at their peak during Lilac Days, a three-week event held every spring at the pioneer farm where Hulda Klager spent most of her life.

lilacs. The petals can be a surprise, too. Lilac florets, which blossom in clusters called panicles, have four distinct petals on each single flower, but some of the cultivars are doubles with two and even three sets of petals. Sometimes the petal is subtly shaded or ringed with another color. And then there's that heady perfume. Each lilac here is rated for its scent: mild, high, very high, and extreme. Late-blooming lilacs use a different system: sweet, spicy, strong, and fragrant. Some have no scent at all—but to me a lilac without scent, no matter how showy the flower, is like a singer without a voice.

A member of the olive family (*Oleaceae*) and native to the Balkan Peninsula, *Syringa vulgaris* was introduced into European gardens via Turkey in the late 1500s. By the eighteenth century, lilacs had made their way to the American colonies. Presidents George Washington and Thomas Jefferson grew lilacs in their gardens at Mount Vernon and Monticello. Like roses, lilacs traveled west with the pioneers, via ship and covered wagon.

So who was Hulda Klager? Known locally as the Lilac Lady, she was the daughter of German immigrants who settled in Wisconsin in 1865 and moved to Woodland, Washington, in 1877, when Hulda was thirteen years old. She'd always had an interest in flowers, but it wasn't until 1903, when she was forty, that a book about pioneering plant geneticist Luther Burbank sparked her interest in

'City of Gresham', with its intense color and unusual florets, is one of the many extraordinary lilacs created by Hulda Klager.

hybridizing plants. She began her experiments with apples, crossing two varieties to create a larger apple that took less time to peel for pies. Then, in 1905, she turned her attention to hybridizing lilacs. She created fourteen new varieties in five years, and by 1920 she had developed so many new varieties that she decided to hold an open house each spring when the lilacs were in full bloom to share her efforts with other lilac enthusiasts. Over the years, she was honored by many organizations—including the State of Washington, the Arnold Arboretum at Harvard, the Federation of Garden Clubs in Washington and Oregon, and the City of Portland, Oregon—for her work as a leading hybridizer of lilacs.

Disaster struck in 1948 when the Columbia and Lewis rivers flooded their banks and destroyed every one of the lilacs Hulda had hand-pollinated, nurtured, and grown in her garden for the past forty years. Undaunted, at age eighty-three, she began to rebuild her garden, obtaining starts from people who had purchased her lilacs in the past.

By 1950 she was able to reopen her gardens for Lilac Week—a practice she continued until her death in 1960 at age ninety-six. This event continues to this day under the sponsorship of the Hulda Klager Lilac Society, a nonprofit volunteer organization. The event is now called Lilac Days and lasts for about three weeks, during which time the early-, mid-, and late-blooming varieties are at their peak. Many of Hulda's hybrid lilacs are for sale at that time, so it's a great opportunity to pick up a unique lilac and support the garden.

The restored farmhouse built by Hulda's parents in 1889, and where she lived with her husband and children, is also open during Lilac Days. It's a handsome, two-story wood structure with large, comfortable rooms loaded with Hulda memorabilia. There's a pretty cottage garden out front and a side lawn shaded by some fine old trees that survived the 1948 flood. You can also see the potting shed where Hulda created lilacs that are now prized specimens in gardens around the world. The lilacs themselves are mostly behind the house, flanking brick walkways. Just follow your nose and you'll find them.

manito park

1702 S Grand Boulevard, Spokane, WA 99203
spokaneparks.org/index.php/Parks/page/88/
Visit in May for lilacs; June and July for roses,
    perennials, annuals

- 📞 (509) 625-6200
- 🕐 Open daily dawn to dusk; Japanese garden closed
  Dec–Mar
- 💲 Admission free
- 🚌 Public transportation
- ♿ Gardens are scattered throughout the park
- 🐕 Dogs on leash

Five different botanical gardens and a conservatory in a historic city park

East of the Cascades, the terrain of Washington State flattens
out to high desert, and the forests change from predominately
Douglas-fir to ponderosa pine. The climate is markedly drier
and hotter in the summer, and colder in the winter. Spokane,
the state's second-largest city, is located in this region called the
Inland Northwest or, because of its boomtown past as a mining
mecca and railroad hub, the Inland Empire. Dating from that
boomtown past is Manito Park, the city's undisputed showplace
for gardens. You can visit all five of its gardens, each stylistically
different, plus the small conservatory, on a leisurely walk (or bike
ride) that takes about ninety minutes. But if the day is clear and
warm, and the air is filled with the pungent scent of pines, lilacs,
or roses, you may be tempted to linger a lot longer.

The 90-acre park, in the South Hill neighborhood, was built
on land deeded to the city in 1904. Initially, it was left mostly as an
undeveloped recreational area, but in 1912 Park Superintendent
John Duncan created the first and most dramatic of Manito Park's
five gardens. Today this classical European Renaissance–style
garden is called the Duncan Garden, but originally it was called
the Sunken Garden because it was built in an area where 42,500

wagonloads of soil had been removed for use in other Spokane parks. Carefully planted with colorful annuals and graced with a central granite fountain, this immaculately maintained garden wouldn't look out of place behind a seventeenth-century palace in France or England. Its size and the strict formality of its bilateral symmetry come as something of a surprise given its roots in pioneer Spokane.

Behind and above Duncan Garden is the Gaiser Conservatory, a relatively new building housing a well-chosen collection of tropical plants and cacti. With its irregularly shaped beds and varied assortment of plants and small trees, the Joel E. Ferris Perennial Garden, located just northeast of the conservatory, serves as an informal counterpoint to the Duncan Garden. It was established in 1930 but has been enlarged and altered over the years. Today, more than three hundred plant species, including several newly

The formal, European Renaissance–style Duncan Garden was created in 1912 and was the first of Manito Park's five gardens.

introduced ornamental grasses, provide color, texture, and fragrance from spring through fall.

In June and July, the captivating scent of roses open and basking in the sun hovers around Rose Hill, the garden to the west of the perennials. The Spokane Rose Society started this hilltop garden in the late 1940s. Shaped like a rectangle with rounded ends demarcated by curving white, colonnaded trellises, the garden is planted with 150 varieties of hybrid tea, floribunda, grandiflora, miniature, and heritage roses.

Earlier in the year, May to be exact, it's the heady perfume of lilacs that drifts through Manito Park. That's when the Lilac Garden, located just northwest of Rose Hill, is in full, fulsome flower. The lilac collection was started in 1912 with 128 named lilac cultivars obtained from a nursery in Rochester, New York, by Park Superintendent John Duncan. Later, in the 1930s, lilacs became to Spokane what roses are to Portland when a group of lilac boosters

Rose Hill, the largest and prettiest rose garden in Spokane, dates from the 1940s and is among the most popular tourist attractions in Manito Park.

John A. Finch Arboretum

In addition to the gardens in Manito Park, Spokane has an outstandingly beautiful arboretum that you might want to visit. Occupying about 65 acres along Garden Springs Creek in the southwest part of the city, the John A. Finch Arboretum was established in 1949 on land once owned by two Spokane pioneers. Few trails traverse the arboretum; instead, some two thousand labeled trees and shrubs representing more than six hundred species and varieties of 120 genera are planted in groves in a green, grassy, parklike setting.

Pick up a map of the self-guided walking tour at the kiosk in the parking lot and give yourself about an hour if you want to make a complete circuit of the grounds. The lilac collection is particularly impressive, but you'll find outstanding examples of beeches, elms, lindens, larches, yews, oaks, dogwoods, walnuts, rhododendrons, crabapples, hawthorns, conifers, maples, and magnolias. The margins of Garden Springs Creek are kept as natural wetlands, and there's a "Touch and See" nature trail as well. No dogs are allowed in the arboretum. 3404 W Woodland Boulevard, Spokane, WA 99224. spokaneparks.org/index.php/Parks/page/99/.

persuaded garden clubs to plant lilacs throughout the city and adopt "the Lilac City" as Spokane's nickname. Today, Manito Park's lilac collection is one of the most important on the West Coast, and the city celebrates its lilac heritage with a Lilac Festival.

Enclosed by a wooden fence and with a separate entrance in the westernmost section of the park, the Nishinomiya Tsutakawa Japanese Garden opened in 1974 as the fifth and most culturally distinct of Manito Park's collection of five gardens. A koi-filled pond forms the centerpiece of this quiet, reflective garden with stone lanterns, clipped pines, and other elements of traditional Japanese garden design.

Herman and Ruth Ohme created a delightful alpine Eden on a barren bluff overlooking the Columbia River near Wenatchee, Washington.

ohme gardens

3327 Ohme Road, Wenatchee WA 98801
ohmegardens.com
Visit April through June

- 📞 (509) 662-5785
- 🕐 Open daily 9am–6pm Apr 15–Memorial Day, and Labor Day–Oct 15; 9am–7pm Memorial Day–Labor Day
- 💲 Admission fee
- ♿ Rustic stairs, steps, and uneven terrain make much of the garden unsuitable for wheelchairs and those with limited mobility
- 🐕 No dogs

A handmade alpine oasis on a bluff overlooking the Columbia River

I wonder if a garden like this one could be created today. Probably not. And that's what makes Ohme Gardens so special: it's a one-of-a-kind wonder that speaks to us about the hard-won beauty that can be achieved when we follow our dreams with persever-ance, endurance, and ingenuity. This garden, now in its seventh decade, was a labor of love, handmade from scratch by two deter-mined people who were not afraid of hard work.

Few big public gardens are found east of the Cascades for the simple reason that the summer weather is too hot and dry to sus-tain them. Without irrigation, not much would grow except for sage, scrub, and drought-tolerant ponderosa pines. It's a different story in the nearby Cascades, where precipitation is plentiful and summer temperatures remain cool. You'll see this shift in climate and vegetation if you approach Ohme Gardens by driving through the Cascades. (For a nice day trip from Seattle, take Highway 2 east over Stevens Pass and return via I-90 and Snoqualmie Pass.)

Once you leave the mountains, you'll start to see fruit and par-ticularly apple orchards (and, of late, a few vineyards). The Leav-enworth and Wenatchee areas have been known for their apples for more than a century. And it was growing apples that became

Herman Ohme's occupation. Son of German immigrants, he'd trained as an iron molder in Illinois but moved west at nineteen for his health. He fell in love with the Cascades and worked as a lumberman but couldn't stand to see all the giant trees being cut. Apples gave him an opportunity to grow trees instead of cutting them down. Eventually he bought 40 acres near the confluence of the Wenatchee and Columbia rivers. He got a good deal on the land because part of the property included a "worthless" rocky bluff that towered 300 feet above the orchard. Herman would climb to the top and exult in the view, an exhilarating panorama that took in the wide Columbia River to the east and the snow-capped Cascades to the west. This is the view that you'll see today from various points in Ohme Gardens, but now the orchards below have unfortunately been replaced by blue industrial sheds.

In 1930 Herman met and married Ruth Orcutt, a stenographer at the local Elks Club. Ruth was the daughter of area pioneers and strong as a horse, though she weighed only 90 pounds. After working in the orchard all day, the two of them would climb to the top of the hill and enjoy the sweeping vista. Ruth fell in with her husband's dream to create a piece of the Cascades on the bare, rocky bluff.

And that's what they did. Neither Herman nor Ruth had any formal training in landscape design or botany. They worked by shared instinct and intuition. They had no money—nobody did, it was the Great Depression—and would drive their battered car into the Cascades to search for pine seedlings and clumps of wild-flowers and ground covers to plant. With no source of water at the top of the bluff, they lugged up 5-gallon watering cans to give their starts a drink. Using a donkey and a board or bucket, Herman reconfigured some areas to make lawns and sylvan pools. He also planned out a series of stairs and pathways using slabs of stone he and Ruth quarried, hauled, and laid themselves. The jutting, jagged basaltic outcrops of the bluff and the smooth stone paths, benches, walls, fireplaces, and pools Herman built by hand serve as a con-stant reminder that rock is the backbone of this alpine oasis.

What Herman and Ruth initially envisioned as a "nice back-yard" for their family and friends to enjoy grew from 4 acres to 9 and began to attract curious visitors—so many visitors, in fact, that in 1940 the garden opened to the public, although it remained the Ohme's private garden. In the 1990s the property was purchased by Washington State and Chelan County and became a self-sustaining public garden.

Alpine wildflowers collected in the Cascades and planted at Ohme Gardens create a tapestry of color in the spring and early summer.

Don't expect elaborate floral displays at Ohme. That's not what this garden is about. The idea was to show flowers, shrubs, and trees in natural-looking surroundings, enhancing what was already there. The gardens unfold along a circuitous path that begins at the Entrance Lawn and winds through tall conifers past a pool, another lawn, and Herman's hand-built benches, picnic tables, and wishing well. The most notable example of his handiwork is the rustic Vista House, an open-sided wood-and-stone outlook that caps the highest point in the gardens. From here the trail continues south along the hillside to the Alpine Meadow. Anchored at its south end by the Hidden Pool and to the west by two smaller pools, with a small waterfall to add sparkle to the scene, the meadow is an undulating tapestry of early-blooming ground covers, including spreading pink phlox, mauve creeping thyme, dianthus, and several varieties of sedum. Elsewhere in the garden look for the orange flowers of *Lewisia*, a sturdy alpine genus native to north-facing cliffs in the Pacific Northwest and named for Meriwether Lewis, who first encountered it in 1806.

Various paths lead back to the entrance. But you might want to linger, or backtrack to an area that caught your fancy. This is not a garden you can rush through. It's picturesque, unpredictable, and quietly inspiring—a unique testament to a partnership that coaxed a dry, barren hilltop into an alpine oasis of color and beauty.

british
columbia

vancouver & vicinity

Dr. Sun Yat-Sen Classical Chinese Garden in Vancouver, British Columbia, takes on a special glow when it's illuminated for evening events.

dr. sun yat-sen classical chinese garden

An entire universe in a small urban space, modeled on a Ming dynasty scholar's garden

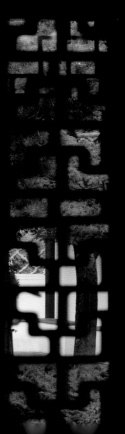

578 Carrall Street, Vancouver, BC V6B 5K2
vancouverchinesegarden.com
Visit spring through fall

· ·

📞 (604) 662-3207
🕐 Open daily May–Jun 14 and Sep 10am–6pm; Jun 15–Aug
   9:30am–7pm; Oct–Apr Tue–Sun 10am–4:30pm; closed
   Dec 25 and Jan 1
$ Admission fee
🚌 Public transportation
🐕 No dogs

An ornate window in a pavilion at Dr. Sun Yat-Sen Classical Chinese Garden looks out to a "leak window" in the garden wall.

Vancouver is home to one of the largest Chinese populations outside of Asia, so it makes sense that the first full-size classical Chinese garden outside of China was built here. The garden's inauguration was timed to coincide with the opening of Expo 86. The garden is named for the Chinese nationalist leader Sun Yat-Sen (1866–1925), who is considered the father of modern China. During his world travels to raise awareness and funds for the nationalist movement, Sun Yat-Sen stayed in Vancouver on three different occasions, and contributions from Chinese nationalists in British Columbia helped finance the Xinhai Revolution that toppled the Qing dynasty in 1911. Sun Yat-Sen subsequently became the first president of the Republic of China.

Like Lan Su Chinese Garden in Portland, Vancouver's Classical Chinese Garden is based on a time-honored type of garden built during the Ming dynasty (1368–1644), the scholar's garden. In 1985, fifty-two master craftsmen from Suzhou came to Vancouver—just as they came to Portland fourteen years later—to build the garden. All the garden materials are from China, from the giant rocks to the little black pebbles used in the paving, and the intricate pavilions and walkways are constructed without the use of nails, screws, or glue.

The walled garden sits within Dr. Sun Yat-Sen Park, a public space built in a Chinese style using Western materials. The park shares the garden's pond, but once you enter the inner garden you are in an entirely different world, characteristic of the private spaces within a Ming scholar's residence. Ming dynasty scholars were the elite of their time and they lived and worked in their gardens, sharing them with friends and family. With its asymmetrical arrangement of rocks and plants, its winding paths and corridors between pavilions, and vistas overlooking its courtyards, Dr. Sun

Yat-Sen Classical Chinese Garden packs an entire universe into a relatively small urban space.

Both architecturally and horticulturally, a classical Chinese garden is meant to be a reflection of the principles of feng shui and Taoism, attempting to achieve harmony through a balance of opposites in the artful use of four main elements: rock, water, plants, and architecture. More overt symbolism takes the form of bats, dragons, and phoenixes, symbols of good luck and regeneration, carved into the elaborate roofs and windows of the garden buildings.

In contrast to Western gardens, Chinese gardens use plants sparingly to set a mood and evoke a landscape. Open spaces are complemented with strong plants like pine and cypress, while confined courtyards are planted with delicate bamboo and miniature rhododendrons. Because the climate in Vancouver is similar to that of Suzhou, many of the same plant varieties are found in this garden and its counterparts in Suzhou. The plants were chosen according to their blossom schedules to emphasize seasonal changes as well as to invoke symbolic, historical, and literary meanings. The "three friends of winter"—pine, bamboo, and winter-flowering plum, which symbolize the human virtues of strength and tenacity, resiliency in the face of adversity, and rebirth—are found in special places throughout the garden.

The large weathered limestone rocks placed like strong, silent guardians throughout the garden were imported from Lake Tai near Suzhou. Chosen for their rough beauty, the rocks are thought to evoke supernatural powers and entice lucky spirits into a scholar's garden. The rocks were also used to create a false mountain at the center of the garden. The hard bones of the garden are counterbalanced by the soft water in the pond. The jade green of the water, symbolizing tranquility, is an intentional effect created by lining the bottom of the pond with clay.

The architecture of a scholar's garden is meant to blend with natural elements, emulating the organic instead of standing apart. The swooping spires of the Yun Wei Ting (Colorful and Cloudy Pavilion) atop the false mountain imitate the boughs of trees, and the zigzagging double corridor is designed to slow visitors' pace so they can more fully appreciate the various landscapes revealed to them along the way. The Han Bi Xie (Jade Water Pavilion) appears to be floating on the jade-green pond whose waters cool it in the summer. The larger pavilions—the Hua Feng Tang (China Maple Hall) and the Bai Chuan Tang (Hall of One Hundred Rivers)—are gathering places where visitors can enjoy the garden's numerous programs and events throughout the year.

To get the most out of your visit, take the free guided tour. The guides will explain this unique urban garden's Taoist yin-yang design principle, and you'll discover the symbolism of the intricate carvings and the subtle, ever-changing views from "leak windows" and covered serpentine corridors. The tours are offered several times a day throughout the year.

Zigzagging paths and covered walkways at Dr. Sun Yat-Sen Classical Chinese Garden invite visitors to slow their pace and enjoy a variety of garden scenes.

Created in an old rock quarry, the Large Quarry Garden in Vancouver's Queen Elizabeth Park is planted with a choice array of trees, shrubs, and perennials.

queen elizabeth park

4600 Cambie Street, Vancouver, BC V5Y 2M4
vancouver.ca/parks-recreation-culture/queen-elizabeth-park.aspx
Visit year-round; May through August for quarry garden
   borders

- ☎ (604) 873-7000; Bloedel Conservatory (604) 257-8584
- 🕐 Park open daily dawn to dusk; Conservatory summer
  Mon–Fri 9am–8pm, Sat–Sun 10am–9pm; winter daily
  10am–4pm
- $ Park admission free, fee for conservatory
- 🚌 Public transportation
- 🐕 Dogs on leash

Horticultural and panoramic showplace on Vancouver's west side

Stanley Park is Vancouver's top tourist attraction, but it's known more for its dramatic forest-and-sea scenery than for its gardens. For those, you need to head to Queen Elizabeth Park, perched atop an extinct volcano called Little Mountain south of downtown on the city's west side. Vancouver's second-most-popular park is a horticultural and panoramic showplace with sunken gardens and elevated views (at 492 feet it's the highest point within Vancouver). There's also a conservatory where brightly colored birds fly freely through a simulated tropical environment.

The 130-acre park occupies land once owned—like much of Vancouver—by the Canadian Pacific Railroad. For years it was quarried for basalt used in road building, but by 1911 it had been stripped bare and was left as a gouged-out eyesore. It took a visit from King George VI of England and his wife, Queen Elizabeth (mother of the present Queen Elizabeth), to get things rolling. When the royal pair visited Vancouver in 1939 to dedicate the

Three Lions Bridge, they also dedicated the overgrown blackberry patch of Little Mountain, which had been given to the Vancouver Board of Parks and Recreation. A year later, the old quarry was christened Queen Elizabeth Park, and Little Mountain began its slow transformation into the popular showplace it is today.

Most of the credit for the park's plantings and landscape design goes to Deputy Superintendent of Parks William Livingstone, a lanky, self-taught plantsman who was the son of one of Vancouver's first nurserymen. In 1948 Livingstone began the task of transforming the site, using the gullies left by the quarry operations as a backdrop for choice plants, trees, and shrubs. By 1949 the slopes were planted as an arboretum, the first civic arboretum in the country, with the long-term goal of displaying every tree species native to Canada. Between 1953 and 1954 the Large Quarry Garden was developed. The Small Quarry Garden was completed and dedicated as part of a series of projects to mark Vancouver's seventy-fifth anniversary in 1961.

The next phase of the park's development began in 1969 when timber magnate and garden aficionado Prentice Bloedel gave more than one million dollars toward the construction of a plaza with covered walkways, fountains, and the domed Bloedel Floral Conservatory. Bloedel capped off his largesse with the gift of a Henry Moore sculpture called "Knife Edge Two Piece." The park's last major project from the original plan was a restaurant (now called Seasons in the Park) perched over the Small Quarry Garden and completed in 1974.

Some thirty-three years later, in anticipation of the 2010 Winter Olympics, the Bloedel-funded plaza was refashioned and redeveloped to include seven covered tai chi arbors, a new pavilion for weddings and special events, a new dancing fountain with seventy jets, and the re-siting of the imposing Henry Moore sculpture to a more prominent position adjacent to the fountains.

The plaza offers views of the Vancouver skyline against the dramatic backdrop of the North Coast mountains. The Bloedel Floral Conservatory with its triodetic dome dominates one side of the plaza. Inside you'll find a lush environment with about five hundred plant species from tropical jungles to deserts, including citrus, eucalyptus, magnolia, fig, and coffee trees, along with epiphytes, euphorbias, bougainvilleas, browallias, gardenias, and hibiscus. The conservatory is also an aviary with some one hundred species of free-flying birds.

From the plaza, winding paths lead down to the two sunken quarry gardens. The Large Quarry Garden, located west of the Bloedel Conservatory, is the one to see. Home to a wide array of trees and shrubs and edged with borders of bright perennials, it's a visual delight. The Small Quarry Garden, below Seasons in the Park restaurant, is planted with annuals. These gardens, and the meandering paths between them, are the favorite spot in Vancouver for weddings and wedding photographs. Sometimes so many bridal parties and photographers are present it becomes a veritable traffic jam.

A favorite gathering spot for families, the plaza in front of the Bloedel Floral Conservatory at Queen Elizabeth Park features a dancing fountain and panoramic views of Vancouver.

stanley park

2000 West Georgia Street, Vancouver, BC V6C 2T1
vancouver.ca/parks-recreation-culture/stanley-park-125.aspx
Visit year-round

- 📞 (604) 257-8400
- 🕐 Open twenty-four hours
- $ Admission free
- 🚌 Public transportation
- 🐕 Dogs on leash

Vancouver's most popular park, a magical interface of forest, sea, sky, and city

Vancouver's evergreen jewel, Stanley Park is a 988-acre temperate rainforest jutting out into the ocean from the edge of the busy West End neighborhood. Created in 1888, the park is filled with towering western red cedar and Douglas-fir trees and countless walking trails that meander through and around it all. The famed seawall running along the park's waterside edge allows pedestrians and cyclists to experience a magical interface of forest, sea, sky, and city. Restaurants, pavilions, soccer fields, playgrounds, beaches, and swimming pools are scattered throughout the park. In short, Stanley Park has something for everyone and can be explored and enjoyed in many different ways—on foot, by bike, on skates, in the water, or in a horse-drawn carriage.

The park is home to lots of wildlife, including beavers, coyotes, bald eagles, blue herons, cormorants, trumpeter swans, brant geese, ducks, raccoons, skunks, and gray squirrels imported from New York's Central Park decades ago and now quite at home in the Pacific Northwest. (No, there are no bears.)

Stanley Park is really more about the urban forest and park than it is about manicured lawns and ornamental gardens, but you may want to include three garden areas in your visit.

Cherry blossoms and
tulips brighten an area
near the Rose Garden
in Stanley Park.

Other Highlights of Stanley Park

For directions, maps, brochures, and exhibits on the nature and ecology of Stanley Park, visit the Lost Lagoon Nature House. On Sundays at 1pm, rain or shine, they offer Discovery Walks of the park (preregistration recommended). stanleyparkecology.ca/education/public-programs/discovery-walks.

The horse-drawn carriage ride operated by AAA Horse & Carriage Ltd. is one of the most enjoyable ways to tour Stanley Park. Carriage tours depart every twenty minutes mid-March through October from the lower aquarium parking lot on Park Drive near the Georgia Street park entrance. The ride lasts an hour and covers portions of the park that many locals have never seen. stanleypark.com.

One of North America's largest aquariums is located in Stanley Park. The Vancouver Aquarium houses some eight thousand marine species, including white beluga whales, sea otters, Steller sea lions, and a Pacific white-sided dolphin. For a substantial extra fee you can have a behind-the-scenes "encounter" (as in feeding) with all of them. The Wild Coast area features a fascinating assortment of fish and sea creatures found in local waters. Vanaqua.org.

The Ted and Mary Greig Rhododendron Garden features an eye-catching collection of about forty-five hundred hybrid rhododendrons and azaleas gifted to the park in the late 1960s and planted around the Stanley Park Pitch & Putt golf course. The rhodies and azaleas are at their peak during the first two weeks of May, but between March and September something is always in bloom. The rhododendron garden is located off Lagoon Drive, accessible from Haro Street in the West End.

The Stanley Park Rose Garden, established in 1920 by the Kiwanis Club, contains more than thirty-five hundred rose bushes as well as arbors with climbing roses and clematis. At its peak in June, the rose garden is part of a larger landscaped garden with seasonal display beds of spring bulbs (March through May) and summer annuals and perennials (June through October). You'll

The magnificent collection of totem poles at Brockton Point in Stanley Park is displayed in an area that recreates the rocky shorelines where the Coast Salish people typically erected their clan markers.

find the rose garden just off Pipeline Road, near the park's main West Georgia Street entrance.

The Shakespeare Garden, between the rose garden and the forest, is an arboretum that includes about forty-five trees mentioned in Shakespeare's plays and poems. Plaques with their identifying quotes are affixed to the trees.

Among the most popular free attractions in the park is the superlative collection of totem poles at Brockton Point. Most of them were carved in the 1980s to replace originals from the 1920s and 1930s. The area around the totem poles recreates the rocky shorelines of sea and river where the Coast Salish First Nations tribes typically erected these clan markers. The totem-pole area isn't a garden per se, but it's far more compelling and atmospheric than all the rhodies and roses combined.

ubc botanical garden

6804 SW Marine Drive, Gate 8, University of British Columbia, Vancouver, BC V6T 1Z4

botanicalgarden.ubc.ca

Visit March through May for rhododendrons, June through September for perennials, October for fall tree color

- ☎ (604) 822-4208
- ⏰ Open daily 9:30am–5pm; closed late Dec–early Jan
- $ Admission fee, but free mid-Oct to mid-Mar; additional fee for Greenheart Canopy Walkway
- 🚌 Public transportation
- 🏷 Parts of the gardens may close during inclement weather; audio tours are available from the Plant Shop
- 🐕 No dogs

An array of special garden areas for serious plant lovers and an elevated trail through the forest canopy

Serious plant lovers will love the University of British Columbia. The prime attraction on campus, besides the must-see Museum of Anthropology, is the 78-acre UBC Botanical Garden. The oldest continuously operating university-based botanical garden in Canada is home to more than twelve thousand species of trees, shrubs, and flowers grouped into Asian, BC Rainforest, Alpine, Food, Woodland Meadow, and Physic (medicinal) gardens. A new attraction, the Greenheart Canopy Walkway, lets you explore the flora and fauna of the forest canopy. This is an unusually attractive place with much to see, and you can easily spend half a day exploring its diverse collections. The garden is divided into north and south segments connected by a tunnel beneath Marine Drive.

The 34-acre David C. Lam Asian Garden is a coastal native second-growth forest underplanted with Asian trees, shrubs, woody vines, and evergreen and herbaceous perennials derived primarily from the Himalayas, Japan, Korea, and China. From Asian Way, the main path, other paths named for famous plant explorers wind through areas where the plant collections are unified by a background of native plants and more than four hundred kinds of rhododendrons.

Centered around a large, shallow pond, the BC Rainforest Garden displays plants that are locally native to the area and region with collections that represent the temperate coastal rainforest of southwestern British Columbia and the Southern Interior "wet belt." Mulched trails and wooden bridges take you through boggy spots around the margins of the pond and into upland forest where you'll see a wide variety of woody and non-woody terrestrial, marginal, and aquatic plants, and plants of ethnobotanical importance to First Nations peoples.

The plants in the Physic Garden at the UBC Botanical Garden were used for medicinal purposes by early European physicians.

Built on a southwest-facing hillside below Thunderbird Stadium, the Alpine Garden is organized geographically with

UBC Museum of Anthropology

One of the finest collections of Northwest Coast Native art in the world is housed at the UBC Museum of Anthropology near the UBC Botanical Garden. Ancient artifacts, argillite sculptures, beaded jewelry, hand-carved ceremonial masks, and a superlative collection of totem poles are on display. Behind the museum, overlooking Point Grey, are two longhouses built according to the Haida tribal style. A number of trails lead down to Vancouver's most pristine beaches. moa.ubc.ca.

Nitobe Memorial Garden

Located on the UBC campus about a mile north of the UBC Botanical Garden, Nitobe Memorial Garden is a traditional Japanese stroll garden that opened in 1960 and is dedicated to Inazo Nitobe (1862–1933), a Japanese diplomat whose goal was to become "a bridge across the Pacific." A little more than 2 acres in size, the garden was inspired by urban gardens in Tokyo rather than the ancient temple gardens in Kyoto, so there is a greater use of open lawn areas that provide an attractive, parklike setting for the cherry trees and mounds of azaleas when they are in bloom. Paths lead visitors through the garden and over bridges to many different viewing points with vistas that open up as you cross each bridge. The garden has numerous lanterns that serve as memorials to Nitobe, each carefully placed to harmonize with the landscape. 6565 NW Marine Drive, Gate 4, University of British Columbia. botanicalgarden.ubc.ca/nitobe.

separate beds representing the mountains of Asia, Africa, North America, Europe, South America, and Australasia. A bounty of interesting and diminutive montane and alpine plants and flowers can be seen here year-round.

Espaliered apple and pear trees partially surround the Food Garden, a formal space where visitors are encouraged to explore their connection to food. Soft fruits are grown in ground-level beds surrounding a series of raised beds where vegetables and culinary herbs are cultivated. Plantings are maintained with organic gardening techniques, without the use of synthetic pesticides.

The Harold and Francis Holt Physic Garden is composed of twelve concentric brick-edged beds arrayed around a central sundial and enclosed by a yew hedge. Many poisonous plants inhabit this garden (as in any traditional physic garden), which explains why the bronze sundial is engraved with the native death camas (*Zigadenus venenosus*) while the gnomon (pointer) has a physician's snake (symbol of Asclepius, god of healing) and a pharmacist's cup of hemlock to represent the medicinal uses of the plants.

Started in 2006, the Carolinian Forest Garden, in the southwest corner of the North Garden, consists of twelve groves planted with hundreds of different tree and shrub species from the eastern deciduous hardwood forests that extend from the Gulf Coast of the United States into southern Ontario. One of the most distinctive features of the plants of the Carolinian Forest—so-called because the plants reach their peak of biodiversity in the Carolinas—

You can see the forest *and* the trees on the Greenheart Canopy Walkway, a unique trail of suspension bridges 50 feet above the forest floor at UBC Botanical Garden.

is autumn leaf color. Maples, oaks, sumacs, tupelos, sweetgums, and sourwoods are all noted for their spectacular effect.

The Garry Oak Meadow and Woodland Garden is designed to be a sustainable landscape where most of the plants are adapted to summer drought, minimizing the need for irrigation. The native Garry oak population in Canada is a threatened ecosystem (only about 15 percent of the original Garry oak ecosystem survives in British Columbia), and this woodland garden serves as a demonstration space to study and view aspects of ethnobotany, biogeography, local biodiversity, conservation, climate change, and horticulture.

Open year-round, the Greenheart Canopy Walkway is an aerial trail system that offers a rare perspective of the Northwest coastal forest canopy ecosystem. The only one of its kind in Canada, the aerial walkway allows access to the upper parts of the forest via eight suspension bridges attached to century-old trees 50 feet above the ground. It's an exciting and adventurous way to interact with nature and the forest with minimal impact on the trees or the habitat. The walkway is open only to prebooked group tours from November 1 through March 31.

vandusen
botanical garden

World-class botanical garden emphasizing entire ecosystems and filled with outdoor sculpture

A serene spot for visitors and a haven for wildlife, Livingstone Lake is one of the many picturesque garden areas at VanDusen Botanical Garden.

5251 Oak Street, Vancouver, BC V6M 4H1
vancouver.ca/parks-recreation-culture/vandusen-botanical-garden.aspx
Visit year-round; spring for flowering cherries; spring through fall for flowering perennials

☎ (604) 227-8335
🕐 Open daily Nov–Feb 10am–4pm, Mar 10am–5pm, Apr 9am–7pm, May 9am–8pm, Jun–Aug 9am–9pm, Sep 9am–7pm, Oct 9am–5pm; closed December 25 and January 1
$ Admission fee
🚌 Public transportation
🐕 No dogs

No question about it: Vancouver's 55-acre VanDusen Botanical Garden is one of the great gardens of the Pacific Northwest. In fact, I'd say it's one of the great gardens of the world. Beautifully designed, impeccably maintained, with endlessly fascinating plant material and lots of intriguing outdoor sculpture, it's a place that will enchant every gardener and garden lover.

Inaugurated in 1975 in the classy Shaughnessy neighborhood, VanDusen always kept a fairly low profile, billing itself as Vancouver's best-kept secret. But with the November 2011 opening of its bold new visitor center, the garden symbolically flung open its gates and dramatically increased its visibility. If you have any interest in sustainable architecture, make a point to visit this LEED-platinum building that uses on-site renewable resources to achieve net-zero energy consumption. The building, with its undulating roof and concrete walls that support a "living roof," uses filtered rainwater for its graywater requirements and treats 100 percent of its blackwater in an on-site bioreactor that is the first of its kind in Vancouver. Inside this impressive building, designed by Perkins + Will Architects of Vancouver, you'll find a restaurant, a café, a gift and seed shop, and a research library.

The VanDusen Visitor Centre acts as a gateway into the gardens. From 1911 to 1960, this site was leased to the Shaughnessy Golf Club by the Canadian Pacific Railway (CPR). When the golf club moved, the CPR proposed a subdivision, but the idea was resisted by locals, who formed the VanDusen Botanical Garden Association to assist the Vancouver Board of Parks and Recreation in saving the site. Eventually, the city and provincial governments, boosted by a big donation from lumberman W. J. VanDusen, purchased the land. Development began in 1971, and the new VanDusen Botanical Garden officially opened four years later.

The outstanding plant collection includes more than a quarter million individual plants from around the world representing more than seventy-five hundred taxa (plant families). Depending on which path you take, you'll be able to view representative flora from ecosystems that range from tropical South Africa to the Himalayas, South America, the Mediterranean, Canada's boreal forests and Great Plains, and the Pacific Northwest. Specific garden areas are planted to illustrate botanical relationships, such as the Rhododendron Walk, or geographical origins, as in the Sino-Himalayan Garden.

But if you just want to enjoy some gorgeously planted display gardens, you have several to choose from, including the Rose Garden, the Fern Dell, the Heather Garden, the Stone Garden,

the Herb Garden, and the Meconopsis Dell, where those famous and finicky blue poppies are cultivated. There's also the Heirloom Vegetable Garden, which illustrates the tasty joys of planting and harvesting your own garden produce.

Although the garden lost hundreds of trees in the 2006 windstorm that also devastated parts of Stanley Park, it remains an impressive arboretum. As you wend your way through the garden, you'll encounter collections of laburnums, oaks, beeches, maples, lindens, bamboos, yews, crabapples, chestnuts, magnolias, ashes, and plenty of conifers, including a grove of giant redwoods. During the annual Cherry Blossom Festival, visitors flock to the Honorable David C. Lam Cherry Grove, where more than a hundred flowering cherry trees representing twenty-four different species and varieties put on a spectacular springtime display. The grove is named in honor of a former lieutenant governor of British Columbia, a gardener with a lifelong passion for the cherry tree.

All these trees and display gardens are set amidst rolling lawns, tranquil lakes, fountains, and dramatic rockwork with vistas of Vancouver's mountains and skyline. There's also a devilishly difficult Elizabethan-style maze.

If you have time to visit only one garden in Vancouver, make it VanDusen. It's an inspiring and enjoyable environment for gardeners of all ages and interests.

Large outdoor sculptures, like this piece by Peter Pierobon, add to the aesthetic pleasures of a stroll through VanDusen Botanical Garden.

victoria
& vicinity

One of Vancouver Island's premier attractions, The Butchart Gardens near Victoria receives about a million visitors a year.

abkhazi garden

1964 Fairfield Road, Victoria, BC V8S 1H4
abkhazi.com
Visit spring and summer

- 📞 (250) 598-8096
- 🕐 Garden open daily Mar–Sep 11am–5pm, Oct–Dec 23 and February 11am–3pm, closed Dec 24–Jan 31; tearoom daily Mar–Sep 11:30am–4pm, Oct–Feb 11am–3pm.
- 💲 Admission fee
- 🚌 Public transportation; if you don't live on Vancouver Island, you will need to take a ferry to Victoria
- ♿ Some steps unsuitable for wheelchairs
- 🐕 No dogs

Small urban garden with dramatic vistas, created by an Englishwoman and a Russian prince

Every garden has two stories to tell. One is visual, narrated with plants. The other is the backstory of the garden's creation and creator(s). This jewel box of a garden tucked into an upscale neighborhood in Victoria and hidden away behind an old hornbeam hedge is extraordinary on both counts.

The Abkhazi Garden was created by an Englishwoman and a Russian prince, both of whom grew up with privilege and wealth but lived through a series of dramatic events and reversals that altered their lives forever. Born in Shanghai, Marjorie (Peggy) Pemberton Carter was orphaned and left destitute until an affluent couple adopted her. Her adoptive mother took Peggy to Paris in the 1920s to broaden her education. There Peggy met Prince Nicholas Abkhazi, a Russian whose family had lost everything in the Soviet Revolution of 1917. To avert a romance between Peggy and the penniless prince, Mrs. Carter took her charge back to Shanghai. When her second set of parents died, Peggy inherited their estate and became a wealthy young woman.

A perfect spot for a spot of tea, the Abkhazi residence—one of the first Modernist structures in Victoria—sits on a rocky outcrop overlooking the garden.

She and Nicholas corresponded but lost touch during World War II—and no wonder, for Peggy, a British national, was incarcerated in a Japanese prisoner-of-war camp in Shanghai (a story she recounts in her book *A Curious Cage: Life in a Japanese Internment Camp 1943–1945*, published in 1961) and Nicholas was imprisoned by the Nazis in Germany. They didn't see one another again—or even know if the other had survived—until 1946, by which time Peggy had moved to Victoria and purchased a 1-acre piece of land, and Nicholas had made his way to New York. They wed, settled in Victoria, and set about creating a landscape garden that takes full advantage of a dramatic site with rocky slopes and lovely vistas. The Abkhazis lived here and refined their garden until their deaths in the 1990s, at which time the garden was threatened by developers who wanted to build townhouses on the site. Garden lovers (as usual) came to the rescue and saved Victoria's most charming and charismatic garden from destruction.

The childless Abkhazis considered the garden their child, and wandering through this serene landscape one can't help but think that it was also a way for them to transform their turbulent pasts into a peaceful, life-affirming future. The garden they spent more than forty years creating was truly a world of their own, both insulating and inspiring.

Visitors enter through the Rhododendron Woodland Garden, where a stand of native Garry oak trees provides shade for a venerable collection of species and hybrid rhododendrons, some of which were already fifty years old when the Abkhazis planted them. This section of the garden is underplanted with woodland perennials that provide a succession of blooms throughout the year: anemones, trilliums, jacks-in-the-pulpit, native bleeding hearts, winter aconites, fawn lilies, and hardy cyclamen. Summer interest is provided by a collection of ferns, hostas, tigridias, and giant Himalayan lilies (*Cardiocrinum giganteum*).

Head west on the path that skirts the South Lawn and reveals the natural rock formations that provide drama to the site and the foundation for the Abkhazis' house. A mixed border of bold architectural plants with silver foliage is set off by the darker backdrop of the original hornbeam hedge and a long sweep of agapanthus. The ashes of Nicholas and Peggy were spread at the base of the rock at the north end of the lawn.

Just beyond the Spanish fir tree (*Abies pinsapo*), separating the lawn from a large rock outcropping, Peggy created a flowing, heather-lined path that she called the Yangtze River because it reminded her of the river near her former home in Shanghai. Side paths lead to three ponds created from natural depressions in the rock and reveal fresh views over the landscape as they rise in elevation.

The Abkhazi Garden in Victoria, British Columbia, is artfully designed to incorporate different garden areas into a small urban setting.

Getting to Abkhazi Garden

Abkhazi Garden is located in Victoria on Vancouver Island. Unless you fly to Victoria or live on the island, you will have to take a ferry to get there. BC Ferries (bcferries.com) offers frequent daily ferry service between Vancouver and Victoria, and the Coho Ferry (cohoferry.com) offers less frequent service between Port Angeles (Washington) and Victoria. Still another option is the Victoria Clipper (victoriaclipper.com), a fast, passenger-only hydroferry service between Seattle and Victoria. Bus 1 from downtown Victoria will take you to Fairfield Road and Foul Bay, near the garden entrance. Do some planning before you go, and don't forget that you will need a passport or other acceptable identification to cross the border into Canada from the United States.

Make your way up to the delightful summerhouse to admire the views from its little porch. Designed by John Wade, a young Modernist architect, the small, perfectly sited structure was completed in 1946 and completely restored in 2002. It was the first building on the property, commissioned by Peggy before she was reunited with Nicholas, and one of the earliest Modernist structures in Victoria.

Continue your tour along the East Path, which follows the contours of the glaciated rock on the north side of the property. Every spring, an original planting of lily-of-the-valley blossoms between the curving path and the outcropping. Views from the top of the path open up to reveal the landscape outside the garden, including the Sooke Hills, the Strait of Juan de Fuca, and the Olympic Mountains.

From here, continue on to the terrace of the Abkhazis' Modernist house perched atop another rocky outcropping. In the summer months, the house is used as a tearoom and gift shop. Step inside to have a look around and enjoy a spot of tea overlooking the garden.

The small, charming house was designed by John Wade, the architect of the summerhouse, and erected in 1947. Though it looks like a modest bungalow to our eyes today, the Abkhazis' house was at the vanguard of architectural design in Victoria at the time, with clean, simple lines that had nothing to do with the faux-English look the town had been cultivating since the 1920s. Constructed of wood and stone, with a view to comfort and utility rather than drama and grandiosity, the house shakes off the past and looks to the future, just like the pair who spent the second half of their lives creating the garden beneath it.

the butchart gardens

800 Benvenuto Avenue, Brentwood Bay, BC V8M 1J8
butchartgardens.com
Visit year-round; April through September for peak blooms

....

- 📞 (866) 652-4422
- 🕐 Open daily 9am to sundown (call or visit Web site for seasonal closing times)
- $ Admission fee
- 🚌 Public transportation
- 🏷 To avoid summertime crowds, try to arrive early or after 3pm; if you don't live on Vancouver Island, you will need to take a ferry to Victoria
- 🐕 Dogs on leash

The Disneyland of gardens, a carefully composed landscape that is the number one tourist attraction on Vancouver Island

If you know of any other garden in North America that receives almost a million visitors a year, I'd like to hear about it. I think The Butchart Gardens is the only garden that can make that claim. It's the Disneyland of gardens—a perfect place where everything performs exactly as it should, or as you think it should.

The fact that this garden is a major tourist attraction and such a huge commercial operation naturally creates high expectations for the visitor. Well-groomed perfection is what you expect and well-groomed perfection is what you get. There are, after all, fifty gardeners and twenty-six greenhouses where a million bedding plants of seven hundred different varieties are grown to ensure uninterrupted seasonal blooms from March through October. Music,

With their geometrically patterned beds and Mediterranean-style plantings, the Italian Gardens at The Butchart Gardens are a paean to the Butcharts' love of Italy.

fireworks, lighting displays, restaurants, and a huge gift store are all part of the garden experience.

The Butchart Gardens is still a family-run operation, and the original gardens—now more than a hundred years old—are on Canada's list of National Historic Sites. The family's fortune derived from cement—or, more specifically, from the limestone that was needed to produce cement. Robert Pim Butchart, a dry-goods merchant born in Ontario, came west and established a limestone quarry at Tod Inlet near Victoria. Cement, and lots of it, was just what the fast-growing West needed. When the limestone was exhausted, Butchart's wife, Jennie, decided to beautify the eyesore quarry by turning it into a garden.

She requisitioned tons of soil from nearby farms, had it hauled over in horse-drawn carts, and created the dramatic Sunken Garden, which remains the centerpiece of the estate and a notable achievement in Canadian gardening history. Located below the Butcharts' residence—a two-story country manor that now serves as an attractive restaurant where you might want to have lunch or afternoon tea—the Sunken Garden is the first stop in a leisurely garden tour that will take you about an hour, depending on how often you stop to snap photos or wait for the crowds to thin at your favorite vistas. The public part of the gardens covers some 55 acres.

As you descend into the old quarry, the painstaking care and meticulous attention to detail that defines The Butchart Gardens comes into sharp focus. Nature becomes almost unnatural in this carefully composed landscape where every bough, leaf, shrub, and flower petal seems to stand at attention and gleam with photogenic perfection. The eye-opening displays of seasonal flowers—masses and masses of them embedded throughout—can sometimes distract you from the less glamorous but more quietly real plants in the garden (like the witch hazels that bloom and scent the air in winter, when nothing else is in flower). Pools and water features enhance the Edenic quality of the scene. The Sunken Garden is the most English of the gardens Jennie Butchart planned or created. It was inspired by gardens of the great country houses in England and completed in 1921.

Above the Sunken Garden on the west side of the property, you'll come to a couple of new attractions that have nothing to do with gardens or gardening. In 2009 the Rose Carousel, with its menagerie of thirty animals beautifully carved out of basswood, started to spin. Farther to the north are two 30-foot totem poles

Getting to The Butchart Gardens

The Butchart Gardens are located northwest of Victoria on Vancouver Island. Unless you fly to Victoria or live on the island, you will have to take a ferry to get there. BC Ferries (bcferries.com) offers frequent daily ferry service between Vancouver and Victoria, and the Coho Ferry (cohoferry.com) offers less frequent service between Port Angeles (Washington) and Victoria. Still another option is the Victoria Clipper (victoriaclipper.com), a fast hydroferry service between Seattle and Victoria. Once on Vancouver Island, if you haven't brought your car or rented one, take the 75 bus from Victoria. Do some planning before you go, and don't forget that you will need a passport or other acceptable identification to cross the border into Canada from the United States.

erected in 2004 to commemorate the garden's hundredth anniversary. To the east of the totem poles, paths skirt the north end of the concert lawn, where Mr. and Mrs. Butchart once hosted symphony concerts for their friends (and where summertime concerts are still held), and bring you to the Fountain of the Three Sturgeons with its ever-changing water displays. The fountain was unveiled in 1964 by Ian Ross, the Butcharts' grandson; they presented the gardens to him on his twenty-first birthday and he was involved in the garden's operations and promotion until his death in 1997.

The fountain marks the northern end of the Rose Garden, planted in 1927 on the site of the Butcharts' vegetable garden. At its fragrant best in June, the Rose Garden contains nearly seven thousand roses displayed around an oval lawn. From here, head back to the fountain and jog northeast to the Japanese Garden. The Butcharts' travels in Japan and Europe introduced them to different gardening styles, and when the Japanese garden designer Isaburo Kishida arrived in Victoria from Yokohama in 1907, they commissioned him to design a Japanese garden for their estate. Though it wasn't completed until many years later, this is one of the earliest Japanese-style gardens in North America.

Italy was another favorite destination for the well-traveled couple. So much so that in the 1920s they named their house Benvenuto (Italian for "welcome") and transformed their tennis court just to the north of the house into the Italian Garden. The design for this handsome space, with its geometrically patterned beds and Mediterranean-style planting, was created by Butler Sturtevant of Seattle and Samuel Maclure, the Butcharts' garden consultant from Victoria. By this time, The Butchart Gardens was already a tourist destination, welcoming some fifty thousand visitors a year.

That figure has grown, and grown, and grown over the decades, as travel to Victoria has become easier. Most of the original garden designs remain intact, and if you find the theme-park atmosphere in the rest of the property uninteresting, just concentrate on the gorgeous trees, shrubs, and flowers. The plants are not labeled, but if something catches your eye and you want to know its name, visit the Plant Identification Center and ask. It's also good to know that the hugely popular Butchart Gardens is keeping up with the times by recycling most of its disposable waste, lowering its energy consumption, and using sustainable methods to keep plant pests at bay and its remarkable gardens watered and fertilized.

milner gardens and woodland

2179 West Island Highway, Qualicum Beach, BC V9K
viu.ca/milnergardens
Visit April through June for bulbs, rhodies, flowering trees

- 📞 (250) 752-6153
- 🕐 Open late Mar–late Apr and Sep 5–mid-Oct Thur–Sun 10–4:30pm, Apr 25–Sep 2 daily 10am–4:30pm; closed mid-Oct–late Mar
- $ Admission fee
- 🚌 If you don't live on Vancouver Island, you will need to take a ferry to get there
- 🐕 No dogs

English-style gardens and ancient forest perched on the edge of an oceanside bluff

At Milner Gardens and Woodland, a picturesque English-style landscape garden exists next to and within an ancient coastal forest, and the result is an intriguing hybrid that is both wild and refined. When you see its unique qualities, you'll understand why Queen Elizabeth and Prince Phillip opted to stay here during a state visit to Canada, and how Prince Charles and Princess Diana used it to snatch a few hours of seclusion away from the media circus that was their honeymoon.

Located in Qualicum Beach on the east coast of Vancouver Island, about 100 miles north of Victoria, this 70-acre estate originally served as a summer retreat for Ray Milner, a prominent Canadian businessman, and his wife, Rina. After Rina's death, the widower Ray married the widowed Veronica FitzGerald, whose husband had been the twenty-eighth hereditary Knight of Glin, County Limerick, Ireland, and whose mother was a first cousin of Winston Churchill. When upper-crust Veronica moved to the remote estate overlooking the Strait of Georgia on Vancouver Island, she set about creating a house and garden that would reflect her talents for gardening and painting.

Part of what made the property so special was 60 acres of coastal forest with Douglas-firs, western red cedars, and grand firs buffering the house from the nearest road. This is one of the last such coastal forests with old-growth trees to survive on Vancouver Island, and as you walk through it from the parking lot to the house, you'll be able to see and appreciate the size of these ancient giants, some of them estimated to be four hundred to five hundred years old.

This leeward side of Vancouver Island sits in a rain shadow created by the Olympic Mountains, which makes it warmer and drier than other parts of coastal British Columbia. It's warm enough in the summer to swim, apparently, for the first developed area you come to on the forest path is the swimming pool and pool house Ray and Veronica installed in the early 1960s. The pool is no longer used for taking a dip—except by native salamanders. It's been filled in and turned into a reflecting pool.

Continuing on, you come to Veronica's enclosed berry garden, still so productive that jams made from its fruits are used for afternoon teas and sold as edible souvenirs. The berry garden is now used as part of Milner's education program for kids, helping them to connect with nature.

The expansive view at Milner Gardens on the east coast of Vancouver Island looks out over the Strait of Georgia to the mountains on mainland British Columbia.

Veronica used the next part of the forest as the setting for an impressive collection of about five hundred varieties of hybrid rhododendrons, creating a woodland garden that erupts into clouds of red, purple, and orange blossoms in the spring.

From the Rhododendron Garden the forest trail emerges into about 10 acres of gardens around the house. Veronica wasn't interested in manicured lawns and instead had natural-looking meadows planted with English daisies, buttercups, violas, scillas, glory-in-the-snow, winter aconites, and daffodils, with spring-time drifts of bluebells, lilies-of-the valley, and forget-me-nots blooming beneath fruit trees in the small orchard to one side of the house. The clover-filled meadow behind the house is edged with plants and shrubbery that give this prominent area a more formal look. Scattered throughout the grounds are specimens of Japanese maple, beech, laburnum, katsura, dawn redwood, birch, Spanish chestnut, and magnolia, along with a dove tree (*Davidia involucrata*) and a Chinese dogwood that puts on an eye-popping display in late June.

Veronica wanted her garden to be a place of serenity and elegance—"in tune with the Infinite," as she said. And there is a sense of the infinite here because the house and gardens sit

Looking misty and mysterious on a maritime morning, the woodland that is part of Milner Gardens is one of the last patches of forest on Vancouver Island where old-growth trees have survived.

Getting to Milner Gardens and Woodland

Milner Gardens and Woodland is on Vancouver Island about 100 miles north of Victoria. If you don't live on Vancouver Island, you can take a ferry to Victoria and rent a car. If you want a shorter drive, you can take a car ferry (bcferries.com) from Tsawassen or Horseshoe Bay, both near Vancouver, to Nanaimo, 30 miles south of Qualicum Beach, where the garden is located. The scenic ferry ride from Horseshoe Bay takes about 90 minutes and passes Bowen Island along the way.

on a clifftop with a magnificent view that puts everything in perspective.

The Milner house, completed in 1931, was designed to resemble a gabled English cottage with elements of a colonial Ceylonese tea plantation thrown in for good measure. That's why it has a large covered verandah and doors leading outside from every bedroom (making it less obtrusive for servants to enter and depart). In the spring, when it's smothered in flowering wisteria vines and surrounded with blooming pink and white camellias, the house looks almost too quaint for words. The interior is appropriately cozy, chintzy, and well bred, with just a touch of unconquerable mustiness to give it character. Veronica's paintings hang on the walls, and an assortment of personal mementos, including photographs of the Queen, adorn various side tables. The bedroom where the Queen stayed for three days (Veronica had to vacate for the duration) has a charming view of the garden through old-fashioned multipaned windows. Veronica continued to live in the house until her death in 1998. She donated the estate to Vancouver Island University.

Since you've come this far, you really should stay and enjoy a proper English tea—on the verandah if the weather is nice. Scones and sandwiches with the crusts cut off seem quite appropriate in this setting.

Before you leave, follow the sloping meadow behind the house to the clifftop overlook and take in the view over the Strait of Georgia. The Coast Range mountains of mainland British Columbia rise in the distance and islands dot the vista to the north. You might see a bald eagle soaring overhead, or blue herons on the rocky shores below. It's a scene that adds yet another layer of quiet magic to this distinctive English-style garden and coastal woodland.

acknowledgments

This book could not have been written without the help of Gary Larson and Tim Kirkpatrick. On my research trips, Gary hauled me around two states and a Canadian province. Tim also accompanied me on research trips and provided innumerable photographs of the gardens we visited. Stephen Brewer, Deborah Mintz, and Lynn Parsons also helped me to reach some of my destinations. To Tom Fischer of Timber Press, a special thanks. He was the one who asked me to write this book, and provided help and encouragement along the way. Franni Farrell must also be thanked for her editorial acumen. Lorraine Anderson edited the book with expert skill and subtlety, for which I thank her. Finally, I'd like to acknowledge all the gardeners I met while working on this book. Sometimes they were the ones who had created the gardens I visited. Sometimes they were the curators. And sometimes they were volunteers who gave their time and labor to keep the gardens alive. All of them were welcoming, enthusiastic, and generous—just what you would expect of a gardener.

photo credits

Page 2, photo by Ron Cooper.
Page 5, courtesy of Rhododendron Species Botanical Garden.
Page 6, photo by Briand Sanderson.
Page 9, courtesy of Portland Parks & Recreation.
Page 10, photo by Tim Kirkpatrick.
Page 12, courtesy of Connie Hansen Garden, photo by Nancy Chase.
Page 16, courtesy of The Butchart Gardens.
Page 25, courtesy of Portland Japanese Garden, photo by Jonathan Ley.
Page 28, photo by Tim Kirkpatrick.
Page 34, photo by Tim Kirkpatrick.
Page 47, courtesy of Portland Parks & Recreation.
Page 49, courtesy of Portland Parks & Recreation.
Page 63, courtesy of Lan Su Chinese Garden.
Page 65, photo by Tim Kirkpatrick.
Page 66, photo by Mary Edmeades.
Page 71, photo by Tim Kirkpatrick.
Page 72, photo by TimKirkpatrick.
Page 76, photo by Tim Kirkpatrick.
Page 79, courtesy of Portland Japanese Garden, photo by Denise Bober.
Page 81, courtesy of Portland Japanese Garden, photo by Larry Klobertanz.
Page 84, photo by Carol Adelman.
Page 97, photo by Ron Cooper.
Page 99, photo by Ron Cooper.
Page 104, courtesy of Schreiner's Iris Gardens.
Page 108, photo by Tim Kirkpatrick.
Page 111, photo by Tim Kirkpatrick.
Page 114, photo by Brad Sick.
Page 117, photo by Marin Kress.
Page 118, photo by Nancy Chase.
Page 124, courtesy of Mount Pisgah Arboretum.
Page 127, photo by Memo Jasso, North Bend, OR.
Page 128, photo by Shirley Bridgham.
Page 132, courtesy of The Arboretum Foundation, photo by Niall Dunne.
Page 139, photo by Richard Brown.
Page 141, photo by Richard Brown.
Page 154, photo by Lynne Harrison.
Page 157, photo by Lynne Harrison.
Page 167, photo by Joan Bell.
Page 168, photo by Joan Bell.
Page 175, Flickr/Brian Holsclaw
Page 176, photo by Ray Pfortner/RayPfortner.com
Page 178, photo by Ray Pfortner/RayPfortner.com.
Page 181, photo by Ray Pfortner/RayPfortner.com.

Page 187, courtesy of The Arboretum Foundation, photo by Niall Dunne.
Page 188, courtesy of The Arboretum Foundation, photo by Niall Dunne.
Page 190, courtesy of Woodland Park Zoo, photo by Ryan Hawk.
Page 193, courtesy of Woodland Park Zoo, photo by Ryan Hawk.
Page 196, courtesy of Chase Garden, photo by Marion Brenner.
Page 198, courtesy of Chase Garden, photo by Marion Brenner.
Page 206, courtesy of Pacific Rim Bonsai Collection.
Page 208, courtesy of Pacific Rim Bonsai Collection.
Page 210, courtesy of Metro Parks Tacoma.
Page 212, courtesy of Metro Parks Tacoma.
Page 215, courtesy of PowellsWood.
Page 217, courtesy of PowellsWood.
Page 218, courtesy of Rhododendron Species Botanical Garden.
Page 221, courtesy of Rhododendron Species Botanical Garden.
Page 223, photo by Kenneth Smith.
Page 225, photo by Kenneth Smith.
Page 227, courtesy of Metro Parks Tacoma.
Page 230, photo by Tim Kirkpatrick.
Page 232, photo by Tim Kirkpatrick.
Page 238, photo by Angel Johnson.
Page 244, courtesy of Ohme Gardens, photo by Bonnie Richmond.
Page 247, photo by Tim Kirkpatrick.
Page 250, courtesy of Dr. Sun Yat-Sen Classical Chinese Garden.
Page 252, courtesy of Dr. Sun Yat-Sen Classical Chinese Garden.
Page 255, courtesy of Dr. Sun Yat-Sen Classical Chinese Garden.
Page 256, courtesy of Vancouver Park Board.
Page 261, courtesy of Vancouver Park Board.
Page 272, courtesy of The Butchart Gardens.
Page 275, photo by Peter Pfann.
Page 276, photo by Peter Pfann.
Page 279, courtesy of The Butchart Gardens.
Page 280, courtesy of The Butchart Gardens.
Page 285, courtesy of Milner Gardens and Woodland.
Page 286, courtesy of Milner Gardens and Woodland.

All other photos are by the author.

index

Main entries for featured gardens appear in bold type.

Abkhazi, Prince Nicholas and Marjorie (Peggy) Pemberton Carter, 274–277
Abkhazi Garden, Victoria, BC, 17, **274–277**
abutilon, 28
acanthus, 129
Adelman, Carol, 85–86
Adelman Peony Garden, Salem, OR, **84–87**
agapanthus, 228
agaves, 28
Ainsworth, Belle, 13, 50
alder, 166
alliums, 205
alpine gardens
    Alpine Garden, Bellevue Botanical Garden, 137
    Alpine Garden, RSBG, 221
    Alpine Garden, UBC, 265–266
    Alpine Meadow, Ohme Gardens, 244–245, 247
    Elisabeth Carey Miller collection, 146–147
alpine shooting stars (*Dodecatheon alpinum*), 116
American bistort (*Polygonum bistortoides*), 116
American elms (*Ulnus americana*), 61
    avenue of, Jenkins Estate, 13, 53
Andrews, Howard E., 191
anemones, 276
anthurium, 183
apple trees, 28–29, 234, 245–246
    Food Garden, UBC Botanical Garden, 266
    Old Apple Tree Park, 234
arboretums
    Brooks Gardens, 87
    Evergreen Arboretum and Gardens, 20, **150–153**
    Hoyt Arboretum, 15, **42–45**
    John A. Finch Arboretum, 243
    Lake Wilderness Arboretum, 20, **200–201**
    Mount Pisgah Arboretum, 112–113, 122, 124
    at Queen Elizabeth Park, 258
    South Seattle Community College Arboretum, **179–181**
    Washington Park Arboretum, 15, **186–189**
architectural components, 11, 52–53. *See also* Butchart Gardens; Queen Elizabeth Park; Stanley Park; *specific gardens*
    bridges, 32–33, 52–53, 78–79, 80, 119, 136, 140, 165, 177, 265, 266, 267

chapel and shrines, 38–41, 209
in Chinese gardens, 19, 62–65, 179, 248–249, 250–255
conservatories, 182–185, 221, 226–229, 241, 258–259
English cottage, Milner Gardens, 287
fort, 232–235
gatehouse, Meerkerk Rhododendron Gardens, 167
gazebos, 46–47, 49, 98, 111, 129, 191, 192–193, 212, 221
grand homes and mansions, 11, 34–37, 50–53, 74–77, 96–99, 102, 138–141, 197–198, 202–205, 282
guesthouse by Paul Kirk, Bloedel Reserve, 140
in Japanese gardens, 15, 25, 78–81, 136, 140, 162–165, 174–177, 212, 243, 266, 282
Mid-Century Modern houses, 137, 198, 277
pergolas, 11, 92–93, 94, 98, 191, 192–193
stone cottage, 66–69
summerhouse and home by John Wade, Abkhazi Garden, 277
sustainable architecture, VanDusen Botanical Garden, 269
teahouses, 11, 51, 52, 64–65, 80, 81, 99, 140, 177
totem poles, 200–201, 263, 281–282
trellises, 103, 242–243
Vista House, Ohme Gardens, 247
Arizona cypress (*Cupressus arizonica* var. *glabra* 'Blue Ice'), 180
Armenian cranesbill (*Geranium psilostemon*), 94–95
arrowleaf groundsel (*Senecio triangularis*), 117
ash tree, 271
aster, 205
astilbe, 40, 129
auricula, 169
avalanche lily (*Erythronium montanum*), 205
azaleas, 31, 80, 129, 136, 174, 177, 183, 187, 200, 212
    Azalea Way, Washington Park Arboretum, 188
    Smith/Mossman Western Azalea Garden, 200

Baird, Marjorie, 201

bamboo, 28, 65, 94, 165, 254
banana trees, 28, 183, 225
banksias, 28
barberry family (Berberidaceae), 110
Beach, Frank E., 48
beaded wood fern (*Dryopteris bissetiana*), 110
Bean, Ormond R., 71
bear grass (*Xerophyllum tenax*), 197
beech trees, 243, 271, 286
Bellevue Botanical Garden, Bellevue, WA, 17, 20,
    134–137
Benedict, Loie, 201
Berger, Thomas, 208
Berrima gold incense cedar (*Calocedrus decurrens*
    'Berrima Gold'), 180
bigleaf (or Oregon) maples, 45, 166, 222
Bingham, George and Willie, 96, 99
birch trees, 61, 140, 165, 286
bird-of-paradise *(Strelitzia reginae)*, 184, 227
Black, Paul, 110
black bat flower (*Tacca chantrieri*), 182
bleeding heart, 40, 117, 225, 276
Bloedel, Prentice, 13–14, 139, 141, 202, 259
Bloedel, Virginia, 139, 202
Bloedel Reserve, Bainbridge Island, WA, 13, 17, 18,
    138–141
bluebells, 169, 286
blue false indigo (*Baptisia australis*), 94
Blue Heron Herbary, Sauvie Island, OR, 29
blue stickseed (*Hackelia micrantha*), 117
bonsai, 17
    Pacific Rim Bonsai Collection, **206–209**
botanical gardens
    Bellevue Botanical Garden, **134–137**
    Elisabeth Carey Miller Botanical Garden,
        146–149
    Leach Botanical Garden, **66–69**
    Oregon Garden, **100–103**
    Rhododendron Species Botanical Garden, 18,
        218–221
    Soos Creek Botanical Garden, **222–225**
    VanDusen Botanical Garden, **268–271**
bougainvillea, 259
boxwood, 72, 98, 99, 129, 204
    allee, Elk Rock Garden of the Bishop's Close, 36
    Scroll Garden at Deepwood Estate, 99
Braille Garden, Jenkins Estate, 52
bromeliads, 228
    Bromeliad House, Volunteer Park Conservatory,
        184–185
Brooks Gardens, Brooks, Oregon, 87

browallia, 259
Brown, Capability, 13
Brown, Clifford and Alice, 96, 98, 99
Bruce, William, 234
bulrushes, 101
bunchberry (*Cornus canadensis*), 204
Bush, Asahel, 98
Bush's Pasture Park, Salem, OR, 98
Butchart, Robert Pim and Jennie, 281
Butchart Gardens, Brentwood Bay, BC, 14, 16–17,
        138, 272–273, **278–283**
buttercups (*Ranunculus gormanii*), 116, 286

cacti, 184, 228
    Cactus House, Volunteer Park Conservatory, 184
Camassia leichtlinii, 12–13
camellias, 40, 61, 65, 68, 141, 187, 225, 287
    Camellia Grove, Washington Park Arboretum,
        188
    Camellia Walk, Bloedel Reserve, 141
candelabra primroses, 140
Cascade Head Trail, OR, 120
Castle Crest Wildflower Garden, Crater Lake
        National Park, OR, 8, **114–117**
catalpa, 224
cattails, 101
ceanothus, 27
Cecil and Molly Smith Rhododendron Garden, St.
        Paul, OR, 18, **88–90**
Chase, Ione and Emmott, 197–199
Chase Garden, Orting, WA, 17, **196–199**
cherry trees, 42, 132–133, 165, 169, 260–261, 271
    Cherry Blossom Festival, Honorable David C.
        Lam Cherry Grove, VanDusen Botanical
        Garden, 271
chestnut trees, 145, 271
Chilean firetree (*Embothrium coccineum*), 94, 204
Chinese dogwood, 286
Chinese empress tree (*Paulownia tomentosa*), 204
Chinese gardens, 19, 62, 64
    classical, elements of, 64, 65, 253
    Dr. Sun Yat-Sen Classical Chinese Garden, 19,
        248–249, **250–253**
    Lan Su Chinese Garden, 19, **62–65**
    principles of yin and yang and, 181, 255
    Seattle Chinese Garden, 19, 62, **178–181**
Chinese stewartia (*Stewartia sinensis*), 118–119
Christie, Scott, 56
Church, Thomas, 194–195, 203, 204, 205, 212
Cistus Nursery, Sauvie Island, OR, **26–29**
citrus trees, 227, 234, 259

City Beautiful movement, 13, 60, 70
clematis, 56, 98, 262
Clematis 'Arctic Queen', 57
Clematis 'Nelly Moser', 224
clivias, 228
coast redwood (*Sequoia sempervirens*), 189
cobra lily or California pitcher plant (*Darlingtonia californica*), 128, 140
coffee trees, 259
Columbian monkshood (*Aconitum columbianum*), 117
common pearly everlasting (*Anaphalis margaritacea*), 117
conifers, 42, 67, 87, 136, 140, 145, 177, 180, 187, 199, 243, 247, 271
    Conifer Collection, The Oregon Garden, 101
    Conifer Garden, Evergreen Arboretum and Garden, 153
    dwarf conifer collection, South Seattle Community College arboretum, 178–180
    Pinetum, Washington Park Arboretum, 189
Connie Hansen Garden, Lincoln City, OR, 12–13, **118–121**
conservatory gardens, 14
    Bloedel Floral Conservatory, Queen Elizabeth Park, 258–259
    Gaiser Conservatory, Manito Park, 241
    Rutherford Conservatory, RSBG, 221
    Volunteer Park Conservatory, **182–185**
    W. W. Seymour Botanical Conservatory, **226–229**
contorted white pine (*Pinus strobus* 'Torulosa'), 180
coral root orchid, 140
coreopsis, 235
cornelian cherry trees (*Cornus mas*), 165
corpse lilies *(Amorphophallus titanum)*, 185
crabapples, 189, 212, 243, 271
Crater Lake National Park, OR, 8, 114–116
crocus, 8, 145
crotons, 183
Crystal Springs Rhododendron Garden, Portland, OR, 18, **30–33**, 59
cycads, 184
cyclamen, 8, 160, 183, 276
cymbidium, 65
cypress, 27, 180, 216

daffodils, 40, 169, 170–171, 286
dahlia, 12, 129, 234, 235

Dahlia Trial Garden, Point Defiance Park, 210–211
    Volunteer Park Dahlia Garden, 185
daisy, 40, 286
Daly, James, 222
Dancing Oaks Nursery, Monmouth, OR, 82–83, **92–95**
daphne, 40
Darlingtonia State Natural Site, Florence, OR, 128
dawn redwood (*Metasequoia glyptostroboides*), 32, 37, 42, 160, 189, 199, 286
daylilies, 40
    Daylily Collection, Lake Wilderness Arboretum, 201
death camas (*Zigadenus venenosus*), 266
Deepwood Estate, Salem, OR, 14, **96–99**
    Erythronium Festival, 99
Denny, Louisa Boren, 192
dianthus, 56, 235, 247
dogtooth violets (*Erythronium dens-canis*), 204
dogwood, 37, 40, 145, 169, 188, 243
Donation Land Act of 1850, 43
Douglas, David, 234
Douglas-fir, 37, 40, 45, 79, 90, 124, 139, 145, 153, 160, 166, 213, 222, 224, 234, 260, 285
    at PowellsWood, 216
    at Rhododendron Species Botanical Garden, 219
    Shade Garden, Lakewold, 203, 204
dove tree (*Davidia involucrata*), 286
Dr. Sun Yat-Sen Classical Chinese Garden, Vancouver, BC, 248–249, **250–253**
Duncan, John W., 45, 240, 242
Dunn, Arthur, 144
Dunn, Edward R., 145
Dunn Gardens, Seattle, WA, 14, 15, 37, **142–145**
dwarf Serbian spruce (*Picea omorika* 'Nana'), 180

eastern white pine (*Pinus strobus*), 224
Eastwood's willow (*Salix eastwoodiae*), 117
Elisabeth Carey Miller Botanical Garden, The Highlands, Seattle, WA, **146–149**
Elk Rock Garden of the Bishop's Close, Portland, OR, 14, 15, 17, **34–37**
    Peter Kerr House, 35
elm trees, 37, 243. *See also* American elms; English elms
English daisies, 286
English elms, 139, 140
English Legend Roses, 91
epimedium, 108–109, 110–111, 200, 204, 216

epiphyllum, 185, 228
epiphytes, 259
erythronium, 145, 204
eucalyptus trees, 26, 27, 259
Eucriphia, 224
euphorbia, 94, 259
European hornbeams, 216
European white birches, 61
Evergreen Arboretum and Gardens, Everett, WA, 20, **150–153**

fawn lilies, 276
ferns, 68, 94, 108–110, 136, 140, 161, 184, 199, 220, 225, 228, 276
    Fern Dell, VanDusen Botanical Garden, 270
    Fern House, Volunteer Park Conservatory, 184
    Fern Wall, Crystal Springs Rhododendron Garden, 33
    Hardy Fern Garden, Lakewold, 205
    Oie Native Woodland, Soos Creek Botanical Garden, 225
    Woodland Garden, PowellsWood, 216
    Woodland Garden and Fernery, Evergreen Arboretum and Garden, 153
Ferry, Clinton P., 229
figs, 228, 259
flannelbush, 189
Foltz, Leonard, 93
Forest Park, Portland, OR, 74
forget-me-nots, 286
forsythia, 40
Fort Vancouver Heritage Garden, Vancouver, WA, **232–235**
Foulkes, Edward T., 76
foxglove, 169
foxtail lilies, 169
French thyme, 52
fringe cup, 225
fuchsia, 57, 68, 94
    Fuchsia Garden, Bellevue Botanical Garden, 137
    Fuchsia Garden, Point Defiance Park, 211
    Perennial Garden, Lake Wilderness Arboretum, 201

gardenia, 259
Garry oak. *See* Oregon white oak or Garry oak
gas plant (*Dictamnus albus*), 94
geranium, 205
giant Himalayan lilies (*Cardiocrinum giganteum*), 276

giant red Indian paintbrush (*Castilleja miniata*), 117
giant redwood, 271
giant sequoia or Sierra redwood (*Sequoiadendron giganteum*), 189
giant yellow skunk cabbage (*Lysichiton americanus*), 140
ginger, 183
ginkgo trees (*Ginkgo biloba*), 177, 199
    Ginkgo biloba 'White Lightning', 94
glory-in-the-snow, 286
golden Japanese forest grass (*Hakonechloa macra* 'Aureola'), 148
golden ninebark (*Physocarpus*), 225
Gordon House (by Frank Lloyd Wright), 101–102
grape, 98
grape hyacinth (muscari), 170–171, 173
Grotto, The, Portland, OR, **38–41**
ground cover, 196–197, 247
    Ground Cover Garden, Bellevue Botanical Garden, 136
gunnera, 28, 224

Hansen, Connie, 119–121
Hansen, Kirk, 109
hawthorn trees, 42, 243
hazelnut bushes, 90
heathers, 121, 145, 196–197
    Heather Garden, VanDusen Botanical Garden, 270
hebes, 28
Heckler, Nancy, 157
Heirloom Roses, St. Paul, OR, 91
Helenium 'Tijuana Brass', 56
hellebores, 40, 216
hemlock, 45, 222
Hendricks, Thomas, 122
Hendricks Park, Eugene, OR, 14, **122–125**
hepatica (*Hepatica nobilis*), 198, 200
herbaceous perennials, 108–111
    Perennial Border Garden, Bellevue Botanical Garden, 134–135, 137
herbs
    Blue Heron Herbary, 29
    Herb Garden, Jenkins Estate, 52
    Herb Garden, VanDusen Botanical Garden, 270
    UW Medicinal Herb Garden, 189
Heronswood, Kingston, WA, **154–157**
hibiscus, 259
Himalayan birches, 140

Himalayan blue poppies (*Meconopsis betonicifolia*), 3, 204, 220
Himalayan lily (*Cardiocrinum giganteum*), 220
Hinkley, Dan, 156, 157
Hogan, Sean, 26–27
holly, 187, 188
Hom, Pam, 153
Hootman, Steve, 219
Horn, Maurice, 56
hornbeam, 154–155, 216
Hoshide, Robert, 207
hosta, 56, 108–110, 276
Hoyt Arboretum, Portland, OR, 15, **42–45**
    Vietnam Veterans of Oregon Memorial, 44–45
Hudson's Bay Company, 233, 234
Hulda Klager Lilac Gardens, Woodland, WA, **236–239**
Huntington, Wallace, 33
hyacinths, 170–171, 205
hydrangea, 52, 56, 57, 136, 183, 216
    Hydrangea Garden, Lake Wilderness Arboretum, 201

Iida, Juki, 175
impatiens, 28
incense-cedar, 124
International Rose Test Garden, Portland, OR, 8–9, 14, **46–49**, 72
iris, 80, 87, 104–107, 171, 174, 176–177, 205
    Heritage Flower Garden, Soos Creek Botanical Garden, 222–223
    Iris Garden, Point Defiance Park, 211–212
    Mid-America Garden, 110
    Schreiner's Iris Gardens, **104–107**
Iris innominata, 68
Iris pallida, 106
Iris variegata, 106

jacks-in-the-pulpit, 276
jade tree (*Crassula ovata*), 184
James F. Bybee House and Pioneer Orchard, Sauvie Island, OR, 13, 28–29
Japanese cherry, 174, 188, 212, 216, 266
Japanese cutleaf maple (*Acer palmatum* var. *dissectum*), 177
Japanese gardens
    at Bloedel Reserve, 140
    elements of, 79, 175, 177, 243
    five styles of, 79, 80
    Japanese Garden, Point Defiance Park, 212
    Japanese Garden, The Butchart Garden, 282
    Kubota Garden, 15, **162–165**

Nishinomiya Tsutakawa Japanese Garden, Manito Park, 243
    Nitobe Memorial Garden, 15, 266
    Portland Japanese Garden, 15, **78–81**
    Seattle Japanese Garden, 15, 164, **174–177**
    Yao Garden, Bellevue Botanical Garden, 136
Japanese iris, 174, 176–177
Japanese laceleaf maple, 80
Japanese larch (*Larix kaempferi*), 161
Japanese maple (*Acer palmatum*), 40, 119, 136, 148, 174, 187, 286, 204
    collection, Lakewold, 204
    collection, Washington Park Arboretum, 189
    Japanese Maple Grove, Evergreen Arboretum and Garden, 153
Japanese maple (*Acer palmatum* 'Goshiki Shidare'), 204
Japanese sasanqua camellia, 98
Japanese snowball shrubs, 37
Japanese snowbell tree (*Styrax japonicus*), 118–119
Japanese striped-bark maple (*Acer capillipes*), 161
Japanese white pine (*Pinus parviflora*), 160
Jekyll, Gertrude, 14, 99, 224, 225
Jenkins, Ralph, 50
Jenkins Estate, Beaverton, OR, 13, 14, 18, **50–53**
John A. Finch Arboretum, Spokane WA, 243
Johnson, Tom, 109, 110
Johnson, Walter, 197
Jones, Robert L., 156, 157
Joy Creek Nursery, Scappoose, OR, **54–57**
juniper, 180, 198

kalmias, 225
Kalmiopsis leachiana, 68
katsura (*Cercidiphyllum magnificum*), 199, 286
Kelley, Lee, 48
Kerr, Peter, 35, 36–37
Keyser, Paul, 31, 32
kinnikinnick, 199
Kirk, Paul, 136, 140
Kishida, Isaburo, 282
Klager, Hulda, 238–239
Knighton, William C., 96
Korean silver fir (*Abies koreana*), 180
Kruckeberg, Arthur and Mareen, 158, 160, 161
Kruckeberg Botanic Garden, Shoreline, WA, **158–161**
Kubota, Fujitaro, 140, 164
Kubota, Tom, 165
Kubota Garden, Seattle, WA, 15, **162–165**
Kuma, Kengo, 81

laburnum, 271, 286
lace fern (*Microlepia strigosa*), 110
Ladd, William Sargent, 31, 58
Ladd's Addition Gardens, Portland, OR, **58–61**
Lake Wilderness Arboretum, Maple Valley, WA, 20, **200–201**
Lakewold, Lakewood, WA, 17, 18, 140, 194–195, **202–205**
Lan Su Chinese Garden, Portland, OR, 19, **62–65**
larch, 189, 243
lavender (*Lavandula*), 29, 52
  Blue Heron Herbary, 29
  Braille Garden, Jenkins Estate, 52
Lawrence, Ellis, 37, 71
Leach, John and Lilla Irvin, 67–68
Leach Botanical Garden, Portland, OR, **66–69**
leptospermum (common manuka or tea tree), 28
Lewis, David, 152, 157
Lewisia, 247
Lewis's monkeyflower (*Mimulus lewisii*), 117
licorice fern, 225
lilac (*Syringa vulgaris*), 236, 238
  Hulda Klager Lilac Gardens, **236–239**
  Lilac Days, 239
  Lilac Festival, Manito Park, 243
  Lilac Garden, Manito Park, 242
  purchasing, 239
  Spokane, WA, and, 242–243
lilies, 128, 129, 140, 169, 183, 205, 220, 276. *See also* daylilies
  ponds, 191, 216
lily-of-the-valley, 277, 286
linden trees, 61, 72, 188, 243, 271
Little, George, 152, 157
little-leaf lindens, 61
Livingstone, William, 258
lodgepole pine, 116
Lord, Elizabeth, 96–98

Maclure, Samuel, 282
madrone, 37
magnolia, 37, 40, 42, 65, 169, 188, 225, 243, 259, 271, 286
Magnolia 'Alexandria', 119
Magnolia campbellii, 188
Magnolia dawsoniana, 188
Magnolia hypoleuca, 220
Magnolia sargentiana var. *robusta*, 220
Magnolia sieboldii, 205
Magnolia sprengeri 'Diva', 33
Magnolia wilsonii, 188

mahonia, 26, 27
maidenhair fern, 184
Manito Park, Spokane, WA, 14, **240–243**
  Duncan Garden, 19, 240–241
maple trees, 42, 61, 90, 145, 161, 177, 243, 271
  Acer Garden, South Seattle Community College Arboretum, 180
marsh mallows, 189
matilija poppies (*Romneya coulterii*), 26, 205
mayapples, 216
Mayer, Father Ambrose, 39
mazes or labyrinths
  The Grotto, 40
  VanDusen Botanical Garden, 271
McLoughlin, Dr. John, 234, 235
Meerkerk, Max and Ann, 167–169
Meerkerk Rhododendron Gardens, Greenbank, WA, 18, **166–169**
Meyer, Adolph, 36
Mid-America Garden, Salem, OR, 110
Miller, Elisabeth and Pendleton, 146, 148
Milner, Ray and Veronica FitzGerald, 284–287
Milner Gardens and Woodland, Qualicum Beach, BC, **284–287**
Miscanthus sinesis 'Gold Breeze', 57
Mische, Emanuel T., 37, 61, 71
Moroccan broom (*Cytisus battandieri*), 225
mosses, 140, 199
  Moss Garden, Bloedel Reserve, 138, 140–141
mountain hemlock, 116, 137
mountain violet (*Viola lutea*), 116
Mount Fuji cherry trees, 204
Mount Pisgah Arboretum, Eugene, OR, 112–113, 122, 124
Mount Rainier National Park, 199
MsK Rare and Native Plant Nursery, Kruckeberg Botanic Garden, Shoreline, WA, 160, 161

native plant gardens
  Northwest Native Garden, Point Defiance Park, 212–213
  Ravine Garden and Oie Native Woodland, Soos Creek Botanical Garden, 225
  Tribal Life Trail, Lake Wilderness Arboretum, 201
  UBC Botanical Garden Rainforest Garden, 265
needle juniper (*Juniperus rigida*), 180
Nicholson, Harold, 67
nicotiana, 235
Nitobe Memorial Garden, Vancouver, BC, 15, 266
Noguchi, Isamu, 185

nurseries, garden shops, and retail growers
    Adelman Peony Garden, **84–87**
    Brooks Gardens, 87
    Connie Hansen Garden, 121
    Dancing Oaks Nursery, 82–83, **92–95**
    Garden Shop, Lakewold, 205
    Garden Shop Nursery, RSBG, 221
    Heirloom Roses, 91
    Heronswood, **154–157**
    Joy Creek Nursery, **54–57**
    lilacs from Hulda Klager Lilac Society, 239
    MsK Rare and Native Plant Nursery, 160, 161
    RoozenGaarde, Mount Vernon, WA, **170–173**
    Schreiner's Iris Gardens, **104–107**
    Sebright Gardens, **108–111**

oak trees, 42, 123, 187, 189, 243, 271
Ohme, Herman and Ruth, 244, 246
Ohme Gardens, Wenatchee, WA, 230–231,
    244–247
Old Apple Tree Park, Vancouver, WA, 234
olive trees, 26, 27
Olmsted, Frederick Law, 15, 44, 228
Olmsted Brothers (John Charles and Frederick
    Law Jr.), 13, 14, 15, 61
    aesthetic of, 144–145
    Dunn Gardens, 142–145
    Elk Rock Garden of the Bishop's Close, 34–37
    Olmsted Interpretive Exhibit, Volunteer Park,
        185
    Portland parks plan, 43, 44
    Seattle parks plan, 185, 186, 229
orchids, 183, 227
    Orchid Trail, Bloedel Reserve, 140
Oregon clover (*Oxalis oregana*), 204
Oregon fawn lilies (*Erythronium oregonum*), 99
Oregon Garden, Silverton, OR, 20, **100–103**
Oregon grape (*Mahonia aquifolium*), 37, 204
Oregon Heritage Tree Program, 42
Oregon white oak or Garry oak (*Quercus
    garryana*), 166, 204, 276
    Garry Oak Meadow and Woodland Garden,
        UBC Botanical Garden, 267
Oregon Zoo, Portland, OR, 48
Oriental paperbush (*Edgeworthia chrysantha*), 136
ornamental grasses, 94
    Joel E. Ferris Perennial Garden, Manito Park,
        241–242
ostrich fern (*Matteuccia struthiopteris*), 220
Owen Memorial Rose Garden, Eugene, OR, 125

Pacific bleeding heart (*Dicentra formosa*), 117
Pacific Coast iris, 205
Pacific dogwood (*Cornus nuttallii*), 204, 224
Pacific madrone, 166
Pacific Northwest gardens, 11–19. *See also
    featured gardens*
    climate and, 10, 20, 26
    first and oldest garden, 12
    first professional gardener, 234
    ice storms' destruction of, 10, 45, 145, 214–215
    Japanese influence, 15–17, 174
    Mid-Century Modern gardens, 17
    the Olmsted influence, 15
    Pioneer Orchard, 13
    the post-pioneer garden era, 13–14
    public works gardens, Great Depression, 14–15
    rainfall and weather, 10
    recent trends, 19–20
    Rhododendron Period, 18
    Rose Era, 14
    topography and, 8, 10
Pacific red elderberry (*Sambucus racemosa*), 117
Pacific Rim Bonsai Collection, Federal Way, WA,
    17, **206–209**, 221
Paeonia lactiflora, 84–86
Paeonia mairei, 220
palm, 28
paperbark maple (*Acer griseum*), 90, 177
pear trees, 266
Peninsula Park Rose Garden, Portland, OR, 14,
    47, **70–73**
penstemon, 56
peony, 84–87, 205, 220. *See also Paeonia*
    Adelman Peony Garden, **84–87**
    Brooks Gardens, 87
    Heritage Flower Garden, Soos Creek Botanical
        Garden, 222–223
Perkins + Will Architects, 269
Persian ironwood (*Parrotia persica*), 204, 224
phlox, 117, 247
phormium, 28
pieris, 40, 225
Pierobon, Peter, 271
pine, 116, 160, 180, 224, 254
pin oak, 152
Pioneers of American Landscape Design (National
    Park Service), 98
Pittock, Georgiana Burton, 14, 75, 77
Pittock, Henry, 74, 75, 77
Pittock Mansion, Portland, OR, **74–77**

plume Japanese cedar (*Cryptomeria japonica* 'Elegans'), 180
Point Defiance Park, Tacoma, WA, 18, **210–213**
poppies, 3, 204, 220
    Meconopsis Meadow, RSBG, 220
Port, Dr. Luke A., 96
Port Gamble S'Klallam tribe, 157
Portland Japanese Garden, OR, 15, 24–25, 48, **78–81**
Portland Rose Festival, 47, 49
Portugal laurel, 216
Povey Brothers of Portland, 96
Powell, Monte, 214, 216
PowellsWood, Federal Way, WA, 20, **214–217**
Price, Charles, 145
pussypaw, 117

Queen Elizabeth Park, Vancouver, BC, **256–259**

rabbitbrush goldenweed, 117
Rainer cherry tree, 224
red alder, 101
red-twig dogwood, 101
rhamnus, 27
rhododendron (*Rhododendron*), 18, 40, 65, 129, 136, 140, 145, 148, 177, 187, 216, 225, 243
    Cecil Smith and, 90
    endangered habitats of, 219
    history in the Pacific Northwest, 31–32
    oldest, 32
rhododendron (continued)
    purchasing, Garden Shop Nursery, RSBG, 221
    wild species, 219
Rhododendron cinnabarinum, 220
Rhododendron 'Cinnamon Bear', 90
Rhododendron 'Cynthia', 32, 119
Rhododendron 'Dame Nellie Melba', 120
Rhododendron 'Fragrantissimum', 204
rhododendron gardens, 18
    Bloedel Reserve, 18
    Cecil and Molly Smith Rhododendron Garden, 18, **88–90**
    Connie Hansen Garden, 118–121
    Crystal Springs Rhododendron Garden, 18, **30–33**
    Henricks Park, **122–125**
    Lakewold, Lakewood, 18
    Meerkerk Gardens, 18, **166–169**
    Point Defiance Park, 18
    Rhododendron Garden, Jenkins Estate, 18, 52–53

Rhododendron Garden, Milner Gardens, 286
Rhododendron Garden, Point Defiance Park, 212
Rhododendron Glen, Bellevue Botanical Garden, 136
Rhododendron Glen, Washington Park Arboretum, 188
Rhododendron Species Botanical Garden, 18, 209, **218–221**
Rhododendron Woodland Garden, Abkhazi Garden, 276
Steuber Rhododendron Collection, 200
Ted and Mary Greig Rhododendron Garden, 262
Rhododendron 'Loderi', 32
Rhododendron macrophyllum, 169
Rhododendron 'Noyo Brave', 90
Rhododendron pingianum, 218–219
Rhododendron rex, 220
Rhododendron russatum, 221
Rhododendron 'Sir Charles Lemon', 120
Rhododendron Species Botanical Garden (RSBG), Federal Way, WA, 3, 18, 209, **218–221**
Rhododendron yakushimanum, 221
Rhododendron 'Yellow Saucer', 90
Roberts, Ebenezer, 211
RoozenGaarde, Mount Vernon, WA, **170–173**
Rosa 'Madame Caroline Testout', 72
Rosa rugosa 'Hansa', 94–95
rose (*Rosa*), 40, 46, 98, 205
    nurseries and retail growers, 91
    Portland as the City of Roses, 14, 47, 48
    Portland Rose Festival, 47, 49, 71, 77
    Portland's official rose, 72
rose gardens
    Heirloom Roses, 91
    Heritage Flower Garden, Soos Creek Botanical Garden, 222–223
    International Rose Test Garden, 14, **46–49**
    Ladd's Addition Gardens, **58–61**
    Owen Memorial Rose Garden, 125
    Peninsula Park Rose Garden, 14, 47, **70–73**
    Rose Garden, Point Defiance Park, 211
    Rose Garden, The Butchart Gardens, 282
    Rose Garden, VanDusen Botanical Garden, 270
    Rose Hill, Manito Park, 242
    Shore Acres State Park, 129
    Stanley Park Rose Garden, 260–261, 262
    Tartar Rose Garden, Bush Pasture Park, 98
    Woodland Park Rose Garden, 14, **190–193**
rosemary, 52

Ross, Ian, 282

Sackville-West, Vita, 11, 67, 224
saguaro cactus, 184
salal, 140
scarlet gilia, 117
Schreiner, Francis X., 107
Schreiner family, 107
Schreiner's Iris Gardens, Salem, OR, **104–107**, 288
Schryver, Edith, 96–98
Schwagerl, Edward O., 228–229
scillas, 286
sculpture, 11
    Beach Memorial Fountain, 48
    at Bellevue Botanical Garden, 136
    at Evergreen Arboretum and Gardens,
        150–151, 152–53
    at The Grotto, 40–41
    by Henry Moore, Queen Elizabeth Park, 259
    at Kruckeberg Botanic Garden, 158–159
    at Lakewold, 194–195
    at UW Medicinal Herb Garden, 189
    at VanDusen Botanical Garden, 270–271
    at Volunteer Park, 185
    water feature at Hersonswood, 157
    at Wright Park, 10–11, 229
    Seattle Asian Art Museum, 185
Seattle Chinese Garden, 19, **178–181**
Seattle Japanese Garden, Seattle, WA, 4–5, 15, 164,
    174–177
Sebright Gardens, Salem, OR, **108–111**
sedum, 28, 247
Sedum moranii, 68
sensory gardens
    Seattle Sensory Garden, 192
    Sensory Garden, Oregon Garden, 102–103
sequoia, 27, 94–95, 101, 161, 189, 225
    Sequoia Grove, South Seattle Community
        College Arboretum, 180
Serazin, Rick, 215
Sersanous, Claude, 31
Seymour, William Wolcott, 226
Shakespeare Gardens
    in International Rose Test Garden, 49
    in Stanley Park, 263
Shasta red fir, 116
Shipman, Ellen, 97
Shore Acres State Park, Coos Bay, OR, 14,
    126–129
Shorts, Cal and Harriet, 136
Siberian iris, 57

silver dollar plants (*Lunaria annua*), 225
Simpson, Aemilius, 234
Simpson, Louis J., 126
Sissinghurst, Kent, England, 11, 13, 67, 98, 224
Sitka spruce (*Picea sitchensis*), 119, 166
Skagen, Maurice, 222, 224
Skagit Valley, WA, 172–173
skunk cabbage, 140, 222
Smith, Cecil and Molly, 90
Smith, Mike, 56
snakebark maple, 225
sneezeweed, 189
snowdrops, 198
soft-shield fern (*Polystichum setiferum*
        Plumosomultilobum Group), 110
Solomon's seal, 40, 199, 225
Soos Creek Botanical Garden, Auburn, WA,
    222–225
Sophora leachiana, 68
South Seattle Community College Arboretum,
    Seattle, WA, **179–181**
South Slough National Estuarine Research Reserve,
    Coos Bay, OR, 129
Spanish chestnut, 286
Spanish fir (*Abies pinsapo*), 161, 276
staghorn ferns, 185
Stanley Park, Vancouver, BC, **260–263**
stewartia (*Stewartia monadelpha*), 160
St. Paul, Oregon, 88–89
Sturtevant, Butler, 282
subalpine fir, 116
sweet briar rose (*Rosa rubiginosa*), 192
sword ferns (*Polystichum munitum*), 110, 225
Syringa 'City of Gresham', 238

tamarisk tree, 225
thyme, 52, 247
tiger-tail spruce (*Picea torano*), 180
tigridias, 276
tillandsia, 185
Tono, Takuma, 78
trident maple (*Acer buergerianum*), 161
trillium, 40, 145, 148, 161, 199, 200, 204, 222,
    225, 276
Trillium grandiflorum, 204
Trillium ovatum, 204
Trillium sessile, 204
Triteleia hendersonii var. *leachiae*, 68
Tsutakawa, Gerard, 165
tulip, 170–173, 260–261
    garden, RoozenGaarde, 170–173

Skagit Valley Tulip Festival, 172–173
twinflower, 225

UBC Botanical Garden, Vancouver, BC, 13,
    264–267
umbrella pine (*Sciadopitys verticillata*), 224
umbrella plant (*Darmera peltata*), 224
University of Washington Arboretum, Seattle, WA,
    175. *See also* Seattle Japanese Garden

vancouveria, 216
VanDusen Botanical Garden, Vancouver, BC, 13,
    268–271
vanilla leaf, 199
Venus flytrap (*Dionaea muscipula*), 184
viburnum, 37, 40, 136, 225
vine maple (*Acer circinatum*), 222
violas, 116, 286
vireyas (tropical rhododendrons), 227
Volunteer Park, Seattle, WA, 185
Volunteer Park Conservatory, Seattle, WA, 14,
    182–185

Wade, John, 277
Wagner, Corydon, 202
Wagner, Eulalie Merrill, 140, 202, 203, 204
Walker Macy architecture firm, 45
walnut trees, 243
Wanker, Maud, 119
Washington Park, Portland, OR, 14, 47, 48. *See
    also* International Rose Test Garden
Washington Park Arboretum, Seattle, WA, 15, 44,
    132–133, **186–189**
water lilies, 100–101
weeping blue Atlas cedar, 37, 92, 94, 165
weeping cherry, 81
weeping giant sequoias (*Sequoiadendron giganteum*
    'Pendulum'), 94–95, 101

weeping Norway spruce, 165
Weisensee, Fred, 93
Welsh onion, 189
western azaleas (*Rhododendron occidentale*), 200
western red cedar, 40, 45, 139, 222, 225, 260, 285
Whidbey Island, WA, 166–167
white-oak, 103, 124
wildflower gardens
    Alpine Garden, Bellevue Botanical Garden, 137
    Bloedel Reserve, 140
    Castle Crest Wildflower Garden, Crater Lake
        National Park, **114–117**
    The Glen, Bloedel Reserve, 140
    meadows at Chase Garden, 196–197
    Oie Native Woodland, Soos Creek Botanical
        Garden, 225
wild tobacco, 189
wingthorn rose (*Rosa sericea*), 225
winter aconites, 276, 286
winter-flowering plum, 254
winter garden
    Joseph A. Witt Winter Garden, 187–188
Wister, John, 107
wisteria, 176–177, 287
Withey, Glen, 145
Woodland Park Rose Garden, Seattle, WA, 13, 14,
    190–193
World Forestry Center, Portland, OR, 48
wormwood, 189
Wright, Charles B., 226–227
W. W. Seymour Botanical Conservatory and
    Wright Park, Tacoma, WA, 10–11, 14,
    226–229

yew, 141, 165, 216, 243, 266, 271
yuccas, 26, 28

about the author

Donald Olson is a travel writer, novelist, and playwright with a longtime interest in gardens and gardening. His travel stories have appeared in the *New York Times*, *National Geographic*, and other national publications, and he is the author of several travel guides, including *Best Day Trips from London*, *England for Dummies*, *Germany Day-by-Day*, and *Frommer's Easy Guide to Seattle, Portland and the Oregon Coast*. An avid gardener himself, Donald has been exploring the great gardens of Europe and the Pacific Northwest for many years, and gardens have played prominent roles in his fiction (*Paradise Gardens*) and plays (*The Garden Plays*). His three most recent novels were published under the pen name Swan Adamson. Donald lives, writes, and gardens in Manhattan and in Portland, Oregon.

SARAH MILHOLLIN